Piano For Dummies®

P9-CRI-793

Cheat Sheet

Glossary of Musical Symbols and Terms

Here's a nice, big list of symbols and terms you may need to know to play music and impress your musician friends.

Accidentals

Sharp   Flat   Natural

Clefs

Treble clef   Bass clef

Crescendo and decrescendo

Crescendo
(Get louder)

Decrescendo
(Get softer)

Dotted notes

Dotted quarter
(1½ beats)

Dotted half
(3 beats)

Fermata

Hold

Notes

Whole note
(4 beats)

Half note
(2 beats)

Quarter note
(1 beat)

Eighth note
(½ beat)

Sixteenth note
(¼ beat)

Octave changes

8*va* - - - - - - - -｜
(1 octave higher)

15*ma* - - - - - - - -｜
(2 octaves higher)

8*vb* - - - - - - - -｜
(1 octave lower)

Rests

Whole rest
(4 beats)

Half rest
(2 beats)

Quarter rest
(1 beat)

Eighth rest
(½ beat)

Sixteenth rest
(¼ beat)

Tie

Time signatures

4/4
4 beats per measure

3/4
3 beats per measure

Triplets

For Dummies™: Bestselling Book Series for Beginners

Piano For Dummies®

The Keys to Success

Rip this page out and place it right above the keys on your piano or keyboard to help you instantly recall the note name for each key.

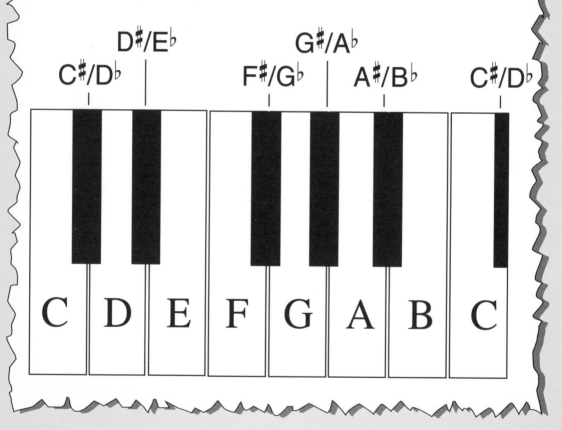

Cheat Sheet $2.95 value. Item 5105-1.

For more information about IDG Books, call 1-800-762-2974.

For Dummies™: Bestselling Book Series for Beginners

TM

References for the Rest of Us!™

BESTSELLING BOOK SERIES

Do you find that traditional reference books are overloaded with technical details and advice you'll never use? Do you postpone important life decisions because you just don't want to deal with them? Then our *...For Dummies®* business and general reference book series is for you.

...For Dummies business and general reference books are written for those frustrated and hard-working souls who know they aren't dumb, but find that the myriad of personal and business issues and the accompanying horror stories make them feel helpless. *...For Dummies* books use a lighthearted approach, a down-to-earth style, and even cartoons and humorous icons to dispel fears and build confidence. Lighthearted but not lightweight, these books are perfect survival guides to solve your everyday personal and business problems.

> *"More than a publishing phenomenon, 'Dummies' is a sign of the times."*
>
> — The New York Times

> *"A world of detailed and authoritative information is packed into them..."*
>
> — U.S. News and World Report

> *"...you won't go wrong buying them."*
>
> — Walter Mossberg, Wall Street Journal, on IDG Books' ...For Dummies books

Already, millions of satisfied readers agree. They have made *...For Dummies* the #1 introductory level computer book series and a best-selling business book series. They have written asking for more. So, if you're looking for the best and easiest way to learn about business and other general reference topics, look to *...For Dummies* to give you a helping hand.

IDG BOOKS WORLDWIDE

1/99

Piano

FOR

DUMMIES®

Piano

FOR

DUMMIES®

by Blake Neely,
Cherry Lane Music

IDG Books Worldwide, Inc.
An International Data Group Company

Foster City, CA ♦ Chicago, IL ♦ Indianapolis, IN ♦ New York, NY

Piano For Dummies®

Published by
IDG Books Worldwide, Inc.
An International Data Group Company
919 E. Hillsdale Blvd.
Suite 400
Foster City, CA 94404
www.idgbooks.com (IDG Books Worldwide Web site)
www.dummies.com (Dummies Press Web site)

Library of Congress Catalog Card No.: 98-87104

ISBN: 0-7645-5105-1

Printed in the United States of America

10 9

1O/QW/QY/QQ/IN

Distributed in the United States by IDG Books Worldwide, Inc.

Distributed by CDG Books Canada Inc. for Canada; by Transworld Publishers Limited in the United Kingdom; by IDG Norge Books for Norway; by IDG Sweden Books for Sweden; by IDG Books Australia Publishing Corporation Pty. Ltd. for Australia and New Zealand; by TransQuest Publishers Pte Ltd. for Singapore, Malaysia, Thailand, Indonesia, and Hong Kong; by Gotop Information Inc. for Taiwan; by ICG Muse, Inc. for Japan; by Intersoft for South Africa; by Eyrolles for France; by International Thomson Publishing for Germany, Austria and Switzerland; by Distribuidora Cuspide for Argentina; by LR International for Brazil; by Galileo Libros for Chile; by Ediciones ZETA S.C.R. Ltda. for Peru; by WS Computer Publishing Corporation, Inc., for the Philippines; by Contemporanea de Ediciones for Venezuela; by Express Computer Distributors for the Caribbean and West Indies; by Micronesia Media Distributor, Inc. for Micronesia; by Chips Computadoras S.A. de C.V. for Mexico; by Editorial Norma de Panama S.A. for Panama; by American Bookshops for Finland.

For general information on IDG Books Worldwide's books in the U.S., please call our Consumer Customer Service department at 800-762-2974. For reseller information, including discounts and premium sales, please call our Reseller Customer Service department at 800-434-3422.

For information on where to purchase IDG Books Worldwide's books outside the U.S., please contact our International Sales department at 317-596-5530 or fax 317-572-4002.

For consumer information on foreign language translations, please contact our Customer Service department at 1-800-434-3422, fax 317-572-4002, or e-mail rights@idgbooks.com.

For information on licensing foreign or domestic rights, please phone +1-650-653-7098.

For sales inquiries and special prices for bulk quantities, please contact our Order Services department at 800-434-3422 or write to the address above.

For information on using IDG Books Worldwide's books in the classroom or for ordering examination copies, please contact our Educational Sales department at 800-434-2086 or fax 317-572-4005.

For press review copies, author interviews, or other publicity information, please contact our Public Relations department at 650-653-7000 or fax 650-653-7500.

For authorization to photocopy items for corporate, personal, or educational use, please contact Copyright Clearance Center, 222 Rosewood Drive, Danvers, MA 01923, or fax 978-750-4470.

About the Author

Blake Neely has been playing piano since he was about 4 years old, although it took a while before real audible music could be detected. His fascination with music led him to other instruments, such as the French horn, guitar, and drums, but the keyboard remains his baby.

Upon graduation from the University of Texas in 1991, he moved to Los Angeles to experience the music business. He licensed music for Hollywood Records and later worked for Disney Music Publishing as editor of all printed music publications.

An award-winning composer and author, he has written symphonies, a piano concerto, and numerous orchestral and chamber works. He is co-author of the acclaimed *FastTrack* series, published by Hal Leonard Corporation.

Blake has worked as a composer, orchestrator, arranger, copyist, engraver, musicologist, and consultant for such prominent figures as Disney, Hal Leonard Corporation, Decca Records, Hyperion Books, composers Michael Kamen and Alan Menken, and the Cincinnati Pops Orchestra.

Currently living in Austin, Texas, Blake spends his free time tuning into his family: wife Elizabeth, daughter Jordan, and son Jacob. Blake is the proud owner of a Kawai grand piano and Kurzweil, Ensoniq, and E-Mu synths and samplers. You can reach Blake via e-mail at BlakeNeely@aol.com.

ABOUT IDG BOOKS WORLDWIDE

Welcome to the world of IDG Books Worldwide.

IDG Books Worldwide, Inc., is a subsidiary of International Data Group, the world's largest publisher of computer-related information and the leading global provider of information services on information technology. IDG was founded more than 30 years ago by Patrick J. McGovern and now employs more than 9,000 people worldwide. IDG publishes more than 290 computer publications in over 75 countries. More than 90 million people read one or more IDG publications each month.

Launched in 1990, IDG Books Worldwide is today the #1 publisher of best-selling computer books in the United States. We are proud to have received eight awards from the Computer Press Association in recognition of editorial excellence and three from Computer Currents' First Annual Readers' Choice Awards. Our best-selling ...For Dummies® series has more than 50 million copies in print with translations in 31 languages. IDG Books Worldwide, through a joint venture with IDG's Hi-Tech Beijing, became the first U.S. publisher to publish a computer book in the People's Republic of China. In record time, IDG Books Worldwide has become the first choice for millions of readers around the world who want to learn how to better manage their businesses.

Our mission is simple: Every one of our books is designed to bring extra value and skill-building instructions to the reader. Our books are written by experts who understand and care about our readers. The knowledge base of our editorial staff comes from years of experience in publishing, education, and journalism — experience we use to produce books to carry us into the new millennium. In short, we care about books, so we attract the best people. We devote special attention to details such as audience, interior design, use of icons, and illustrations. And because we use an efficient process of authoring, editing, and desktop publishing our books electronically, we can spend more time ensuring superior content and less time on the technicalities of making books.

You can count on our commitment to deliver high-quality books at competitive prices on topics you want to read about. At IDG Books Worldwide, we continue in the IDG tradition of delivering quality for more than 30 years. You'll find no better book on a subject than one from IDG Books Worldwide.

John Kilcullen
Chairman and CEO
IDG Books Worldwide, Inc.

Eighth Annual
Computer Press
Awards ≥1992

Ninth Annual
Computer Press
Awards ≥1993

Tenth Annual
Computer Press
Awards ≥1994

Eleventh Annual
Computer Press
Awards ≥1995

Dedication

This book is dedicated to anyone who has ever dreamed of being a musician but had no idea where to begin. If a little guy from Paris, Texas can do it, so can you.

Author's Acknowledgments

Special thanks to Cherry Lane Music, Ted Piechocinski, and John Cerullo for thinking of me; to Keith Mardak for being Keith Mardak (I said your name twice!); to Brad Smith for the connections; to Richard Slater and Tom Johns for the photos; to Rick Walters for rearranging his schedule; to Jason Frankhouser at Digital Lane for mastering the CD; and to Susan Borgeson for getting me started in the business.

Additional thanks to Sandy Morgenthal at E-Mu, Joe Kramer at Ensoniq, Brian Chung at Kawai, Larry Harms at Roland, and Ray Reuter at Yamaha for the consultations and information about their toys.

Extra special thanks to Mary Goodwin, my patient and kind editor at IDG Books; to Stacey Mickelbart for catching all those darn passive verbs; to Paul Kuzmic for downloading all those files; to Mark Butler for taking a chance with this book; to Jonathan Malysiak for help with the cover; and to the inspiring Jeff Sultanof, my technical editor/researcher/friend/therapist, for his wealth of ideas, knowledge, encouragement, and humor.

Personal thanks to my piano teachers for making me less of a dummy; to my parents for enduring long hours of practice and dinner delays; to my sister for playing piano duets with me; to my brother for finally opening my ears to jazz; to my in-laws for letting their daughter marry a crazy musician; and to J.S. Bach for the genius that he was and inspiration that he is.

Never-ending thanks to my wife, Elizabeth, for her constant love and support; and to my kids, Jordan and Jacob, for making the sun shine every day.

Publisher's Acknowledgments

We're proud of this book; please register your comments through our IDG Books Worldwide Online Registration Form located at http://my2cents.dummies.com.

Some of the people who helped bring this book to market include the following:

Acquisitions, Editorial, and Media Development

Senior Project Editor: Mary Goodwin

Acquisitions Editor: Mark Butler

Acquisitions Coordinator: Jonathan Malysiak

Editorial Coordinator: Maureen F. Kelly

Copy Editors: Stacey Mickelbart, Stephanie Koutek, Billie Williams

Technical Editor: David Cartledge, Indiana University School of Music

General Reviewer: Jeff Sultanof

Editorial Manager: Kelly Ewing

Editorial Assistant: Paul Kuzmic

Production

Project Coordinator: Valery Bourke

Layout and Graphics: Lou Boudreau, Linda M. Boyer, J. Tyler Connor, Kelly Hardesty, Angela F. Hunckler, Todd Klemme, Heather N. Pearson, Lindsay Sandman, Brent Savage, Janet Seib, Rashell Smith

Proofreaders: Christine Berman, Kelli Botta, Chris Collins, Nancy Price, Rebecca Senninger, Janet M. Withers

Indexer: Sharon Hilgenberg

General and Administrative

IDG Books Worldwide, Inc.: John Kilcullen, CEO

IDG Books Technology Publishing Group: Richard Swadley, Senior Vice President and Publisher; Walter R. Bruce III, Vice President and Publisher; Joseph Wikert, Vice President and Publisher; Mary Bednarek, Vice President and Director, Product Development; Andy Cummings, Publishing Director, General User Group; Mary C. Corder, Editorial Director; Barry Pruett, Publishing Director

IDG Books Consumer Publishing Group: Roland Elgey, Senior Vice President and Publisher; Kathleen A. Welton, Vice President and Publisher; Kevin Thornton, Acquisitions Manager; Kristin A. Cocks, Editorial Director

IDG Books Internet Publishing Group: Brenda McLaughlin, Senior Vice President and Publisher; Sofia Marchant, Online Marketing Manager

IDG Books Production for Branded Press: Debbie Stailey, Director of Production; Cindy L. Phipps, Manager of Project Coordination, Production Proofreading, and Indexing; Tony Augsburger, Manager of Prepress, Reprints, and Systems; Laura Carpenter, Production Control Manager; Shelley Lea, Supervisor of Graphics and Design; Debbie J. Gates, Production Systems Specialist; Robert Springer, Supervisor of Proofreading; Trudy Coler, Page Layout Manager; Troy Barnes, Page Layout Supervisor, Kathie Schutte, Senior Page Layout Supervisor; Michael Sullivan, Production Supervisor

Packaging and Book Design: Patty Page, Manager, Promotions Marketing

◆

The publisher would like to give special thanks to Patrick J. McGovern, without whom this book would not have been possible.

◆

Contents at a Glance

Cartoons at a Glance

By Rich Tennant

"Get me the ant spray, honey. My B flat just became an F sharp!"

page 5

"C'mon! Allegro vivace! Allegro vivace! We're selling ice cream not coffins!"

page 79

"These are your custom sound buttons. There's an 'oink-oink' here and a 'gobble-gobble' there, here a 'quack', there a 'moo'..."

page 239

"Normally, a cross-hand technique is used for reaching upper register notes. But what you're doing is fine, as long as it doesn't hurt."

page 121

That's very good, Martin. Except after the fooosamento section you're forgetting to look out at the audience and give them a wink and a smile.

page 171

"This piece comes with accidentals already in it? You mean I don't produce enough on my own?"

page 35

Yeah-barrel-house boogie-woogie!! Go Stuart, go! Make that harpsichord growl!!

page 267

Fax: 978-546-7747 • E-mail: the5wave@tiac.net

Table of Contents

· ·

Part V: Technique Counts for Everything 171

Chapter 13: Dressing Up Your Music 173

Chapter 14: Great Grooves 191

Introduction

* *

*W*elcome to *Piano For Dummies*. Come on in and don't be nervous about wanting to play the piano. The piano is just a big, lazy piece of oversized furniture with a bunch of black and white keys on it. By selecting this book, you're taking the appropriate action to keep your piano from becoming a giant dust collector.

If you've never seen or put your hands on a piano or keyboard, no problem. This book starts at the very beginning and walks you through everything you need to know to tame that beast and make it sing sweet music. You'll also have fun along the way — I promise.

Why This Book Is for You

I assume that you are looking at, or considering the purchase of, a keyboard to go with this lovely book. Most likely, your keyboard will have at least 25 black and white keys, may or may not plug into the wall, and will have cost you as much as you could justify as a "legitimate and necessary" business expense on your tax return.

Because you are in possession of (or plan to be in possession of) a piano or keyboard, you may need this book to figure out how to play it. Or you may want to read music. Maybe you already know how to play, and you want to improve your playing skills or develop your style. Could be you're interested in knowing more about pianos and their performers. Or you may need some help buying a keyboard or finding a teacher. For any of these reasons, this is the book for you.

You can use *Piano For Dummies* as a teaching aid or just as a reference book. Even if you already know how to play music, you may run across some new tricks or techniques in these pages.

Of course, you should continue to seek knowledge about your instrument long after you tire of my jokes. Piano teachers and method books shouldn't be forsaken forever for *Piano For Dummies*. But, hey, what a revolutionary way to start playing the piano — by having fun with a great book!

How to Read (and Listen to) This Book

Don't think you must start reading *Piano For Dummies* from the beginning. This isn't *Gone With the Wind*. There's no cliffhanger in Chapter 4. You can open up and start reading from any page or chapter that interests you. If you need to know something from a chapter you skipped, just flip back to that chapter, read what you need to know, and then flip ahead.

Also, this book is smaller in size than most piano books, so you can easily set it atop your piano, keyboard, or airline pull-out tray as you read. Just ask the flight attendant to hold your drink and peanuts for you.

You have eight different parts to read. Take your pick, starting anywhere you wish.

Part I: Warming Up to the Keyboard

Part I serves as your introduction to the family of keyboards, how they work, where to sit to play them, which hands to use, and how to operate all those black and white keys.

Part II: Getting Sound Down on Paper

In this part, I explain the many symbols, lines, and dots that most people call "music," and I also show you how to translate those symbols, lines, and dots into actual songs.

Part III: One Hand at a Time

Everything comes together in Part III, which shows you how to play the melodies of lots of well-known songs. I also talk about the importance of scales and how they can help you master the piano. At the end of this part, I get the other guy involved — the left hand.

Part IV: Living in Perfect Harmony

In this part, you can discover the world of harmony — what it is, how it's made, and how to use it to fill out the sound of the songs you play.

Part V: Technique Counts for Everything

Read this part to help dress up the music you play with some neat tricks, techniques, and styles. Beware: After word gets out that you've read this part of the book, people will always ask you to play the piano at their parties.

Part VI: So Many Toys, So Little Time

This part is your guide to selecting, buying, and caring for your keyboard, whether your instrument is brand new or a family heirloom. The excitement you experience from this part may lead to breaking open your piggy bank and going shopping.

Part VII: The Part of Tens

This part offers a few lists to help you have more fun with the piano. I tell you about some of the great masters, past and present, of the instrument. I also show you some avenues to pursue if you want to expand your interest beyond the scope of this book. I end the part with a list of tips to help you find a teacher who's right for you.

I also throw in a glossary of musical terms and an appendix to tell you about the CD that comes with this book. What? The book comes with a CD? You thought that round thing attached to the back of the book was a cool little drink coaster? Sorry, you'll have to find a napkin instead. This CD features recordings of every song in the book, as well as other fun audio examples. The appendix gives you a complete track listing of what awaits you on the CD.

Icons Used in This Book

Specific icons alert you to information you may want to pay closer attention to, skip past as fast as you can, or tell your Mom and Dad all about.

When you see this icon, you know some handy-dandy information follows that can save you time, save you money, save your memory, or save you from electrocuting yourself.

Some of the information in this book gets a little more advanced. You may find yourself skipping these parts to keep your brain power to a minimum, or you may be surprised by how fascinating and fun you find it.

Sometimes I get really excited about a particular CD, book, or other musical paraphernalia I enjoy. This icon alerts you to those things you should check out at a store or library near you.

On the CD, you can hear every song example in this book and other fun audio clips. You can play along or hear how the song sounds before playing it yourself. Take a listen when you see this icon.

When I digress into the swamp of technical jargon, I give you fair warning with this icon. Don't tear the page in your haste to flip past if you don't care for technical jargon.

Pay attention to these icon occurrences. You can thank me later for showing you how to avoid mistakes or even accidents.

Things that make you say "Wow!" are preceded by this icon. These little gems are funny, odd, and sometimes even useful.

Part I
Warming Up to the Keyboard

"Get me the ant spray, honey. My B-flat just became an F-sharp!"

In this part . . .

*B*efore you play a keyboard, you should know what it is, what makes it tick, where to put your hands and feet, and what all those keys are for. No, you don't need a license, and you won't have to parallel park for me.

Chapter 1 introduces the keyboard family to you, with its strange cast of characters. Chapter 2 shows you how to sit and what to touch. After Chapter 3, you're sure to know the name of every black and white key on the piano. Guaranteed!

Chapter 1

Meeting the Keyboard Family

. . . .

In This Chapter

▶ Discovering what makes a keyboard tick

▶ Comparing acoustic to electric keyboards

▶ Distinguishing a piano from an organ from a pig squealing

. . . .

To be perfectly clear, when I say *keyboard* I mean the type that produces musical sounds. I don't mean a keyboard with the letters QWERTY on it that is connected to a computer, typewriter, or NASA space launch. So, did you purchase the right book? Good.

Be it a piano, organ, or synthesizer, your keyboard is a wonderful and miraculous instrument. You have chosen your instrument wisely.

Keyboards come in all shapes and sizes. They can have many keys or just a few; they can be huge pieces of furniture or small little boxes. Whatever the size, shape, or makeup, the instrument is probably a keyboard if any of the following happens:

♪ Musical sound is produced via the pressing of a key or button.

♪ Blowing, bowing, strumming, or plucking it doesn't do much good.

♪ Anyone in the room says, "Hey, dude, nice keyboard!"

If you haven't yet purchased a keyboard, read this chapter, decide what kind of keyboard interests you, then see Chapter 16 for tips on buying your instrument. You may discover a keyboard at the store that you find even more exciting, but at least the ones I mention in this chapter will give you a starting point.

The Acoustic Ones

Acoustic means *non-electric*. So, acoustic keyboards are great for starving musicians, because even when you can't pay the electric bill, you can keep playing.

The inner workings

Each key on most acoustic keyboards corresponds to a string, or set of strings, housed inside the body of the instrument. When you press a key, it triggers a fancy mechanism to "play" the strings associated with that key. The string begins to vibrate very, very rapidly. The entire vibration process occurs in a split second — think hummingbird wings' speed. Your ear picks up these vibrations and you hear music.

To get an idea of just how fast this all happens, go to a piano and touch a key. At the exact same time, you hear a musical note. That's pretty darn fast.

To keep the strings from vibrating all the time, another mechanism called a *damper* sits over the strings inside the keyboard. Dampers are made of cloth or felt, which mutes the strings by not allowing any vibration. When you press a key, in addition to triggering the mechanism that vibrates the string, a piano key also lifts the damper.

The basic difference between each type of acoustic keyboard is the type of mechanism used to vibrate the strings. The different mechanisms can produce very different overall sounds.

Back when no one bathed

A long time ago (in a century far, far away), an early keyboard was in the form of a *hydraulis*, or *water-organ*. Featured in Roman circuses ("In the center ring, see the dancing hydraulis!"), the pipes were sounded by moving a slider, rather than pressing keys.

Soon after came a small *portative organ*, which had buttons instead of keys, followed by your basic *pipe organ* (also known as a *church organ*) with a set of keys to play a series of pipes.

As early as 1435, Henry Arnoult de Zwolle began designing various keyboard instruments affixed with strings that were vibrated by the trigger of a key. These early designs included one for the *clavichord*, which led to the birth of the *harpsichord* later that century. These two *chord* instruments differed by the process and mechanism that played each string.

Early versions of keyboard instruments had very few keys — 10 to 20 — a feature that was easily expanded with each successive new model. This marked the birth of an ever-popular sales strategy in the musical instrument industry: making products obsolete in order to sell more next year.

Pianos

Pianos, the most popular acoustic keyboard, come in three appropriately named packages:

- ♪ **Grand piano (see Figure 1-1):** You may need a living room the size of a grand ballroom to house one of these instruments. If you don't live in a castle, you may want to consider a baby grand, the smaller version of the grand piano.

- ♪ **Upright piano (see Figure 1-2):** These relatively small instruments sit upright against your living room wall.

- ♪ **Baby grand piano:** The offspring of the first two types of piano — kidding! This is simply a smaller version of the grand.

Figure 1-1:
Owning one
is so grand.

You can hear the marvelous sounds of a piano on Track 1 of the CD. First, you hear an excerpt from Erik Satie's classical work "Three Gymnopédies," followed by a sampling of Scott Joplin's "Maple Leaf Rag."

Figure 1-2:
Upright, not
uptight.

Thousands of pieces have been written for piano. For a small sampling of various piano styles, check out the following recordings:

♪ Alan Feinberg, *Fascinatin' Rhythm* (Argo)

♪ Dave Grusin, *The Firm – Soundtrack* (MCA/GRP)

♪ Franz Schubert, *Piano Sonata in A minor*, Alfred Brendel (Philips)

♪ George Winston, *December* (Windham Hill)

Lids

The grand piano has an enormous lid that you can prop open with a stick that comes with the piano. By propping open the lid, you can see lots of metal strings and other components, maybe even those car keys that you misplaced last month.

Because the sound of a piano comes from the strings inside the instrument, you get a louder and more resonant sound when you leave the lid of a grand piano open.

The keyboard: Master of all instruments

Many people regard keyboards as music's most versatile instruments. I can back up this big, broad (and slightly biased) statement with some facts:

♪ They are capable of a great range of volume — from very soft to very loud.

♪ They can sound more than one note at a time.

♪ They are *toned*, or *pitched*, instruments (capable of producing different musical notes, compared to unpitched drums and cymbals).

♪ They have the widest *pitch range* of any instrument from very low to very high.

♪ They can be played as solo or accompaniment instruments.

♪ They're capable of playing by themselves.

Sure, your neighbor can (unfortunately) play his clarinet very loud to very soft, but he can only play one note at a time. Your friend with the violin can play two or three notes at once, but she can only play half the notes a keyboard can play. And, yes, the Pearl Jam concert on Friday night *did* feature a drum solo, but was it very hummable?

The upright piano also has a lid — and some even have a stick to prop it open — but only piano tuners actually use the stick to help them keep the lid open while they tune the strings. Because an upright's sound is not dramatically changed by opening the lid, you can instead try pulling the piano away from the wall a bit to make the sound less muffled.

String layout

In the grand piano, the strings are horizontal; in the upright, the strings are vertical. The strings must be set diagonally — with the treble strings crossing the bass strings — to fit in the smaller upright case.

The difference in the string layout affects the resulting sound of the two pianos in the following ways:

♪ The strings in an upright are perpendicular to the ground, thus the sound travels close to the ground.

♪ The strings in a grand piano are parallel to the ground, thus the sound travels upward from the ground and fills the room.

♪ The strings in an upright are mostly behind wood casing that can't be opened, causing a more muffled sound.

♪ The strings in a grand are directly under a lid that can be opened to allow a more resonant sound.

Keys and hammers

Most acoustic pianos today have a row of 88 black and white keys. If you have 87, 89, or 32, you may have been cheated! Each of the 88 keys is connected to a small, felt-covered *hammer,* the mechanism that plays the string, shown in Figure 1-3. Press a key and the correct hammer strikes a string, or set of strings, tuned to the appropriate musical note.

Figure 1-3:
Hammering
out your
ideas.

Courtesy of Kawai America

Ol' Bart needed more volume

Contrary to popular belief, the inventor of the piano was not named Steinway, nor was it Alec, Billy, Steve, or any other famous Baldwin brother. No, the piano was invented by an 18th-century Italian harpsichord-maker named Bartolommeo Cristofori (1655-1731).

It seems that one day in 1709, after a long day polishing his umpteenth harpsichord, Mr. Cristofori thought to himself, "Hmm, instead of each key causing a string to be plucked, what if each key caused a string to be struck?" Rather poetic, don't you think? (I'm paraphrasing, of course, because I wasn't there, and I don't know Italian.)

Not one to sit still for long, ol' Bart quickly set out to expand his business with the new hammered harpsichord. The marketing pitch? Unlike a harpsichord, which played the same volume no matter how darn hard you hit the keys, the new instrument would play all volume levels. Thus, the new invention was christened *pianoforte,* which is Italian for "soft loud."

Why the name dropped *forte* over the years is probably about as exciting and informative as why you shorten Robert to Bob. Suffice it to say that 18th-century Italians were pretty trendy. Heck, why say a five syllable word when three syllables will do?

The piano was not an instant success. Wine and cheese parties at the time were all a-buzz with heated debates over the "dullness of tone" and "lack of an escapement" in the new piano. (Oh, my kingdom for a time machine!)

After many improvements and many years, such prominent composers as Beethoven, Haydn, and some guy named Mozart were abandoning all logic and writing for the crazy instrument.

Harpsichords

The number of households in the U.S. with a harpsichord is roughly the same as the number of households with a mural of Beethoven on the front door. Harpsichords are so rare today, it's hard to believe that harpsichords were once all the rage in Europe.

If you happen to find a harpsichord — perhaps at a university or bingo parlor — you'll notice that harpsichords look a lot like pianos (see Figure 1-4). But check out the ornate lid on the harpsichord. Today, keyboard players have to suffice with plain old black boxes.

Figure 1-4:
The ornate harpsichord.

Some harpsichords even have the color of the keys reversed — as do some old pianos. I'm sure there was a good reason for this switch to more white keys than black ones — perhaps a surplus of ivory.

The harpsichord may bear a striking resemblance to the piano in many ways, but strike a key on the harpsichord, and you'll notice the difference between it and a piano immediately.

Track 2 of the CD, an excerpt of Bach's "The Well-Tempered Clavier," lets you hear the different sound of the harpsichord.

The harpsichord achieves its different sound because of the way the strings are played inside the instrument. Instead of a hammer, the keys on a harpsichord connect to small *hooks,* or *quills,* which sit very close to the strings. Pressing a key causes the corresponding hook (also called a *plectrum*) to pluck the string — much like a hillbilly would pluck a banjo — tuned to the correct musical tone.

Many harpsichords have more than one keyboard, also called a *manual.* This was a quick solution to the instrument's one big problem: No matter how hard you hit the keys, the volume stays the same. By adding a second keyboard and a few other fancy mechanisms, the melody can be played slightly louder — on the lower keyboard — than the accompaniment.

Listen to harpsichord music as it was meant to be heard . . . on the harpsichord:

♪ Domenico Scarlatti, *Sonatas,* Trevor Pinnock (Archive)

♪ Antonio Vivaldi, *The Four Seasons,* Nigel Kennedy and the English Chamber Orchestra (EMI); this piece doesn't feature the harpsichord as much as the violins, but you can hear the harpsichord plunking away in the background.

♪ Johann Sebastian Bach, *Concerto in D minor for Harpsichord,* Igor Kipnis with Sir Neville Marriner and the London Strings (CBS)

Is that a Ruckers in your salon?

Next time your snobbish violinist friend utters the words, "Darling, I only play a Stradivarius" (arguably the finest violin crafter in history), step up to the challenge with "Well, I insist on a Ruckers." Then ask her for some Grey Poupon.

Hans Ruckers (around 1555-1623) is considered to be the greatest harpsichord-maker the world has ever known. At the young age of 20, this Flemish-born (where the heck is Flemland, anyway?) began building his own keyboards

of unsurpassed quality. He even managed to moonlight as an inventor, being credited with adding a second keyboard to the instrument.

Sadly, few of his creations survive. It seems that their casings were so beautiful — the paintings and wood designs — that art dealers began buying, dismembering, and selling pieces of Ruckers harpsichords all over Europe . . . including in Flemland.

What is that term again?

A *concerto* is a composition written for orchestra and one or more featured instruments. So, in a concerto you hear the whole orchestra playing frantically, followed by a solo by a pianist, harpsichordist, or kazoo player.

A *sonata* is a composition written in a specific form for a solo instrument. You can find sonatas for piano, harpsichord, violin, you name it.

Other terms like *fugue, passacaglia, mazurka, bagatelle,* and many others appear in the titles of keyboard works. To understand more about these and other classical music terms, hop in your car or on your bike and head to the bookstore to buy your very own copy of *Classical Music For Dummies,* by David Pogue and Scott Speck, published by IDG Books Worldwide, Inc.

Pipe organs

As I explain earlier in this chapter, *acoustic* means *non-electric*. It does not mean *having strings*. Therefore, I must quickly point out — lest you call me a liar — that a pipe organ is also an acoustic keyboard. It does not, however, have any strings. Instead, it has . . . *pipes*.

You won't find a pipe organ in many of your neighbors' homes. Well, maybe if your neighbor has the last name Gates, but that's another story. You can find pipe organs at churches, synagogues, universities, and some concert halls.

Pipe organs are the world's largest and most complex acoustic instruments. They are great monsters with many, many different-sized pipes. Each pipe has a unique sound. Several pipes played in combination can produce other, non-organ sounds — a trumpet, a flute, a violin, a pig squealing. Okay, so maybe not a pig squealing, but you can get a large variety of sounds.

 Sound is created by blowing air through the various-size pipes. Unless your organist enlists the help of about a hundred hot-aired music enthusiasts, a giant air bag (called *bellows*) sits under the organ loft — hidden from public view and kids carrying sharp objects. The bellows push air through the pipes. The longer the pipe, the lower the sound.

Most pipe organs have several rows of keyboards. Any single key on a keyboard can trigger one to a hundred pipes. Which pipes a key triggers is controlled by little knobs called *stops,* located on a panel near the keys.

If you have the chance, put your hands on a pipe organ and — as they say in show business — pull out all the stops. Any (and I mean *any*) note you play will sound wonderful and terrifying all at once. But not as terrifying as the organist shouting, "Who did that? Show yourself!"

Listen to Track 3 of the CD to hear the ominous sounds of a pipe organ, playing an excerpt from Bach's terrifyingly magnificent "Toccata and Fugue in D minor."

If you like the sounds of a pipe organ, listen to other classics written specifically for this complex and impressive instrument.

♪ Johann Sebastian Bach, *Toccata and Fugue in D minor*, E. Power Briggs (CBS); *Passacaglia and Fugue in C minor*, Virgil Fox (RCA)

♪ Camille Saint-Saëns, *Symphony No. 3 (Organ)*, Peter Hurford with Charles Dutroit and the Montreal Symphony (London)

♪ Andrew Lloyd Webber, *Phantom of the Opera - Broadway Cast Album* (Polydor)

Other wooden boxes with funny names

The centuries have seen the rise and fall of such ridiculously named instruments as the *psaltery*, the *virginals*, the *spinet*, the *hurdy-gurdy*, the *ottavina*, and the *harmonium*. Sounds like you're reading from a Dr. Seuss book, doesn't it? All of these acoustic keyboards were boxes of strings triggered in one way or another by a set of keys. Please send me an e-mail at blakeneely@aol.com if you have one.

The Electric Ones

For considerably less money than you shell out for an acoustic keyboard — not to mention no delivery fees — you can own an electric keyboard that can sound like just about any other instrument on the planet (including an acoustic keyboard).

The nuts and bolts (and knobs and buttons)

Without taking a screwdriver or welding torch to the body of your electric keyboard, you can probably surmise that there are no vibrating strings inside like the strings you find in an acoustic keyboard (see "The Acoustic Ones" in this chapter for more information).

Instead, a little thing called an *oscillator* produces a sound source that gets amplified over a loudspeaker. I won't get too technical, but the loudspeaker *does* vibrate, sending vibrations to your eardrum, causing you to hear the sound.

The electronic sound source is manipulated by a series of knobs, buttons, and sliders (more formally known as *knobs, buttons,* and *sliders*) which change the shape of the sound's *waveform*. I won't even begin to explain the scientific process of waveforms any further. Just trust me — you plug in your keyboard, hit a key, and it makes a sound.

Synthesizers

Like bakers, dancers, and burglars, synthesizers derive their name from the work they perform — they *synthesize* sound. (Burglars burgle, by the way.) Synthesizers can imitate virtually any instrument or sound effect you can think of plus tons of generic hums and buzzes that sound cool. Heck, you can make your synthesizer sound like the entire Vienna Philharmonic is in your living room — and without bringing in coffee or extra chairs.

A synthesizer, commonly known in this hip music industry as a *synth,* has a bunch of buttons, knobs, switches, and sliders that subtly change the shape of the waveform produced by the oscillating . . . oh, never mind. It has a bunch of doogies that change the sounds.

You want to hear some cool sounds? You got it. Track 4 features various bleeps, bloops, and blunders from various synthesizers. One of them even sounds like an orchestra.

If you create some really neat synthesizer sounds, you probably want others to hear them, right? That's what these artists do.

- ♪ Wendy Carlos, *Switched-On Bach,* (CBS)
- ♪ Kraftwerk, *Computer World,* (Elektra)
- ♪ Jean-Michel Jarre, *Oxygene,* (Dreyfus)
- ♪ Maurice Jarre, *Witness – Original Motion Picture Score* (Varése Sarabande)
- ♪ Vangelis, *Chariots of Fire – Original Motion Picture Score* (Polydor)

A major Mager contribution

Not too long after Thomas Edison discovered how to light up Times Square, others began putting electricity in musical instruments (careful with that oboe!).

In 1924, Jörg Mager made some attempts at synthesizing sounds. His creations were capable of imitating an infinite number of sounds by slightly altering the sound through a series of knobs and buttons.

The world's been oscillating ever since. Although modern synthesizers are far more complex (and, thankfully, more user-friendly) than Mager's early feats, the principle remains the same.

Electronic pianos and organs

If you were alive in the 1980s, you may have experienced an unavoidable shopping mall phenomenon I like to refer to as the "Organ in Every Home" craze. As Mom shopped for shoes, you were with the salesman at the organ shop, pushing knobs and buttons and playing rock song riffs by Journey and Bon Jovi. So was I.

Electronic pianos and organs became a huge success. Simply plug 'em in and have the kids gather 'round. Each comes in a compact size, even smaller than an upright piano, loaded with 10 to 20 different sounds — including piano, organ, trumpet, violin, and banjo.

Given their ability to imitate the sounds of other instruments, these keyboards are close relatives of the synthesizer. In fact, they use the same "brains" as a synthesizer. The difference, however, is that you can't change the sounds. Sure, you can change between a trumpet and piano sound, but you can't change the particular sound of the trumpet.

But thousands, even millions, of customers are not concerned with programming sounds. They are happy with the sounds they have and just want to play music, thus the electronic piano and organ craze continues.

Many of these electronic instruments feature a bonus *rhythm section*. With the push of a single button, you have a non-stop-always-on-the-beat drummer accompanying you on "Yankee Doodle." (Bossa nova, anyone?)

Hear an electronic organ at work, playing "Here Comes the Bride" on Track 5 of the CD, complete with the rhythm section. It's quite alright if you feel the need to dance or shout, "I do! I do!"

Read more about the types of electric keyboards, synthesizers, electronic organs, and their many wealthy manufacturers in Chapter 16.

Chapter 2

What Your Parents Never Told You About Posture

Good posture, including how you sit and how you hold your hands, keeps you comfortable at your keyboard for hours on end.

Practicing good posture while you play also helps you avoid cramped hands, a tired back, and even more serious medical problems like carpal tunnel syndrome. After you're a famous concert pianist, you can look back fondly on Chapter 2 of this book and remember how it helped prepare you for a career with the keyboard.

To Sit or Not to Sit

Depending on the type of keyboard — and sometimes the type of stage — that you are playing on, you can either sit or stand while you play.

As a general rule, concert pianists sit at the piano, but many rock keyboardists stand behind their boards. I've never been quite sure why on the latter. Perhaps rock keyboardists are jealous that the guitarist and singer can run around on stage. Maybe they want the audience to have a better view of them playing. Or maybe they're just tired of sitting from all those days on the tour bus.

As a beginner, however, I advise that you begin your musical endeavors in a seated position. No matter what kind of keyboard you play, sitting brings you closer to the keys, which makes picking out unfamiliar notes a little bit easier.

Whether sitting or standing, you should be comfortable at all times. Your feet should rest firmly on the floor. Your hands should have a nice relaxed arch to them. The keys should be at an appropriate height so that your hands and forerams are parallel to the ground, as shown in Figure 2-1. That's my hand and arm. Lovely, yes?

Figure 2-1:
Positions,
everyone.

Make sure your back is straight and that you are not slumping, slouching, or hunching over. Not sitting up straight leads to backaches — the kind that discourage you from practicing.

Chairs versus benches

If you choose to sit, you have a few options: a chair, a bench, or a devoted teacher or fan who will hold you. I don't advise the last option, because the adoring devotee tends to drop you when overcome by the need to applaud during your big solo. Needless to say, this is not the ideal time to fall to the floor.

So, now you're down to either a chair or a bench. Both are acceptable, and both are readily available at most piano stores and concert halls. Of course, either one you choose has its pros and cons.

Chairs

When I say *chair*, I'm not talking about a recliner with flip-out footrest and side pockets for the TV remote. I'm talking about standard-issue piano chairs, which are usually plain, black chairs. Many have a padded seat, and a few offer a mechanism to raise or lower the height of the seat just a bit.

The back on a chair does provide some added support, but the back may cause you to slump more just because you can. As Mom and Dad always told you, slumping isn't very attractive or good for your back. Also, the extra wood on chair backs often tends to creak, which is not a pleasant sound during a performance of Debussy's *Clair de Lune*.

But paradoxically, the back on a chair is also its main advantage. The extra support is good for young, sometimes fidgety students, because they feel a bit more secure on a chair than on a backless bench. Heck, strap on a booster seat for the young child prodigy. Plus, like it or not, admit it or not, everyone slumps occasionally. Late at night, as you continue to practice diligently, I won't tell anybody if you slump against the back of the chair a little bit. Who can complain when at least you're practicing!

In my opinion, the biggest drawback of a chair is the inability to accommodate a duet partner. Many pianists enjoy playing duets with friends, where you sit side-by-side and play the keyboard in two parts: one of you playing the lower notes, the other playing the upper notes. Sure, you can just pull up another chair, but where's the romance in that?

Benches

The standard piano bench, which you see in Figure 2-2, measures approximately 2 feet high by 3 feet wide. The width allows ample room for shifting your "seat" to reach higher or lower notes while you play, as well as for the addition of a duet partner.

Height is an important function of whatever you choose to sit on while playing. However, many piano benches are not adjustable, forcing you to lean up into the keyboard or to sit on top of phone books. The nicer benches come with big round knobs on the side, used to adjust the stool's height for a more personal fit. The better benches also offer padding, which you begin to appreciate after a few hours of hard practice.

Unlike a chair, a bench provides no back support, leaving you to keep a straight spine throughout the performance. This can be a good thing, though, as it forces good posture during your playing. However, no back support also means no protection from falling backwards when you become too excited during the climax of a Bartók concerto or your jamming rock solo.

The coolest thing about piano benches is that some have hinged seats, allowing you to open the seat and store sheet music, books, or even a mid-concert snack. Just don't forget what you leave in there. I once lost my car keys for a week!

Figure 2-2:
Your typical
piano
bench.

Stands and racks

Keyboard stands (see Figure 2-3) come in all shapes and sizes. Some are multi-tiered for adding more and more keyboards as your career or bank account grows. Keyboard stands are also offered in different colors. If you don't like the colors, you can always buy a can of spray paint.

Nearly every stand is adjustable, because the manufacturer is never exactly sure just how tall their client base is. This adjustment also allows you to spread multiple keyboards farther apart on the stand to allow easy access to the various buttons and knobs on each. You can also adjust the height of the keyboard so that you can sit or stand, depending on your mood. Just make sure that the keys are at the proper height (refer to Figure 2-1).

Adjust the height of each keyboard so that your hands are comfortable and all knobs and sliders are easily accessible. If your keyboard has a lighted display, make it clearly visible from where you sit or stand, not hidden by the keyboard or a hanging plant.

Figure 2-3:
Take a
stand.

—The stand

In addition to a stand, you may also need a *rack*. This is a wooden or metal box with holed brackets along the edge into which you can screw various components, samplers, effects processors, mixers, or even drawers. (See Chapter 16 for more on the various types of keyboard accessories.) Racks can be stationary or on rollers, according to your personal needs and desires.

It's All in the Hands

I can't stress enough how important hand posture and comfort are while playing the piano or keyboard. Poor hand posture can cause your performance to suffer for two reasons:

♪ **Lack of dexterity:** If your hands are in tight, awkward positions, you can't access the keys quickly and efficiently. Your performance will sound clumsy and be full of wrong notes.

♪ **Potential for cramping:** If your hands cramp often, you won't practice often. If you don't practice often, you won't be a very good player.

Cut those nails

When I was a kid, I had a piano teacher with fingernails so long that all I could hear was the clicking of her nails against the keys as she played. I felt like Mom was taking me to typing class every Tuesday, rather than piano lessons.

My point is simple: Keep your fingernails short, or at least at a reasonable length. Your audience wants to hear beautiful piano music, not clickety-click-click.

Arch those fingers

When you place your hands on the keys, you must keep your hands arched and your fingers slightly curled at all times. It feels weird at first, but you can't improve your playing technique until you get used to holding your hands this way. Arching your hands and fingers pays off with the following benefits:

- ♪ Your hands don't get tired as quickly.
- ♪ Your hands are less likely to cramp.
- ♪ You can quickly access any key, black or white.

If you know how to type, you have already assumed this arched-hand position — you hold your hands exactly the same way on the keyboard. If you're lucky enough not to be familiar with typing, find two tennis balls (or similarly sized balls) and hold one in each hand, as demonstrated with my beautifully manicured right hand in Figure 2-4. This is how your hand should look when you play the piano . . . of course, minus the ball.

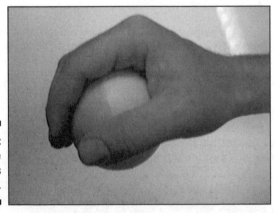

Figure 2-4:
Arch those
hands
proudly.

Pick a finger, any finger

Correct *fingering* — using the best finger to play each note of a song — is always a very important part of piano playing. Some pieces, even the easy ones, have fingerings marked in the sheet music. These fingerings help you plan which fingers to use to execute a particular musical passage most efficiently and comfortably.

The fingerings you see in music correspond to the left- and right-hand fingering you see in Figure 2-5. Think of your fingers as being numbered 1 through 5. Begin with the thumb as number 1 and move towards the little finger, or pinkie.

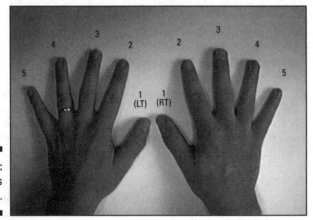

Figure 2-5:
Numbers and digits.

While you get used to thinking of your fingers in terms of numbers, you may find it helpful to write these numbers on your hands. I advise using non-permanent markers or fingernail polish. Otherwise, you'll have to explain those numbered fingers to your date on Friday night, your boss on Monday morning, or your homeroom teacher.

A Serious Pain

Poor posture can lead to the beginning of serious and painful problems in your piano career. The sports claim "no pain, no gain" has no validity when applied to piano playing. Simply put, if you hurt, you won't play. If you don't play, you won't be very good.

Feeling cramped

Even if your posture is absolutely perfect, your hands will inevitably begin to cramp at some point. Cramps are your body's way of saying, "Hey, let's go do something else for a while." By all means, listen to your body.

Generally, you'll experience hand cramps long before you experience any other kind of body cramp during practice. Your back and neck may become sore from poor posture, but your hands begin to cramp simply from too much use.

If your hands hurt, take a long break and do something that creates a completely opposite hand action. For example, throwing a ball to your dog is an opposite hand action; typing is not. If your whole body hurts, hire a masseuse or take a luxurious cruise in the South Pacific. You deserve it.

Carpal tunnel syndrome

Much has been said about a career-oriented injury called *carpal tunnel syndrome (CTS)*. Without getting into its technical definition (because, frankly, I'm no doctor), suffice it to say that it is produced by overstraining the muscles and ligaments in your wrist through a constant, repetitive action. Piano playing is a constant, repetitive action.

As you can probably imagine, many a keyboardist and secretary experience CTS during their careers. Unfortunately, many wait until it's too late for a simple remedy. What starts out as a dull pain in the forearms, wrist, and fingers is ignored until it becomes a severe pain whenever the hands are in motion. Severe CTS requires surgery to remedy, but the results are not always 100 percent effective. Piano players need 100 percent of their hand motion, so don't let any pain go unnoticed.

If you are concerned by pains in your wrist, no matter how minor, consult your physician for ways to reduce or prevent it. You may get lucky and be sent home from school or work to watch TV, eat ice cream, and recover.

Of course, if you already have CTS, talk with your physician about your piano playing goals and ask what steps to take to prevent any further damage or pain. Your doctor will probably ask how you got interested in the piano, giving you an excellent opportunity to wholeheartedly endorse this book.

Recipe for a "squishy"

Keeping a "squishy" nearby to squeeze can supply some relief whenever you feel a hand cramp starting. Follow the recipe and make your own, or look for something similar at your local drug store. To make a squishy, you need the following ingredients.

♪ Two latex balloons

♪ Two handfuls of very small pebbles, sand, or rice

♪ One permanent marker

In a medium-sized bowl, stir the sand, rice, or small pebbles until they are the consistency of sand, rice, or small pebbles. Carefully pour or insert the batter into one of the latex balloons. Continue until the entire balloon is full.

Tie a knot in the end of the full balloon. Put the full balloon inside the other balloon for an added layer of latex and tie a knot at the top of the outer balloon. Take a marker and draw a big smiley face or your favorite band logo on the fat side of the balloon.

Let your squishy chill until cramping begins. Squeeze it to your heart's desire to alleviate cramping.

Chapter 3

Eighty-Eight Keys, Three Pedals, Ten Fingers, and Two Feet

. . . .

In This Chapter

▶ Exposing the ebonies and ivories

▶ Picture this: Blake's E-Z Key Finder

▶ Putting the pedals to the metal

. . . .

*Y*ou're staring at all these keys, trying to make sense of the whole thing, and wondering why you didn't just buy a pair of cymbals and call it a day. I've been there. It seems quite intimidating, but to paraphrase the Jackson Five: It's as easy as A-B-C, 1-2-3.

In this chapter, I help you get acquainted with all the finer features on the piano, including the keys and the pedals.

Blake's E-Z Key Finder

The first thing you notice on your keyboard is the not-so-colorful use of black and white keys aligned from left to right. The black ones are slightly raised and appear to be set further back than the white ones, as you can see in Figure 3-1.

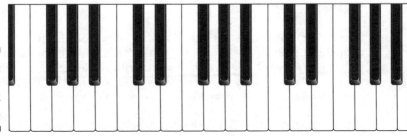

Figure 3-1: Your basic set of black and whites.

If the black and white keys are reversed, you're either playing a very old keyboard — I worry about you walking home from the museum at night — or the manufacturer messed up and you got an enormous discount. Congratulations!

Each key on the keyboard represents a specific musical note. These notes use a very complex naming system — the alphabet. Even more complex, I say tongue-in-cheek, is the use of only seven of the alphabet's letters: A-B-C-D-E-F-G. I have no easy way for you to remember these seven letters, except start with A and don't say H.

The names of the keys correspond to the names of musical notes. (Chapter 4 explains note names.) For now, just realize that a G key plays a G note, an A key plays an A note, and so on.

I know what you're thinking: "I'm looking at 88 keys but I only have seven alphabet letters to name all those keys! How do I name all the other keys?" For all 88 keys, the basic set of seven letter names repeats over and over.

In the following sections, I show you how to use my E-Z Key Finder technique to locate the different notes on the keyboard. After you read my technique, you'll have an unforgettable way to find any key on the board.

The white keys

To make things really easy, the seven note names (A-B-C-D-E-F-G) are all on the white keys. The black keys have names of their own, but for now you can use the black keys as landmarks to find the correct white keys . . . even in the dark!

You read that correctly. Ladies and gentlemen, boys and girls, penguins and parakeets, I present to you the first instrument ever equipped with a sort of musical Braille system: The raised black keys help you locate any white key quickly and precisely.

You may observe fairly quickly that the black keys always appear in consecutive groups of two and three. There are never two sets of two black keys or two sets of three black keys in a row. This distinction of twos and threes is important and makes the job of finding white keys even easier — as easy as eating.

Use your imagination and think of any set of two black keys as a pair of chopsticks. Think of any set of three black keys as the tines on a fork. (Take a glance at Figure 3-2.) *Chopsticks* starts with the letter "C" and *fork* starts with the letter "F." This handy memory-device forms the basis of my E-Z Key Finder technique for finding the white keys on the keyboard:

  ♪ To the left of the *chopsticks* (two black keys) is the note *C*.

  ♪ To the left of the *fork* (three black keys) is the note *F*.

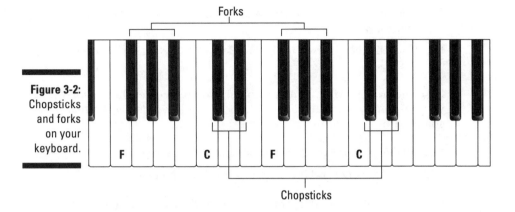

Figure 3-2: Chopsticks and forks on your keyboard.

Forks

Chopsticks

Allow that to sink in, and you won't forget it. But what about the other white keys, you ask? You know the alphabet fairly well, don't you? Look at the alphabet letters again:

A-B-C-D-E-F-G

Notice what letters surround C and what letters surround F. The same advanced logic applies to the white keys surrounding C and F. Moving up from C you have the notes D, E, F, G. When you get to G, think "Go" as in "go back to the beginning of the alphabet." The alphabet pattern repeats over and over again on the keyboard, as many times as you see chopsticks and forks on the keyboard.

To practice finding notes, take your chopsticks and fork and play every C and F on the keyboard, from bottom to top. Then locate every D and G. Test yourself by playing all the other white keys while reciting the names of the keys. With the aid of your utensils, you'll never forget a key's name.

The black keys

Play A, then B, then the black key in between A and B. You'll notice that it sounds like a different musical note. You're correct: Black keys do represent separate musical notes.

However, because no alphabet letter comes between the letters A and B, the black key between these two can't be given a logical alphabet name. "What do we do?" pondered the old key namers, a respectable but short-lived profession.

Not much for originality — the key namers only worked with the first seven letters of the alphabet — the black keys were assigned the same name as the closest white key but with one of the following suffixes added on:

♪ The suffix *sharp* is used for a black key to the *right* of (or *higher* than) a white key.

♪ The suffix *flat* is used for a black key to the *left* of (or *lower* than) a white key.

I use another culinary metaphor to help you remember these suffixes. At your imaginary musical place setting, a white key represents a plate. (Hey, some plates are white!) Here you go:

♪ A knife is *sharp* and lays on the *right* side of the plate.

♪ A napkin is *flat* and lays on the *left* side of the plate.

Put it to the test: Find the D plate (key). To the right is a sharp knife, D-sharp. To the left is a flat napkin, D-flat. Easy enough? Just remember chopsticks and forks, knives and napkins, and you'll never forget the names of the keys . . . but you may feel a little hungry.

You quickly see that because each of the black keys lies between two white keys, each black key has two names, depending from which white key you are approaching it. For example, the black key to the right of C is C-sharp. But wait — it is also D-flat. The split personality of each black key (note) seems odd at first, but after you get the hang of seeing each key from two different perspectives, it isn't that awkward.

You probably already noticed, and puzzled over, the fact that no black keys reside between B and C or E and F. Before you demand a full refund from your local keyboard dealer, you should know that this is no mistake. Theoretically, C is also B-sharp and, similarly, E is also F-flat. But this is way too much needless theory. Suffice it to say that there are no notes between B and C or E and F. You'll survive without knowing why.

Pedal Power

When you play the keyboard, your hands are busy picking at the keys; introducing *pedals* (down there by your feet) to control other aspects of the music.

Most pianos have two or three pedals, while synthesizers can have even more. Pipe organs often incorporate an entire keyboard of pedals to be played by the feet. I won't go into the details of the pipe organ pedals — if you play a pipe organ, you can find a whole host of teachers at your disposal to help you figure out the pedals (see Chapter 1 to understand how rare, and expensive, pipe organs are).

The various pedals on your instrument allow you to achieve effects with your music, which I list later in this section. Most of the time, the composer of a musical piece tells you when to use which pedal, but you should feel free to experiment with the pedals and the interpretations they can bring to your music.

Piano pedals

Most pianos come equipped with three pedals, shown in Figure 3-3. To the far right is the *damper pedal* (or *sustain pedal*). When you hold this pedal down, the *dampers* — mechanisms which mute the strings — are moved away from the strings, allowing the strings to ring until (a) you release the pedal, (b) the sound gradually fades away, or (c) you fall asleep and fall off the bench.

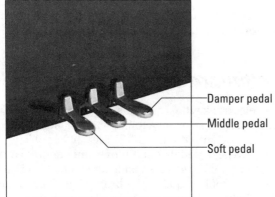

Damper pedal

Middle pedal

Soft pedal

Figure 3-3:
Fun with pedals.

Most musicians, and even non-musicians who purport to know something about music, refer to the damper pedal as "the pedal." This is either because it's the most popular and most frequently used pedal, or because no one can remember the real name.

You don't have to use the damper pedal every time you play a note. Actually, each key has its own damper. When you play a key, the damper for that key moves away and allows the strings for that key to vibrate (sound) until you release the key. Dampers for any keys you aren't playing stay in place and mute their respective strings. The damper pedal lifts the dampers away from all of the strings at once.

To the far left you have the *soft pedal.* This pedal actually shifts the entire set of 88 keys and hammers ever-so-slightly to the right. This shift causes the hammers to strike a *key's string,* or set of strings, in a different spot and create a softer sound.

On many pianos you see a third pedal in the middle: the *middle pedal.* Unlike the damper pedal, which sustains all notes being played, the middle pedal allows you to sustain a specific note, or group of notes, while you continue playing other notes normally. Play a key on the piano and at the same time (not before) hold down the middle pedal . . . the sound sustains. Now, quickly play other notes and you'll notice they do not sustain. Pretty cool, right? Well, pretty difficult, too — especially in the midst of playing Rachmaninoff's *Piano Concerto No. 3.* Many piano manufacturers now opt to save money and delete this feature.

On some upright pianos, the middle pedal has an entirely different function: It inserts a layer of felt between the hammers and strings to make the sound much softer and more muffled. This allows you to practice late at night without disturbing others. You might call it the "good neighbor" pedal.

Electric keyboard pedals

The most common electric keyboard pedals are the sustain pedal (which performs the same function as on an acoustic piano) and volume pedal (which makes your music softer and louder). Nearly every keyboard comes with one or the other. These pedals don't move any dampers or shift any keys, because there are no real strings inside an electric keyboard. Instead, the pedal sends an electronic signal to the brain of your keyboard, telling it to "keep oscillating, baby." (Chapter 1 tells you more about the brain of an electric keyboard.)

Other pedals you can add to your electric keyboard control such things as *vibrato* (which makes the note sound as if it is warbling), program changes, special effects, acceleration . . . no, I'm sorry, that last one is for a car.

You can sample these various pedals and decide which one's right for you at your local electric keyboard dealer. The salesperson will be more than happy to show you a whole line of different pedals, hoping that you want to spend even more money. (See Chapter 16 for more helpful information on shopping for keyboards and accessories.)

Part II
Getting Sound Down on Paper

The 5th Wave   By Rich Tennant

"This piece comes with accidentals already in it? You mean I don't produce enough on my own?"

In this part . . .

When you travel to a foreign land, you should bone up on the local language so that you can easily ask for directions, order a cheeseburger, and translate what the people on the elevator are saying about you.

When you travel to your piano to play some music, it's not only advisable but *critical* to understand the language of music. That's what this part is all about — understanding what all those lines and symbols mean and how they translate into the songs that you love to hear and play. *Parlez-vous musique?*

Chapter 4

Following Horizontal and Vertical Lines

In This Chapter

▶ Figuring out all those lines

▶ Deciphering what those doo-hickeys stand for

▶ Discovering how written notes relate to the keyboard

Bees buzzing, computers humming, and power tools (um) power tooling are all sounds that can't be easily deciphered and written down on paper. In frustration, humans decide that these noises mean nothing to them and move on with their lives. But humans are incapable of being so blasé when it comes to two other types of sound: speech and music. Because this isn't *Speech For Dummies,* I'll cut to the chase.

To play music, you have to know what note to play and when. A piano has 88 keys to play, each sounding a different musical note. (Chapter 3 tells you all about those 88 keys on the keyboard.) With a bunch of lines and dots, a composer tells you which notes to play, which of the 88 keys to press, and how long to play each note. In this chapter, I get you started on how each of these elements is written down in music.

Thou Art with Me, My Clef, My Staff, and My Notes

When you look at a piece of printed music, like "Humoresque," the first thing you may notice are a bunch of dots and circles. These dots and circles represent *notes*. Each written note tells you two essential things:

♪ What key to play

♪ How long to play that key

Humoresque

It won't take you long to notice that the notes aren't out there on the page by themselves. Look at the lines the notes sit on. Without these lines, the notes are . . . well, just dots and circles.

Employing a staff of five

Writing on lines keeps things looking neat and pretty. Unlike the ruled-paper notebooks you use in school or for your journal, the lines on a music page aren't there just to make the notes straight.

Figure 4-1 shows a set of the parallel lines you find in music. Count 'em — you should count five, in all. Now count the spaces in between the lines and hopefully you get the number four.

Figure 4-1:
Music's
parallel
lines.

Together, these five lines and four spaces comprise a musical *staff*. It's an appropriate name, because a composer "employs" his staff to hold the notes he's writing. And what a staff to have! No complaining, no vacation time, no tardiness excuses — just some inanimate lines and spaces.

Each line and space represents a specific musical note. The notes are named with the first seven alphabet letters, A-B-C-D-E-F-G, just like the white keys on the keyboard. (You can read more about the letters assigned to each of the keyboard keys in Chapter 3.) Each line and space is also named one of these letters. That way, when you see a note on the G line, you know to play the G key. See how everything is lining up?

Looking at your keyboard, you can see that there are several of each of the seven notes. For example, you see several separate G keys on the keyboard. Obviously, five lines and four spaces aren't enough to accommodate all 88 keys. Before you panic, realize that you have a few more options.

Hanging from a clef

Rather than adding more lines and spaces to accommodate all the occurrences of each of the seven notes, you get a symbol to help out with the job. Think of it as your secret decoder ring, Captain Music Maker. Look at Figure 4-2 and notice the little squiggly thing at the far left of the staff. This ornamental creature is called a *clef*.

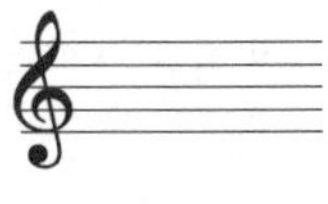

Figure 4-2:
The clef.

The clef's sole purpose in life is to tell you the names of the lines and spaces on the staff. If the clef could talk, it would say something like, "For this set of notes the lines and spaces represent these keys." But how weird is a talking clef?

Music uses several different clefs, but as a keyboard player you're in luck — you only need to know two of them. Think of it as having a clef for each hand.

Treble clef

Generally, the *treble clef* (refer to Figure 4-2) signals notes to be played by the right hand. This clef is also called the *G clef,* for the following two reasons:

♪ It looks like a stylized G (very stylized).

♪ It circles around the second staff line which (not coincidentally) represents the note G.

It's also possible to think of this clef as a stylized T for "treble," but don't quote me on that in any snobbish music circles.

The G line encircled by the treble clef isn't for just any old G key. It's the G that is closest to the middle of your keyboard (see Figure 4-3 for a guide). After you've found this G, reading the other lines and spaces on the staff is as easy as reciting the alphabet.

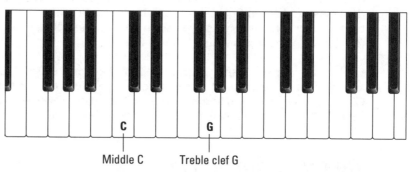

Figure 4-3: Gee, finding the G wasn't too hard.

Middle C   Treble clef G

If you're close to a keyboard, put a right-hand finger on this G key. (If you're not close to a keyboard, then refer to the keys you see in Figure 4-3.) The next white key up (to the right) of the G is represented by the next space up on the staff. According to my E-Z Key Finder in Chapter 3, G stands for "Go back to the beginning of the alphabet," so the next white key on the keyboard and the next space up on the staff correspond to the note A.

Continue up and down the staff and you get the musical notes you see in Figure 4-4.

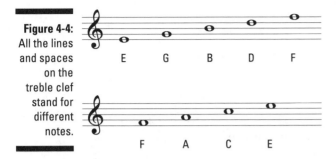

Figure 4-4:
All the lines and spaces on the treble clef stand for different notes.

You may be wondering why none of the black keys is represented by the lines and spaces. Chapter 3 explains that the black keys are sharps and flats. Instead of adding more lines and spaces to show the sharps and flats, a much simpler approach places these sharps and flats on the same lines or spaces as their "root" note but with a little symbol next to the note. So, B-flat sits on the B line with a little flat symbol next to it, as shown in Figure 4-5.

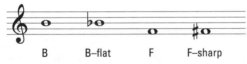

Figure 4-5:
Flats and sharps are marked by these symbols.

Bass clef

Most often, your left hand plays the lower notes on the keyboard, which are also called *bass* notes. For the record, that's pronounced like "base," not like the fish you lied about catching last weekend.

The rules of equality demand that the left hand get its own clef, too. Introducing the *bass clef* (see Figure 4-6). Like the treble clef, the bass clef surrounds a particular line that represents a particular note — the note F. You can remember the special relationship between the bass clef and the note F by thinking about the following two things:

♪ The bass clef looks like a stylized F (use your imagination).

♪ The bass clef's two dots surround the staff line that represents the note F.

You can call the bass clef the *F clef,* if you like, or think of it as a stylized B — the dots are the humps — for "bass." Again, you didn't hear that from me when Professor Uppity asks.

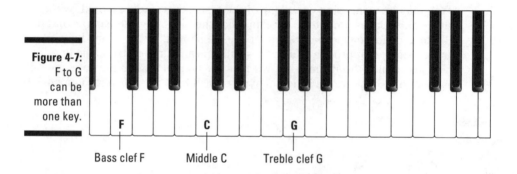

Figure 4-6:
The bass
clef.

Don't think that the bass clef surronds the F just below the treble
clef G. It doesn't! Instead, this F is one set of keys lower on the
keyboard (see Figure 4-7).

Figure 4-7:
F to G
can be
more than
one key.

Bass clef F   Middle C   Treble clef G

To read the notes on the bass clef, simply start with the F line and travel
down, or backwards, and up, or forwards, through the alphabet. Figure 4-8
shows you the notes on the bass clef staff.

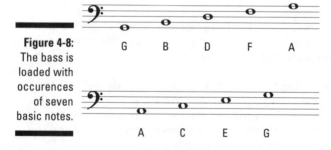

Figure 4-8:
The bass is
loaded with
occurences
of seven
basic notes.

G   B   D   F   A

A   C   E   G

On both the treble and bass staff, notice that the bottom line and top space
have the same letter name. Same goes for the bottom space and top line on
each staff. Figure 4-9 illustrates my point beautifully.

Mnemonics help you remember the mnotes

Having trouble remembering the names of the lines and spaces for each staff (and consequently, the notes they represent)? Use a *mnemonic,* a word or phrase created from the letter names of these lines and spaces, to help you remember.

I like the following mnemonics, but feel free to make up your own. Unless otherwise noted, these mnemonics start on the bottom line of each staff and go up:

Treble clef lines (E-G-B-D-F):

♪ **Traditional (but sexist):** *Every Good Boy Does Fine*

♪ **Musical:** *Every Good Band Draws Fans*

♪ **Pianistic:** *Even Gershwin Began (as a) Dummy First*

♪ **Culinary:** *Eating Green Bananas Disgusts Friends*

♪ **Shameless:** *Every Good Book (is a) Dummies Favorite*

Treble clef spaces (F-A-C-E):

♪ **Traditional:** *FACE* (like the one holding your nose)

♪ **Musical:** *Forks And Chopsticks Everywhere* (See Chapter 3.)

♪ **Laundry (start with top space):** *Eventually Colors Always Fade*

Bass clef lines (G-B-D-F-A):

♪ **Recreational:** *Good Bikes Don't Fall Apart*

♪ **Musical:** *Great Beethoven's Deafness Frustrated All*

♪ **Musical:** *Grandpa Bach Did Fugues A lot*

♪ **Painful:** *Giving Blood Doesn't Feel Agreeable*

Bass clef spaces (A-C-E-G):

♪ **Musical:** *American Composers Envy Gershwin*

♪ **Animal:** *All Cows Eat Grass*

♪ **Revenge (start with top space):** *Get Even, Call Avon*

Read enough of these, and you'll be hard-pressed to forget them. Of course, if you do happen to forget these helpful mnemonics, simply find the line encircled by the clef and move up or down the alphabet from there.

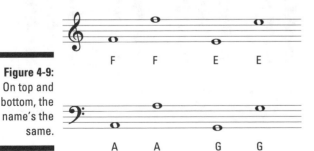

Figure 4-9: On top and bottom, the name's the same.

Double Your Staff, Double Your Fun

Sooner or later, on either staff, you run out of lines and spaces for your notes. Surely the composer wants you to use more of the fabulous 88 keys at your disposal, right? Here's a solution: Because you play piano with both hands at the same time, why not show both *staves* (plural form of "staff") on the music page? Great idea!

Grand staffing

Join both staves together and you get one *grand staff* (it's really called that), as shown in Figure 4-10. This way, you can read notes for both hands at the same time.

Figure 4-10:
Ain't these
staves
grand?

Why all the wasted space between the two staves? I'm glad you asked. Look at the treble (top) staff and name the notes downward from G. You'll notice that you only get to E before running out of lines. What to do?

Now go to F on the bass (bottom) clef and name the notes upward. You only get to A. What about the remaining B, C, C-sharp, D, and D-sharp in between A and E, shown in Figure 4-11?

Figure 4-11:
Where are
the lines
and spaces
for these
little guys?

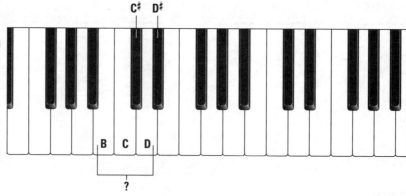

The grand staff has an "imaginary" solution. Imagine, if you will, another line running between both staves. This line creates spaces that can hold three extra notes and the applicable sharps and flats for each, as shown in Figure 4-12.

Figure 4-12:
Making
room for
more notes.

Notice what this line does to the grand staff — it makes it practically impossible to read. Instead, the staves are spread apart and a very small line is used in the middle for C — just wide enough to hold the note — as shown in Figure 4-13. You call this a *ledger line,* often spelled without the "d" as *leger,* but that just looks wrong.

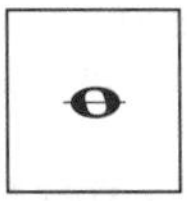

Figure 4-13:
A thin little
line to hold
more notes.

Squeezing in the middle

The note C that occupies the ledger line in between the staves is called — drum roll, please — *middle C.* Coincidentally, middle C is the white key located just about dead center on your piano. On some pianos, the middle C is labeled "C4," because it's the fourth C from the bottom.

To remember the name of this ledger line note forever, just think of it as the note floating in the *middle* of the *sea* (C) between the staves. And my, how this note does float! Middle C "floats" to one of two positions between the staves, depending on which hand you use to play the note. Figure 4-14 shows middle C in its two positions. When it's closer to the treble clef staff, you play it with your right hand; if it appears closer to the bass clef staff, you use your left hand.

The notes B and D can also float around, depending on which hand plays them. That is, D can either cling to the bottom of the treble clef staff, or it can sit on top of the middle C ledger line. Similarly, B can sit on top of the bass clef staff or attach itself to the bottom of the middle C ledger line. Figure 4-15 illustrates these floating note positions.

Figure 4-14:
Floating
on the C.

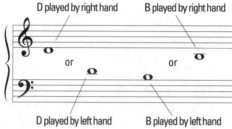

Figure 4-15:
Playing the
same note
with
different
hands.

D played by right hand   B played by right hand

or   or

D played by left hand   B played by left hand

Climbing up the staff and beyond

Middle C may be powerful, but it isn't the only note to receive the coveted ledger line award. Other ledger lines come into play when you get to notes that won't fit on the lines and spaces created by the treble and bass clefs.

For example, the top line of the treble staff is F. Just above this line, sits the note G. After G, a whole new set of ledger lines waits to bust out.

A similar situation occurs at the bottom of the bass staff. Ledger lines begin popping up after the low G line and low F that's hanging on to the staff for dear life. Figure 4-16 illustrates all of this ledger line fun.

Remembering these ledger lines is simple: Both sets of three ledger lines (on either staff) spell "ACE." Once you know them, you too will be an ace.

Solving the mysteries that lurk between the clefs

For me, and hopefully for you, the existence of middle C clears up some very big questions about the staves — what I call Staff Line Mysteries (soon to be an Agatha Christie paperback):

♪ If it's so important, then why isn't G on the middle line of the treble staff?

♪ Likewise, why isn't F on the middle of the bass staff?

The answer to both of these mysteries is, of course, that the staff positions of G and F are determined by their distance from middle C. You might say middle C has some power in the musical world.

Rising (or falling) to the occasion

Composers can't use ledger lines to notate all the notes that fall outside the boundaries of the treble and bass clefs — if they did, each staff would take up an impractical amount of space on the printed page. Instead, composers use abbreviations to point you to the appropriate notes.

The abbreviation *8va* tells you to play the same note but one key set higher. For example, when you see *8va* above the note F on the top line of the treble staff, it means to play the next F up on the keyboard.

When you see *8vb* below a note, you play the same note but one key set lower. Think of the "b" in *8vb* as meaning "below." For example, *8vb* under the note G on the bottom line of the bass staff instructs you to play the next lower G key.

If the composer wants a really, really high or low note, you see the abbreviation *15ma* or *15mb*, which means to play two sets of keys higher or lower. Don't ask me why 2 times 8va equals 15ma. The laws of musical math are just funny that way.

Figure 4-16: Bustin' out the ledgers.

Lines Heading North and South

In addition to horizontal lines, music employs some verticals, too. These vertical lines help you keep track of where you are in the music, sort of like punctuation in a written sentence.

Reading this paragraph is a bit difficult it has no punctuation it is like one long sentence never ending that's because without capital letters or punctuation marks it is difficult to understand the phrasing of a sentence music is like that too.

Think of the single or grand staff as one very long musical paragraph. The notes are the words. The vertical lines are the commas and periods, breaking up the musical paragraph into intelligible musical phrases. An example of these vertical lines is shown in Figure 4-17.

Chapter 5 tells you more about these vertical lines and the important function they play when it comes to rhythm.

Figure 4-17:
Vertical
lines that
divide the
staff.

Don't Stop 'Til You Get Enough

As you read this book, you can instantly see that each page has several lines of text. You don't stop reading when you get to the edge of the page or the end of a line. Rather, your eyes continue to read from left to right, reaching the end of one line and immediately falling to the beginning of the next line. You keep reading until you get to the end of the book, the end of the sentence, or until dinner's ready.

Reading music is similar. You play the notes on the staff from left to right. When you get to the end of the staff, or edge of the page, you drop down to the beginning of the next staff, or set of staves, and keep playing. (This applies to reading from either a single staff or a grand staff.) Figure 4-18 shows you what I mean. Notice that the appropriate clefs appear on every new line of music.

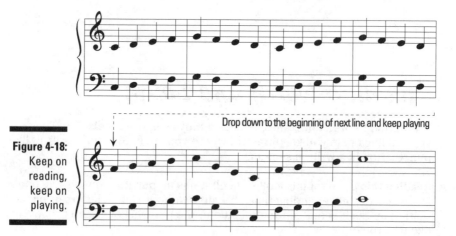

Drop down to the beginning of next line and keep playing

Figure 4-18:
Keep on
reading,
keep on
playing.

Chapter 5

Joining the Rhythm Nation

● ●

In This Chapter

▶ Making some notes last longer than others

▶ Recognizing note shapes

▶ Measuring music without a ruler

● ●

Music is not just a series of long, sustained, droning tones. Sure, this description may apply to a few 20th century classical pieces — and that stuff bagpipers play — but you probably want to play some songs that make people dance or, at the very least, make them stay awake.

In this chapter, I show you just how important the timing of your notes is when playing the piano. As they say, timing is everything.

The Beat Goes On

When you listen to music played on the keyboard, or any other instrument for that matter, you hear notes of different lengths. Some notes sound as long as a fog horn; other notes are quite short, like a bird chirping; and others are of a medium length, like the ring of a telephone.

Depending on how long the notes in a musical piece are played, the music can sound fast, slow, or somewhere in between. These varying lengths of the different notes combine to form the *rhythm* of the music. Whether it's a fast-paced dance song or a slow love song, the rhythm provides the groovy groove to the music.

Measuring the beat

Rhythm is measured out in *beats*. Like heartbeats, musical beats are measured over time. A certain number of beats occur in music (and in your heart) every minute. If you're like me, when a doctor tells you how fast your heart is beating, you think "Who cares? I don't know what those numbers mean." But when a composer tells you how many musical beats occur in a specific length of musical time, you can't take such a whimsical attitude — not if you want the music to sound right.

To help you understand beats and how they're measured, look at a clock or your watch and tap your foot once every second. Hear that? You're tapping beats — one beat per second. Of course, not all beats last one second. Look at the clock again and tap your foot two times for every second.

How fast or how slow you tap these beats is called *tempo.* For example, when you tap one beat for every second, the tempo is 60 beats per minute, because there are 60 seconds in one minute. Tap two beats per second and the tempo becomes twice as fast, or 120 beats per minute.

Okay, that's enough math, but this example can help you to understand the relationship of music and rhythm to time. Think of a music staff as a time line. (Chapter 4 tells you all about the music staff.) In the same way that the face of a clock can be divided into minutes and seconds, the music staff can also be divided into smaller units of time. These smaller units of time help you count the beat and know where you are in the song at all times.

Breaking things up with vertical lines

A short three-minute song can have 200 separate beats or more. To keep from getting lost in this myriad of beats, it helps to count the beats as you play. But rather than ask you to count up into three-digit numbers, the composer groups the beats into nice small batches called *measures* (or *bars*).

Each measure has a specific number of beats. Most commonly, a measure has four beats. This smaller grouping of four beats is much easier to count: Just think "1, 2, 3, 4" and then begin again with "1" in each subsequent measure.

The composer decides how many beats to put in each measure and then marks each measure (or bar) with a vertical line called a *barline,* as shown in Figure 5-1.

Why does it matter how many beats are in each measure? If the composer wants every fifth beat emphasized, a measure with four beats helps you keep track of which beats to emphasize.

Figure 5-2 shows a staff with several measures of beats. The slash marks represent each beat. Clap these beats as you count out loud. The first time you try it, don't emphasize any of the beats. The next time, emphasize the first beat of each measure a little more than the other three by clapping louder. Notice how this emphasis adds a little pulse to the overall rhythm.

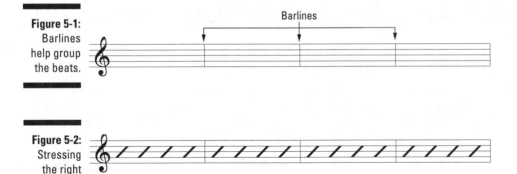

Figure 5-1:
Barlines
help group
the beats.

Barlines

Figure 5-2:
Stressing
the right
beats.

Clap: 1, 2, 3, 4   1, 2, 3, 4   1, 2, 3, 4   1, 2, 3, 4

Shopping for barlines

Like jeans, barlines are available in various styles. In piano music, the different styles of barlines give you directions on how to play the music.

The four main styles of barlines tell you to do the following things:

♪ **Single (one thin barline):** Go on to the next measure.

♪ **Double (two thin barlines):** Go on to the next section of the song, which will have a change of some kind, whether it's a new tempo, new grouping of beats per measure, or just a new set of lyrics.

♪ **Repeat (one thin and one thick barline, plus two dots):** Repeat the music from the beginning of the song or from the beginning of the section.

♪ **End (one thin and one thick barline):** You've reached the end of the song, so stop playing. Of course, you can keep humming if you like — no one's stopping you.

Figure 5-3 shows you the four styles of barlines.

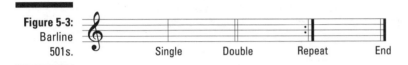

Figure 5-3:
Barline
501s.

Single   Double   Repeat   End

Note Lengths: Serving Some Musical Pie

Piano music uses lots of different symbols and characters. Perhaps the most important symbols to know are those that tell you the length of each note.

Each note you play lasts for a certain number of beats, or a fraction of a beat. Don't worry — math doesn't exactly thrill me either. So, I'm pleased to tell you that the fractions you use in music are no more complex than the fractions you use when you carve up a fresh pie.

Picture yourself at the ultimate dessert table, staring at hundreds of freshly-baked, meringue-topped pies. I'll take the coconut cream one, thank you. Now, pretend that each pie represents one measure of music.

Your master chef (the composer) tells you at the beginning of the dessert (music) how many equal pieces to cut each pie (measure) into. Each resulting piece of pie represents one beat. You can eat the whole piece of pie, or just a part of it, depending on how hungry you are (how the music should sound). At this point, I recommend taking a few antacid tablets before continuing with your musical dessert.

One piece at a time

Most pieces of music have four beats per measure. In essence, your master chef asks you to cut each pie into four equal pieces. When you divide something into four, you get quarters. When you divide a measure into four parts, you also get quarters — *quarter notes*.

A quarter note is represented by a black rounded notehead with one long *stem*. For some unknown preferential reason, the quarter note has become the most popular — and, hence, most recognizable — note of all musicdom. Look at the notes in Figure 5-4. Recognize them? I told you so.

Figure 5-4:
The wonderful quarter notes.

Try playing these quarter notes on your piano. Begin by tapping your foot to the beat at a tempo of one tap per second. Count out loud "1, 2, 3, 4." Each time your foot taps the floor, play the next quarter note on the piano. When you reach the barline, continue playing, tapping, and counting the next measure.

Half the pie

Returning to the dessert table, if you cut each pie into quarters and you eat two pieces, you end up eating half a pie. Likewise, if you cut up a measure of music into four beats, and you play a note so that it lasts for two beats, you can surmise that the two beats equal a *half note*.

Figure 5-5 shows you a few measures with half notes and quarter notes. Notice that a half note looks similar to a quarter note with its rounded notehead and long stem, but the half note's notehead is white instead of black.

Figure 5-5:
Save half
for me.

Try playing the notes that you see in Figure 5-5. For every half note hold the key down for two beats, or two foot taps, before playing the next note. Keep counting "1, 2, 3, 4" to help you know when to play and when to hold.

The laws of staff gravity

You may have noticed that sometimes a note's stem points up and sometimes it points down. Thanks to the laws of staff gravity, any notes on or above the middle line of a staff point downwards. This applies to all notes with stems.

Sir Isaac Newton would have been proud, don't you think?

The whole pie

Get those stomach muscles ready: If you eat all four pieces of a pie that's been cut into four pieces, then you eat the whole pie. I hope it was a small one. If you play a note that lasts for all four beats of the measure, you are playing a *whole note*.

For obvious oblong reasons, this note is sometimes referred to by (non-athletic) musicians as a "football." Like the half note, the whole note's notehead is white, but its shape is slightly different — more oval than round. See Figure 5-6 to check out some whole notes.

Figure 5-6:
Eating the
whole pie
in one
big gulp.

Count: 1, 2, 3, 4   1, 2, 3, 4   1, 2, 3, 4

The art of playing whole notes is an easy one. Play the notes in Figure 5-6 and hold the key for four beats, or four foot taps. You then go across the barline and immediately play the next measure, since a whole note lasts for the *whole* measure. Remember to count all four beats as you play, which helps you maintain a steady rhythm.

Mixing up the pieces

After you know how to count, play, and hold the three main types of notes, try playing Figure 5-7 (Track 6) with all of the different note lengths mixed up. Listen to Track 6 before you play, so that you can hear how long each note lasts. Okay, I agree that the song's melody doesn't exactly bring a tear to the eye — I used the same note throughout the "song" to help emphasize the rhythm created by combining the three note lengths.

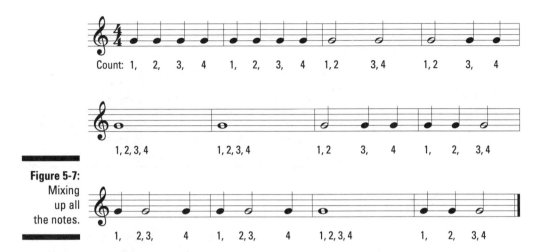

Count: 1, 2, 3, 4   1, 2, 3, 4   1, 2   3, 4   1, 2   3,   4

1, 2, 3, 4   1, 2, 3, 4   1, 2   3,   4   1,   2,   3, 4

Figure 5-7:
Mixing
up all
the notes.

1,   2, 3,   4   1,   2, 3,   4   1, 2, 3, 4   1,   2,   3, 4

Faster, Faster, Alley Cat

Just because a measure has four beats in it doesn't mean that it can only have four notes. Unlike quarter, half, and whole notes (which I talk about in the preceding section), some notes last only a fraction of a beat. The smaller the fraction, the faster the music sounds, because you hear more notes for every beat, or foot tap.

Listen to Track 7 on the CD. Each beat — represented by the steady clicking sound — is the length of one quarter note, which creates a *quarter note feel*. However, the shorter note lengths make the music sound like it's getting faster and faster.

Actually, the speed of the music doesn't change at all. Rather, in each successive measure, the length of the notes is a smaller and smaller fraction of the beat. Dividing the beat like this allows you to play more notes in the same amount of time, as well as giving the music a slightly different, perhaps more danceable, rhythm.

If you find it difficult to play these faster notes, simply slow down the tempo by tapping a slower quarter-note beat. This allows you to play these faster note patterns at a slower tempo. You can increase the tempo as you become more familiar with the music.

A note by any other name

Other English-speaking countries (and a few snobbish music circles in the U.S.) use different names for lengths of notes. For example, in the United Kingdom, New Zealand, and Australia, you hear the quarter note referred to as a *crotchet,* the half note as a *minim,* and a whole note as a *semibreve.* Never fear — the notes, by any name, all have the same values.

Eighth notes

When you cut four pie pieces in half, you get eight pieces. When you cut the four beats in a measure in half, you get *eighth* notes. It takes two eighth notes to equal one beat, or one quarter note. Likewise, it takes four eighths to make one half note. It takes eight . . . you get the idea.

You can write eighth notes in two different ways, shown in Figures 5-8. By itself, one eighth looks like a quarter note with a flag (also called a *flag* in many elite music circles). When two or even four eighth notes are present, a *beam* replaces their flags and groups the notes. This beam groups the eighth notes, making it much easier to spot each beat.

Figure 5-8:
Eight isn't
enough.

Count: 1 - and 2 - and 3 - and 4 - and

To play the eighth notes like the ones in Figure 5-8, count the beat out loud as "1-and, 2-and, 3-and, 4-and," and so on. Every time your foot taps down, say a number; when your foot is up, say "and." If anyone is nearby, change "and" to "grand" so they think you're counting money. Won't they feel silly when they ask to borrow some? "Sure," you say, "you can have an eighth note."

Sixteenth notes and more

By dividing one beat, or quarter note, into four separate parts, you get a *sixteenth note.* Two sixteenth notes equal one eighth note, so it takes four sixteenth notes to equal one beat, or quarter note.

As with eighth notes, you can write sixteenth notes in two different ways: with flags and beams. One sixteenth note alone gets two flags, while grouped sixteenth notes use two beams. Most often you see four sixteenth notes "beamed" together, because four sixteenth notes equal one beat. And frequently, you see one eighth note beamed to two sixteenth notes, also equaling one beat. Figure 5-9 shows examples of flagged and beamed sixteenth notes plus eighth notes joined to sixteenth notes.

Figure 5-9:
Sixteen
going on
sixteen.

Count: 1　e　and　a　2　e　and　a　3–e　and　a　4　e　and–a

To count sixteenth notes, divide the beat by saying "1-e-and-a, 2-e-and-a," and so on. You say the numbers on a downward tap; the "and" is on an upward tap, and the "e" and "a" are in between. It's also fun to count sixteenth notes as "1-banana, 2-banana," and so on. Try it at the supermarket and listen as the clerks announce over the loudspeaker, "Crazy person in aisle three!"

Sixteenth notes aren't so difficult to play at a slow ballad tempo, but try pounding out sixteenth notes in a fast song and you sound like Jerry Lee Lewis — and that's a good thing! (You can read more about Jerry Lee Lewis in Chapter 18.)

I could divide the beat even more, and some composers do until there's virtually nothing left of the beat. Figure 5-10 shows that from sixteenth notes you can divide the beat into 32nds, then 64ths, and even 128ths. But really, Professor Over-the-Top, this is getting a bit ridiculous.

Figure 5-10:
Chopping
into
oblivion.

1&,　2e　&　a,　oh　my　gosh　you　must　be　jok – ing　!　!　!　!

If you happen to encounter very small, very short note lengths, simply slow the tempo way, way down and count out the fraction of the beat in a way that makes sense to you. Then speed the tempo back up and try to play it. Or you can just play a different song without such small note lengths.

Triplets love chocolate

Most notes divide a beat neatly by some factor of two. But every now and then, you may want to play slightly faster than eighth notes but slightly slower than sixteenth notes. That means playing three notes per beat, aptly called a *triplet.*

The most common triplet pattern is the *eighth-note triplet,* which looks like three beamed eighth notes. To help you spot these triplets quickly, composers add a little number "3" above the beam. The second most common triplet pattern is the quarter-eighth triplet, which looks like (get this) a quarter note and an eighth note but with a little bracket and a number "3." Figure 5-11 shows you both types of triplets.

Figure 5-11:
Congrats!
You have
triplets.

Count: 1,   2,   choc - o - late, choc - o - late   1,   choc-o-late, choc-'late, 4

You can hear an example of these triplets on Track 8 before you try to play them yourself from Figure 5-11. To count these triplets, tap your foot and say "tri-pl-et" or (because I like food metaphors) "choc-o-late" for every beat.

Metric Conversions

Never fear, I have no idea how many kilometers are in a mile either. This section involves a different kind of metric system.

Each measure of music receives a specified number of beats. (See "The Beat Goes On" in this chapter for more information on beats.) Composers decide the number of beats per measure early on and convey such information with a *time signature,* or *meter.*

The two numbers in the time signature tell you how many beats are in each measure of music. In math, the fraction for a quarter is 1/4. So, 4/4 would mean four quarters. Thus, each measure with a time signature of 4/4 has four quarter note beats. Each measure with a 3/4 meter has three quarter note beats, and so on, as shown in Figure 5-12.

Figure 5-12:
Buying time
with a
quarter.

Please understand that 4/4 meter doesn't mean that each measure has only four quarter notes. It means each measure has only four *beats*. These beats might contain half notes, quarter notes, eighth notes, whatever the composer wants, but all note lengths must combine to equal no more or less than the specified number of beats per measure.

Common time (4/4 meter)

The most common meter in music is 4/4. It is so common that its other name is *common time*. Did I mention how common it is? It's so common that the two numbers in the time signature are often replaced by the letter "C." You know, for "common." (See Figure 5-13.)

Figure 5-13:
Another
common
way to
write
4/4 meter.

In 4/4, the stacked numbers tell you that each measure contains four quarter note beats. So, to count 4/4 meter, each time you tap the beat, you are tapping the equivalent of one quarter note. To hear an example of 4/4 meter, play Track 9. Notice how the 4/4 meter creates an emphasis on beat 1 of each measure, as I explain earlier in the section, "Breaking things up with vertical lines."

TRACK 9

A Hot Time in the Old Town Tonight

When you hear them old bells go ding ling ling.

All join 'round and how sweet-ly you must sing. And when the

verse is through, in the cho-rus all join in: "There'll be a

hot time in the old town to - night."

Waltz time (3/4 meter)

In the second most common meter, 3/4, each measure has three quarter note beats. Of course, this doesn't mean that only quarter notes exist in this meter. You may have one half note and one quarter note or you may have six eighth notes, but either way, the combinations equal three quarter note beats.

In 3/4 meter, the first beat of each measure is usually the emphasized beat, though it is also quite common to hear emphasis on the second or third beats instead, like in many country music songs.

Another name for 3/4 meter is *waltz time,* because emphasizing every third beat is the rhythm used for waltzing. Listen to Track 10 and play "The Beautiful Blue Danube." Notice the emphasis on beat 1 of each measure. You could say that 3/4 was probably composer Johann Strauss's favorite meter, because he is known as the "Waltz King."

TRACK 10

The Beautiful Blue Danube

March time

Chop a 4/4 meter in half and you're left with only two quarter note beats per measure. Not to worry, though, two beats per measure is perfectly acceptable. In fact, you find 2/4 meter in most famous marches. The rhythm is similar to the rhythm of your feet when you march: "Left-Right, Left-Right, 1-2, 1-2."

Track 11 is a good example of 2/4 meter. It's a famous dance by Jacques Offenbach, called "Can Can," but played on a synthesizer for a more modern sound. Play along, or just dance to the CD.

TRACK 11

Can Can

Time keeps on slipping

No rule says that a song has to remain in one meter all the way through. Nothing is carved in stone when it comes to the rules of music. Heck, music really has no rules.

A song that begins in 4/4 might shift to 3/4 later on down the road. This change in meter can really liven up the song and keep the listener attentive. Call it music's "element of surprise."

Any time the meter changes in a song, the composer alerts you to the change by placing the new meter just to the right of the barline where the change takes place.

Track 12 on the CD gives an example of changing meter in a little song called "Changing It Up." Notice how the change in measure 9 shifts the emphasis on beat 1 (in 4/4 meter) to an emphasis on beat 2 (in 3/4 meter).

This type of meter change is considered abrupt, because the entire rhythmic pulse suddenly changes. A more subtle change in meter is simply to extend a musical phrase by one or two beats to accommodate a new lyric or added melodic tones.

"Add-ons" (Track 13) illustrates this subtle approach. The first time you hear the melody, it's in 4/4. The next time you hear it, you expect the same ending, but this time the melody is extended by the addition of one beat in measure 15. The new meter of 5/4 (five quarter note beats per measure) then returns to 4/4 to end the song. The effect makes the ending more dynamic.

TRACK 12

Changing It Up

TRACK 13

Add-ons

No notes, just rhythm

Some songs are so well-known that you can recognize them by their rhythm alone. For example, the holiday favorite "Jingle Bells" has a unique rhythmic pattern. After hearing it in every shopping mall and grocery store from November to January each year, you can't help knowing that quarter-quarter-half, means "Jingle Bells." On the other hand, many songs with memorable melodies use fairly generic rhythms.

Rhythm is a vital component of a song, sometimes even the defining characteristic of that song. Too often, you are tempted to take rhythm for granted and rely solely on the melody. Melody and rhythm rely on one another. Melody without rhythm is just a nondescript series of musical tones. Rhythm without melody is, well, a drum solo.

Chapter 6

Changing the Beaten Path

● ●

In This Chapter

▶ Knowing when to rest

▶ Tying and dotting your notes

▶ Picking up the missing beats

▶ Playing off the beat

● ●

As soon as the music starts, you hear beats as a constant, ever-present force. But you don't have to play a new note on every darn one of those beats.

This chapter shows you some ways to interpret the beat, whether it's holding notes longer, playing off or around the beat, or even not playing at all.

Taking a Rest

No matter how much you enjoy something, you can't do it forever. Most composers know this and allow you places in the music to rest. It may be resting the hands or simply resting the ears, but rest is an inevitable — and essential — part of every piece of music.

A *musical rest* is simply a pause in which you play nothing. The beat goes on — remember it's a constant pulse — but you pause. This pause can be as short as the length of one sixteenth note or as long as several measures. (Chapter 5 tells you about the lengths of different notes and measures.) However, a rest is usually not long enough to order a pizza or do anything else very useful.

During a rest, you should get your fingers and hands ready to play the next set of notes. Don't put your hands in your lap or your pockets. Keep them on the keys, ready to play whatever may follow.

For every note length, a corresponding rest exists. And, as you may guess, for every rest there is a corresponding symbol. Here they are for the taking.

You can leave your hat on

When you see a whole note F, you play F and hold it for four beats. For a half note, you play and hold the note for two beats. (Chapter 5 tells you all about whole and half notes.) A *whole rest* and *half rest* ask you to pause, not play anything, for the corresponding number of beats.

Figure 6-1 shows both the whole and half rests. They look like little hats, one "on" and one "off." This hat analogy, and the rules of etiquette, make for a good way to remember these rests:

♪ If you rest for only half of the measure (two beats), the hat stays on.

♪ If you rest for the entire measure (four beats), take off your hat and stay for a while.

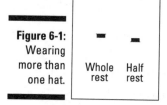

Figure 6-1:
Wearing more than one hat.

These hats, er, rests always hang in the same positions on both staves, making it easy for you to spot them in the music. A half rest sits on the middle line, while a whole rest hangs from the fourth line up, shown in Figure 6-2.

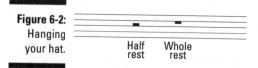

Figure 6-2:
Hanging your hat.

To see whole and half rests in action, take a peek at Figure 6-3. In the first measure of Figure 6-3, you play the two A quarter notes, and then the half rest tells you not to play anything for the next two beats. In the next measure, the whole rest tells you that you're off duty — you rest for four beats. In the third measure, you put down your donut and play two G quarter notes, two beats of rest, and finally, the whole show ends in the next measure with a whole note A.

Figure 6-3:
Rocking
and resting.

Count: 1, 2, (3, 4)   (1, 2, 3, 4)   1, 2, (3, 4)   1, 2, 3, 4

Quarter rests and more

Composers also use rests to tell you to stop playing for the equivalent of quarter notes, eighth notes, and sixteenth notes. Figure 6-4 shows you the musical squigglies that correspond to each of these resting periods.

Figure 6-4:
Quarter,
eighth, and
sixteenth
rests.

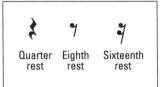

Quarter   Eighth   Sixteenth
rest   rest   rest

I like to think of the *quarter rest* as an uncomfortable-looking chair. Because it's uncomfortable, you won't rest too long. In fact, you don't rest any longer than one beat in this chair.

The *eighth rest* and *sixteenth rest* are easy to recognize: They have the same number of "flags" — although slightly different in fashion — as their note counterparts. An eighth note and eighth rest each have one flag. Sixteenth notes and rests have two flags.

Quarter rests are easy to count — they last only one beat. Eighth rests are a bit harder to count simply because they happen faster. When you play eighth rests, count out loud "1-and, 2-and," and so on. Doing so helps you place the eighth rests more precisely, and may even cause others to sing along.

Figure 6-5 gives you a chance to count out some quarter and eighth rests.

Figure 6-5:
Counting
smaller
rests.

Count 1&, 2&, (3&)   4 &   1&, 2&, (3) &, 4&   (1&) 2 (&) 3 &, 4&

Sixteenth notes also have a corresponding rest, but these are very tricky to play, except at very slow tempos. Until you get into more advanced music, you really don't need to know much more about these rests than what they look like (refer to Figure 6-4).

For an example of how a composer incorporates all of the various-sized rests into one song, listen to Track 14. With so many rests, I call this one "Waiting for a Note." The tune's still pretty catchy, though, don't you think? Play along when you're ready.

TRACK 14

Waiting for a Note

Pick Me Up at Four

You've heard the old adage "everything starts from nothing." Well, some songs actually begin with rests. That's right: The performer walks out on stage, sits at the piano, and rests for a few beats before hitting a single note. Why can't they all do this resting in the dressing room? I could give you a long and boring explanation of why some music starts with rests — but instead, I hope it will suffice to say that there are good reasons to do so.

A song like "She'll Be Coming Round the Mountain" actually starts with a couple of rests, and the first melody notes come in on beats 3 and 4. These melody notes are called *pickup notes,* I guess because they pick up the beat and start the song. How nice of them! To play "She'll Be Coming Round the Mountain," you count "1, 2, She'll be . . .," as shown in Figure 6-6.

Figure 6-6:
Pickup
notes.

Rather than "play" a bunch of rests at the beginning, the composer can opt to use a *pickup measure,* which contains only beats that actually play notes. Figure 6-7 shows you the different notation in a song with a pickup measure.

Figure 6-7:
She'll Be
Coming
Round the
Mountain in
a pickup.

To play songs with pickup measures, follow three easy steps:

1. **Notice the meter.**

2. **Rest for the number of "missing" beats.**

3. **Play the pickup notes and away you go.**

Hundreds of songs begin with pickup measures, including "When the Saints Go Marching In" (Track 15) and "Oh, Susannah" (Track 16). Listen to the CD and get a feel for these great songs. Play along with the CD if the mood strikes you!

TRACK 15

When the Saints Go Marching In

1   Oh, when the   saints   go march-ing in.

5   Oh, when the   saints   go   march - ing   in,

9   Oh Lord, I   want   to   be   in   that   num -   ber,

13   when the   saints   go   march - ing   in.

TRACK 16

Oh, Susannah

1   Oh, I   come from Al - a - bam- a with a   ban- jo on my   knee.   And I'm

6   goin' to Lou' - si - an - a my Su - san- na for to   see.

Adding Time to Your Notes with Curves and Dots

Plain-patterned, monochromatic clothing can be dreadfully boring or terribly hip. To avoid the former, you might "dress things up" with a little design or other accessory. For a plain black suit, add a tie. If you're Bozo the Clown, add some polka dots.

Ties? Polka dots? What a great idea! This book may not be billed as *Fashion For Dummies,* but after you see how ties and dots fit into music, you may begin to have your doubts.

What I'm really talking about is a set of symbols, specifically some curves and dots, that add more time or length to your notes. A quarter or half note doesn't quite cut it? Need to play the note a little bit longer? Just throw in some of these rhythmic elements to extend the length of your notes.

Ties

Half notes and whole notes last longer than one beat. (Chapter 5 gives you the full scoop on half and whole notes.) But say you want to hold the note over to the next measure of music. What can you do? Of course, music has a solution. Introducing a curvy little line called the *tie*.

The tie does just what it sounds like: It ties two notes together, causing one continuous-sounding note. For example, a half note tied to a quarter note lasts for three beats. Likewise, a quarter note tied to an eighth note is held for one and a half beats. Figure 6-8 shows you a few notes that are all tied up, as well as how to count them.

Listen to Track 17 and try to play these rhythms. This example helps you quickly understand the function of a musical tie, other than being a cheesy last-minute gift for your musician friends. Please don't send me one; I already have four!

Figure 6-8:
Tying up the
notes.

Dots

Another way to extend the length of a note, not to mention to make it look a little fancier, is through the use of a *dot*. A dot on any size note or rest makes that note or rest last 50 percent longer.

Dotted half notes

Probably the most common dotted note in music is the dotted half note, which gets a total of three beats, as shown in Figure 6-9.

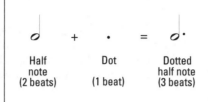

Figure 6-9:
Dotting the
note.

Half note (2 beats)   Dot (1 beat)   Dotted half note (3 beats)

You find dotted half notes scattered throughout waltzes and other songs in 3/4 meter, like the theme from Rimsky-Korsakov's "Scheherazade" (Track 18). (Chapter 5 tells you all about 3/4 meter.)

Notice in "Scheherazade" that you can combine the use of ties and dots. The tie simply adds even more time to the dotted half note. For example, in measure 4, you hold the note B for four beats.

Dotted quarter notes

When you add a dot to the quarter note, you get a great hybrid note that lasts for $1\frac{1}{2}$ beats. Because these notes equal $1\frac{1}{2}$ beats, they nearly always require a dance partner, another eighth note, to finish out the second beat.

"I've Been Working on the Railroad" (Track 19) provides a classic example of the dotted-quarter-followed-by-an-eighth rhythm. Listen to it over and over until you get the feel and can't help climbing on board.

Scheherazade

TRACK 19

I've Been Working on the Railroad

I've been work-ing on the rail - road all the live - long day. I've been work-ing on the rail - road just to pass the time a - way. Can't you hear the whis - tle blow - in'? Rise up so ear - ly in the morn. Can't you hear the cap - tain shout - in' "Di - nah, blow your horn!"

Dotted eighth notes

The dotted eighth note equals 1½ eighth notes, or three sixteenth notes. As you know, it takes four sixteenth notes to make one quarter note (or one beat). So, a dotted eighth note usually attaches itself to a sixteenth note. What a leech! When this happens, the normal eighth note beam connects the two notes and the sixteenth note gets a shortened second beam.

You hear dotted eighth notes in all types of music, but especially dance tunes. Composer Stephen Foster made good use of this long-short, long-short rhythm in his classic tune "Swanee River." Listen to Track 12 a couple of times before trying to play the new rhythm yourself.

TRACK 20

Swanee River

Bad musical joke

Q: What is Lawrence Welk's favorite rhythm?   A: Polka-dotted eighth notes.

Playing Off the Beat

The beat may go on and on, but music can be quite dull if every note you play is on the beat. By changing up the rhythm a bit and playing some notes off, around, or in between the main beats, your songs take on a whole new life.

As you read the following sections about playing notes off the beat, tap your foot along to the examples. That way, even when you don't play a note right on the beat, you won't lose the beat.

It's pure coincidence that all three of these rhythmic variations — swing, shuffle, and syncopation — start with the letter "S." As lyricist Ira Gershwin might say, "'swonderful, 'smarvelous." You'll feel the same way, too, after knowing these "fascinatin' rhythms."

Swing and shuffle time

I could write paragraphs and paragraphs expounding the virtues of the *swing beat*. However, I'll spare you (and my editor) that little treat; the best way to understand a swing beat is to hear it.

Figure 6-10 shows four measures of music. I play these four measures twice on Track 21. The first time, I play it as written — straight quarter and eighth notes. The second time, I play the rhythm with a swing beat. The notes are the same, but with a slightly different, swingin' feel.

Figure 6-10:
Swinging a
straight
beat.

Instead of straight eighth notes played as "1-and, 2-and," you hear a long-short, long-short rhythm. The real way to notate this long-short rhythm is with a quarter-eighth triplet. (See Chapter 5 for more on triplets.) But rather than write a ton of triplets, the composer gives you a big "heads up" on the first measure telling you to "Swing," either in plain English or with a little symbol like the one in Figure 6-11.

Figure 6-11:
The symbol
for a swing
beat.

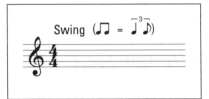

 Like I said, the best way to understand the swing beat is to hear it. So popular is this classic American rhythm that it has its own type of bands and dance moves. Ever seen the movie *Swingers?* Ever heard the band Cherry Poppin' Daddies? Both feature tons of music in a swing beat.

 Although swing music is extremely popular, some temperamental rock stars find it just too uncool to write a 1920s word like "swing" on their great heavy metal anthems. So, another name is given to the exact same rhythmic feel . . . but don't tell the egomaniacs it's the same beat. *Shuffle feel* has the same long-short feel as swing, but this beat is more readily associated with — and accepted by performers of — rock and blues-style music.

Syncopation

One of the most common forms of playing off the beat is a little rhythmic concept called *syncopation.* To understand syncopation, you first have to get to know *downbeats* and *upbeats.*

Start tapping your foot to any beat, and count eighth notes "1-and, 2-and, 3-and, 4-and." Every time your foot goes down to the floor you say a number; when your foot goes up you say "and." In this example, the numbers are downbeats while the "ands" are upbeats. Get it? Your foot goes *down* on the downbeats, *up* on the upbeats.

Downbeats are the beats that are normally emphasized in a song. But through the miracles of syncopation, you emphasize some (or all) of the upbeats instead. By "emphasize," I mean to play those notes a little bit harder, or louder, than the others.

 You can syncopate any melody. Listen to Track 22 while you follow along with the music to "The Kitchen Sync." The first eight measures are played on the beat. The last eight measures are the same melody but with a syncopated rhythm. Keep your foot tapping the beat throughout the entire 16 measures and notice the emphasized notes on the upbeats (when your foot is up).

TRACK 22

The Kitchen Sync

Have I piqued your interest with this keen new syncopated rhythm? For more on syncopation, read Chapter 15, which explores various ways to make a plain vanilla melody into something special with this offbeat rhythm.

Part III
One Hand at a Time

The 5th Wave — By Rich Tennant

Harriet's First Gig

"C'mon! Allegro vivace! Allegro vivace! We're selling ice cream, not coffins!"

In this part . . .

Take off the training wheels and put the pedal to the metal. I show you how to play songs, real songs! You start with the right hand in Chapter 7.

In addition to melodies, scales are very important, so I devote Chapter 8 to them. In Chapter 9, you get to screw your left hand back on and play with both hands at once.

Chapter 7

Playing a Melody

● ●

In This Chapter

▶ Observing which fingers to use

▶ Discovering song-playing hand positions

▶ Moving your hands all over the keyboard

● ●

Melodies create a wonderful transformation in music: Melodies turn a whole bunch of random notes into songs that entertain, please your ear, and sometimes get stuck in your head. It would be safe to say that you aren't really playing music unless you're playing a melody.

In order to really get the most out of this chapter about melodies, you need to have the following skills under your belt, er, fingers:

♪ Naming all the keys, both white and black (Chapter 3).

♪ Naming all staff lines and spaces (Chapter 4).

♪ Counting rhythms from whole notes to sixteenth notes (Chapter 5).

♪ Recognizing rests, ties, and dots (Chapter 6).

If you are missing any of these key ingredients, please leave now and head to the store . . . that is, the first five or six chapters of this book. Without these fundamentals, attempting to play songs may lead to frustration.

Let Your Fingers Do the Walking

In order to play a melody correctly, you need to control the way your hands make contact with the keyboard. If you don't develop this control, you'll find it hard to reach the notes you need to play — and your playing will look and sound more like the Keystone Cops than Chopin.

Think of your fingers as being numbered 1 through 5, with the thumbs being 1. In many chapters in this book, I refer to your fingers by number and to your hands by ultra-hip abbreviations: RH and LH. So, when I say RH 1, that means the thumb on your right hand.

In Figure 7-1, RH 2 plays D. Notice the relaxed but arched position of the hand and fingers. See, too, how the other four fingers are poised and ready to play the next note, whatever it may be. Of course, because it's a photo, these fingers will never, ever play another key. (Chapter 2 tells you more about how to hold your body and hands at the keyboard.)

Figure 7-1:
Playing a
key.

With correct hand position and fingering, your fingers literally walk along the keys. Practice enables them to walk faster and faster and without much thought on your part.

As you play a melody, your fingers should travel gracefully up and down the keyboard. You aren't typing a letter or playing video games, so don't punch or slap the keys.

Positions, Everyone

So, you're at the keyboard, your back is straight, the lights are on, and the music's waiting. Where does your hand go? Good question. You need to get into position.

Position is a common term you hear regarding any musical instrument. Several positions exist for each musical instrument, giving the player points of reference all along the body of the instrument. The keyboard is no exception.

Using positions diligently is vital to playing the keyboard well. From each designated position, you can easily access certain notes, groups of notes, chords, or even other positions.

When you sit down to play, survey the music and locate the first set of notes. After you find these, decide which of the following two positions is the more accommodating.

C position

Many tunes start at middle C or close to it, so you often find yourself in *C position* at the beginning of a song. To get to C position, put your thumb on middle C and place your fingers on the five successive white keys, as shown in Figure 7-2. That is, RH 1 should be on C and RH 5 on G with the other three fingers in the middle. If the other three aren't in the middle, you've got something very amusing going on with your fingers.

Figure 7-2: Getting into C position.

With your right hand in C position, which is sometimes also called *first position,* try to follow along with "Frere Jacques," playing one note at a time. To make the song easy to grasp, I chose a tune that's recognizable and has almost all quarter notes. It may be helpful to just listen to Track 23 a couple of times before you attempt to play along.

TRACK 23

Frere Jacques

Be sure to observe the numbers above the notes. These numbers are called *fingerings* because they tell you which finger to use for each note. Most players appreciate these fingerings because they represent the best possible finger pattern for executing the notes. Of course, being the wunderkind that you are, you may invent other custom fingerings. For now, though, I recommend you follow the fingerings I show you. Otherwise, I'll see you after class.

Not too painful, right? Try another song that uses C position. In "Ode to Joy" (Track 24), the melody begins on RH 3, travels up to RH 5, then dips all the way down to RH 1. Beethoven, himself, was a pianist, so no doubt he knew just how well this melody would play under beginning fingers.

TRACK 24

Thumbing a ride to B

As you can probably imagine, not all songs use the same five notes. Eventually, you must come out of your safe little shell of five white keys, take a good stretch, and extend certain fingers up or down. A good finger to start with is your thumb.

An opposable thumb is what sets us apart from other animals. I know — some people argue that it's the invention of language, or art, or the splitting of atoms. No, it's the existence of an opposable thumb. Imagine buttoning a shirt, turning a page, or hitching a ride without one. I'd like to see a kangaroo try to do one of those things.

From C position, your thumb can extend down to B. As you play B with your thumb, you can simply leave your other fingers exactly where they are.

For "Skip to My Lou," simply move your thumb to the left in measure 3 to play the Bs. Don't forget you can also play along with the CD on Track 25.

TRACK 25

Skip to My Lou

Good stretch, pinky!

From C position, RH 5 (your pinky) can reach out and play A. In the camp-fire classic "Kum-bah-yah," you anticipate the extension up to A by shifting fingers 2 through 5 to the right from the very start. Notice this shift in the fingerings above the notes. Instead of playing D with RH 2, you play E with RH 2 this time. You can hear "Kum-bah-yah" on Track 26.

Don't take this word "stretch" too literally. I don't want you to injure yourself. It's quite all right to allow fingers 1 through 4 to move toward RH 5 as you reach up to play A.

TRACK 26

Kum-bah-yah

Stretching C position to the limits

In many songs that begin from C position, you must shift your fingers, or stretch both your pinky and your thumb, to hit the desired notes. "Chiapanecas" is one such song. Try to play this Latin American song as it was meant to be heard: hot and spicy. You may want to listen to Track 27 before trying it yourself.

Always, always remember to notice the time signature before you start playing. You don't want to be thinking "1, 2, 3, 4" if the song is in 3/4 time. And, by the way, "Chiapanecas" *is* in 3/4 time.

 TRACK 27

Chiapanecas

G position

To get into *G position,* move your hand up the keyboard so that RH 1 rests on the G occupied by RH 5 in C position. Figure 7-3 shows you this new position, as well as the staff notes you play in it. Notice that RH 5 now rests all the way up on D.

Figure 7-3:
Gee, I
like it!

Just like in C position, you can extend your thumb and pinky east and west to access other keys. In this case (G position), you can reach out and play E and F, respectively.

Give this position a whirl by playing "This Old Man," a song known to many a tormented parent as the Barney theme song. Watch the fingering in this song and shift your fingers where appropriate. You can also listen to "This Old Man" and play along with the CD (Track 28).

TRACK 28

This Old Man

This old man, he played "one," he played knick-knack on my thumb, so I

slapped him on his knuck-les real-ly hard. Now he keeps his dis-tance far.

Getting more out of your positions

Knowing two positions is great, but you really only get five or six notes in each position. I know what you're thinking: *"How do I play those modern 12-tone pieces with only six keys?"* Whoa there, Tex, save the virtuosic pieces for later.

Combining the use of different positions in the same song allows you to play a few more notes. To combine two positions, you have to switch between them mid-song, which takes a bit of practice. One way is to simply shift your hand upward or downward when the music gives you the chance.

For example, in Figure 7-4 you play the first two measures in C position. During the two beats of rest in measure 2, you can move your hand up and get ready to play B in measure 3 with RH 3. Ta-da! You've just shifted to G position.

Figure 7-4:
Moving from one position to another.

Cross your fingers and hope it works

Shifting positions can be smooth and easy when rests are involved, but when the melody doesn't stop, you must find alternative ways to move between positions. The best way is to use a little maneuver called *finger crossing*.

Why cross over fingers when you can just move your hand? In C position, the thumb *can* sometimes extend to play B. But not always. For example, you may need to play B followed immediately by middle C. If you extend and contract your thumb back and forth between these two keys, it sounds clunky. And, by George, you don't want clunky! Instead, you cross RH 2 over your thumb to play B, as shown in Figure 7-5.

You can watch the keys when you cross over or under, but with practice you should easily feel where the keys are without looking. But whether you look or not, it's important to keep a relaxed arch in the hand even when crossing fingers over or under.

Figure 7-5:
Crossing
over to play
more notes.

Bach's little gem "Minuet" (Track 29) requires your RH 2 to cross over your thumb. You shift positions briefly in measures 3 and 11, but the main focus here is on the finger cross to B in measures 7 and 15.

TRACK 29

Minuet

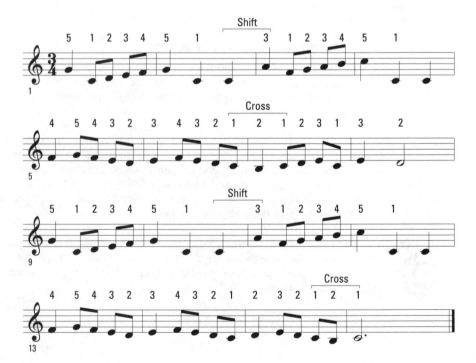

Cross over to a new position

Sometimes the finger cross can help move your hand to a new position entirely. For example, you can begin with your hand in C position and play C, D, E in C position before crossing your thumb (RH 1) under to play F. After a stretch, you'll end the song by playing the last two measures in C position again.

Figure 7-6:
From C to
shining C.

Don't try to make your hand, wrist, fingers, or arm do something impossible. I don't want any broken ligaments here. When you cross your fingers between positions, it's important to also shift your hand and arm to the new position after the finger cross.

The song "Row, Row, Row Your Boat" (Track 30) gives you another, more musical chance to try out this little switch-o-rama between positions. You start with your right hand in C position (middle C to G), but as you approach measure 4, you cross your thumb under RH 3 and play the G with RH 2. You then continue measure 5 with your hand closer to G position. As you play downward from the C in measure 5, your hand will naturally shift back to C position by measure 6, where you then stay to finish the song.

TRACK 30

Row, Row, Row Your Boat

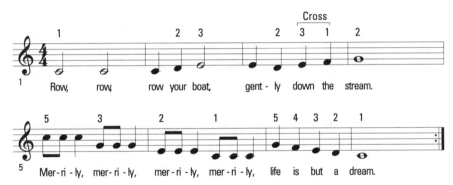

Chapter 8

Scaling to New Heights

· ·

In This Chapter

▶ Getting to know scales

▶ Building all kinds of scales

▶ Improvising melodies using scales

· ·

*H*ave you ever heard the following from your musician friends?

> ♪ "Scales are boring!"
>
> ♪ "Scales are difficult."
>
> ♪ "I never play scales."
>
> ♪ "The scales in my bathroom read 10 pounds more than I actually weigh."

These statements are all lies, including the last one. For various selfish reasons, your friends don't want you to know the truth: Scales are easy, scales can be fun, every musician plays scales, and your friend actually put on a few pounds over Spring Break.

You can use scales to do some great things on the piano — like playing entire songs. Okay, I admit that not all scales are songs. But it's true that all songs *are* created from scales, be it an entire scale or just a few notes from the scale. Remember the "Do-Re-Mi" song from *The Sound of Music?* The whole darn song was *about* scales, and those kids had fun!

In this chapter, I show you that it's well worth your while to give scales a chance. Besides using scales to understand the notes in a song's melody, you can use scales to beef up your finger power on the piano. Plus, the more scales you know, the easier it becomes to play the piano.

You've probably heard this a thousand times before now, but it's true: practice makes perfect. Later in this chapter, I show you several different types of scales. Pick the ones you like and play through them five to ten times a day. This warms up your fingers and builds finger dexterity. Think of it like shooting baskets every day before the big basketball game. You wouldn't want to go out on the court without a little practice, would you?

Building a Scale, Step by Step

Put simply, a musical *scale* is an arrangement of notes in a specific, consecutive order. Most scales have the following attributes:

♪ They are eight notes long.

♪ The top and bottom notes have the same name.

♪ They are made up of notes that are side by side (or at least very close), which are played in order, one after another.

Each scale has a different, whacky sounding name, like *C major*. A scale derives its name from the following two things:

♪ The scale's bottom note, or *root note*

♪ The *step pattern* used to create the scale

What's a step pattern, you ask? First, you need to understand *steps*. Music is made up primarily of two types of steps: *half steps* and *whole steps*. These steps are the building blocks of scales.

Look at your keyboard, or Figure 8-1, and notice that some white keys have a black key in between and some white keys are side by side. The layout of the keys leads to the following terms:

♪ Two keys side by side (whether black or white) are one half step apart.

♪ Two keys separated by another key are a whole step apart.

♪ Two half steps equal one whole step.

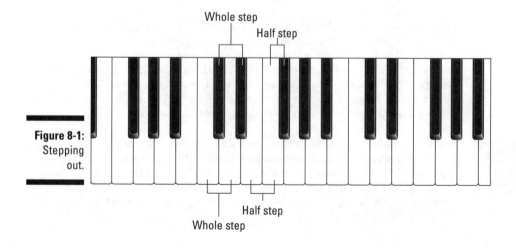

Figure 8-1: Stepping out.

Whole step

Half step

Half step

Whole step

In Chapter 3, I explain how the suffixes *sharp* and *flat* are used to name the black keys. Half steps help define sharps and flats. For example, find any D on your keyboard. Move one half step higher and play the black key to the right, D-sharp. Now play one half step lower than D, or D-flat.

After you understand steps, you can build any scale starting on any root note, simply by applying the correct step pattern (or combination of whole and half steps). These step patterns, which I discuss in the following section, give scales (and therefore songs) wildly different sounds.

Minor Renovations, Major Innovations

The two most frequently used, most popular, and most famous scales in Western music are the *major* and the *minor* scales. You can make a major and a minor scale starting with any note on the piano — think of it as getting two scales for the price of one. The difference between the two types of scales is the combination of whole and half steps (step pattern) that you use to build them. (Check out the previous section if you need to brush up on steps.)

Generally speaking, major scales sound happy and minor scales sound sad. It's safe to assume that even in olden times, when the names for scales were first thought up, the terms major and minor were a bit more marketable than "happy scales" and "sad scales."

Major scales

Every major scale is built the same way. Don't let a scale salesman try to sell you a new and improved major scale. There is no such thing. Actually, you should turn and run from anyone proclaiming to be a scale salesman.

The step pattern used by all major scales on the planet is:

Whole-Whole-Half-Whole-Whole-Whole-Half

For example, you can form a C major scale by starting on C and applying this pattern. Play any C and play the pattern of whole steps and half steps all the way to the next C. Figure 8-2 shows you the way. Starting with C, the layout of the white keys follows the pattern exactly, so you play the entire C major scale on white keys only.

You must cross over with your finger in the appropriate spot in order to play all eight notes that make up the scale. See Chapter 7 for tips on this finger-crossing business.

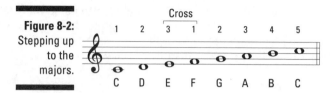

Figure 8-2:
Stepping up
to the
majors.

When playing most scales backwards (from top to bottom), it is important to realize that the step pattern is exactly reversed. Don't think about it too hard — just remember which keys you played going up and play the same ones in reverse order going down.

Now for something slightly different: Start on G and apply the major scale step pattern. When you get to the sixth step, you notice that a whole step from E requires playing a black key, F-sharp. I never said that *all* major scales were playable on white keys only. Figure 8-3 shows you the G major scale in all its glory.

Figure 8-3:
The G major
scale
employs
one sharp.

The root note and step pattern dictate which sharps and flats (black keys) to use. G major uses one sharp. How about a major scale that uses one flat? Start on F and apply the pattern, as shown in Figure 8-4, and you have built yourself the F major scale.

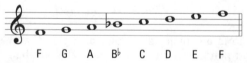

Figure 8-4:
F major
uses B-flat.

How do you know it's B-flat and not A-sharp? Excellent question. The easy answer is that in a scale, every letter name has its turn. Because the third note of the scale represents A, it would show nothing but favoritism to call the fourth note A-sharp. So, the fourth note represents B with its flat version, B-flat, one half-step higher than A.

Take this newfound major scale knowledge and see how it applies to a song. The classic "Danny Boy" uses all of the notes from the F major scale, even the note B-flat.

TRACK 31

Danny Boy

Oh, Dan-ny Boy, the keys, the keys are call-ing:

"Come play a song. Don't let us col-lect dust."

So you sit down and play a song like "Dan-ny Boy,"

It's not too hard, but prac-tice is a must.

Turning ugly scales into beautiful songs

You can play the exact same notes of the C major scale in a different order, but instead of a scale you have a melody. For example, if you jump around and play C-G-F-E-A-B-D-C, the notes no longer sound like a scale — the notes have become a melody. And you have become a composer.

Another scale, another song. Try playing Bach's little masterpiece "Jesu, Joy of Man's Desiring" (Track 32), which is based on the G major scale (and a lot of triplets, which you can read about in Chapter 5). All of the notes from the G major scale are used. Yes, even F-sharp.

Jesu, Joy of Man's Desiring

Minor scales

Some people think of major scales as sounding "happy" and minor scales as sounding "sad." Well, grab a hanky, because this section is all about the minor (sad-sounding) scales.

I must clarify something right away: Minor scales are no less important or any smaller in size than major scales. They just have an unfair name.

Like major scales, minor scales have eight notes with the top and bottom notes having the same name. But unlike major scales, minor scales use the following step pattern:

Whole-Half-Whole-Whole-Half-Whole-Whole

Sure, it may look similar to the major scale's pattern, but this slight rearrangement of half and whole steps makes all the difference in the world. The best way to understand this sonic difference is to play and hear a major and a minor scale side by side. Figure 8-5 shows the C major scale, followed immediately by the C minor scale.

Figure 8-5:
Major and minor C scales.

Hear the difference? Try something else: Figure 8-6 demonstrates the scaly song "Joy to the World." The first time the melody uses the C major scale. The second time, the melody is constructed on the C minor scale. Notice the difference in the sound.

Figure 8-6:
Joy (and sadness) to the world.

Minor scales can use both sharps and flats. Apply the step pattern to the root note A and you get a minor scale on all white keys. But apply the step pattern to other root notes and you encounter some minor scales with sharps (like E minor) and some with flats (like G minor), as you can see in Figure 8-7.

The notes from minor scales make great, memorable melodies, too. "House of the Rising Sun" is based on the E minor scale. Play this song along with Track 33 and you'll hear how a minor (but not less important) melody sounds.

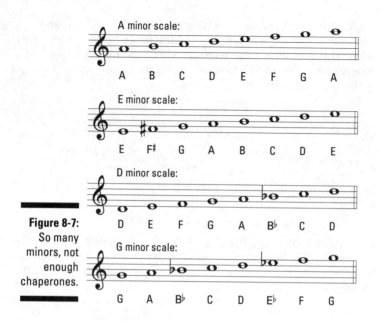

Figure 8-7:
So many minors, not enough chaperones.

TRACK 33

House of the Rising Sun

Breaking the rules

Of course, the composer of a song is not obligated to use every note from a scale in the melody. The composer simply uses the scale notes as a menu to choose from. "The Farmer in the Dell," for example, is based on the F major scale, but it does not use the note B-flat. Listening to Track 34, or playing the song on your piano, I bet you don't even miss the omission.

 TRACK 34

The Farmer in the Dell

Not only can the composer leave out notes from a scale for a song's melody, he or she can also use notes that aren't even part of the scale — just to spice things up a bit. I told you that music has no rules. Play "Greensleeves" (Track 35) and hear what I mean. The song is based on the A minor scale, but that G-sharp and F-sharp sure aren't part of the A minor scale, are they?

Greensleeves

Alternative Scales

Major and minor scales are definitely the most popular scales, but they aren't the only ones. Come on, admit it — you've experimented a little bit with the step patterns of the major and minor scales. Curiosity begs you to insert a half-step in place of a whole-step here and there to hear what happens.

Well, what happens is that you begin to form other scales, neither major nor minor. Some sound great, some sound horrible, and some sound sort of exotic. Creating your own scales is not only acceptable — it's recommended. Fresh new scales inevitably give birth to fresh new melodies and harmonies.

People have experimented with scale patterns since the dawn of music. Although most experimental scales take a back seat to major and minor scales, some music styles use the inventions as the basis for captivating melodies.

Harmonic minor scales

The *harmonic minor* scale differs from the normal minor scale by only one half step, but in doing so you achieve a whole new sounding scale. To play the harmonic minor, follow these steps:

1. **Start out playing a normal minor scale.**

2. **When you get to the seventh note, raise it one half-step (or *sharp it*).**

   This change makes the next to last step a $1^1/_2$ step, but I think your fingers can handle it.

If you do this correctly, the resulting pattern for a harmonic minor scale will be the following:

Whole-Half-Whole-Whole-Half-$1^1/_2$-Half

Play and compare the normal minor scale in Figure 8-8 with the harmonic minor scale next to it. Sounds rather exotic, doesn't it? You'll encounter this scale in lots of classical piano music (which you can read more about in Chapter 15).

Figure 8-8:
The A minor and A harmonic minor scales.

Melodic minor scales

Another variation on the minor scale is the *melodic minor* scale, also commonly known as the *jazz minor,* because it seems to find its way into most of the jazz music you hear. Of course, long before the advent of jazz music, other composers like Bach and Mozart used this scale as a basis for their works of art.

Whether jazz, classical, or some other style of music, the following is the step pattern for a melodic minor scale:

Whole-Half-Whole-Whole-Whole-Whole-Half

I also like to call this scale the *fickle scale,* because it can't decide whether to sound major or minor. Look at the step pattern again and notice that the first four steps are the same as in the minor scale pattern, while the last four steps are just like the major scale pattern. Whatever you call it, Figure 8-9 shows you how to play a melodic minor scale.

Figure 8-9:
Make a
decision.
Are you sad
or happy?

A minor scale:

A B C D E F G A

A melodic minor scale:

A B C D E F♯ G♯ A

Blues scale

A scale that I personally love is the *blues scale.* You can hear it in rock, country, jazz, and of course . . . blues-style music.

This scale is a real rebel, practically throwing the rules of scale building out the window. Of course, there aren't really any hard-and-fast "rules" to scale building, but this scale is rebellious anyway:

♪ It begins with a 1¹/₂ step.

♪ It has only seven notes.

♪ It favors one of the letter names of the notes, using the third note's natural and sharp name.

The step pattern for this seditious little scale is:

1¹/₂-Whole-Half-Half-1¹/₂-Whole

To clear up this confusion, play the scale in Figure 8-10.

Figure 8-10:
Getting the
blues.

Where else have you seen a scale with two half steps in a row? Where else
have you seen a scale using F and F-sharp? Not in this book, I tell you. But
after you know the blues scale, playing it is as addictive as eating peanuts.
You can use blues scale notes for all kinds of little riffs and melodies like the
one in Figure 8-11.

Figure 8-11:
Using the
blues scale
for a cool
melody.

Using scales any which way you like

Okay, okay — scales are important, scales
help you improve your playing, scales make
you happy, scales make you rich, blah, blah,
blah. But how can you use scales now — *right
now?*

What are you waiting for? You don't need me
to tell you to break all the rules, push the
boundaries, and explore the mystical world of
scale patterns. Make up your own scales with
their own step patterns. Improvise melodies
or left-hand bass patterns by using just a few
notes of a scale (see Chapter 9 for more

information on bass patterns). Print out hundreds of scales and wallpaper your kitchen.
Basically, just do what you want with scales.

The bottom line is this: Let scales help you in
whatever way you need them. It doesn't
matter how you use scales — limbering the
fingers with some fast E-flat majors, discovering a cool left-hand groove through the
inspiration of a G harmonic minor, or just
impressing your friends with a rhythmic
F-sharp blues scale. Scales are fun — get out
there and play.

Chapter 9

Hey, Don't Forget Lefty!

In This Chapter

▶ Using the left hand

▶ Playing notes from the bass clef

▶ Accompanying a right-hand melody with the left hand

*W*ant to know an industry secret? Many a pianist who plays with a band never even uses the left hand. Oh sure, you think the left hand is playing, because it's moving up and down the left side of the keyboard and you're hearing lots of bass lines and chords. But *au contraire, mon frére.* The bass player fills in the bass notes; the guitarist covers the chords. The not-so-good pianist just fakes it.

Playing with your left hand, or both hands together, is considerably more difficult than just right-hand playing. But you have no need to fake your way through a career. You can show those phoneys how a real player does it! In this chapter, I tell you how to get both hands jamming together. Save your band some money: Fire the bass player.

In this chapter, I refer to your fingers with the numbers 1 through 5. Your right and left hands are abbreviated as "RH" and "LH." I'm not quite sure how much space these abbreviations save, but I do know that my editors are really, really happy about it.

Exploring the West Side

If you consider middle C the middle of the piano, you can think of the keys to the right of middle C as the East Side and the keys to the left of middle C as the West Side. (Turn to Chapter 4 if you need help locating middle C.) It's time to turn and head west.

To explore the lower keys, acquaint yourself with the bass clef. Chapter 4 has some easy ways to remember the lines and spaces on this often neglected staff. But the best way to figure out this staff is to dig in and start playing. You soon recognize each line and space by sight, without even thinking about it.

Moving into position

In Chapter 7, I show you two positions for the right hand: the *C* and *G* *positions*. These positions are the same for the left hand, but this time, C position has LH 5 (pinky) occupying the C below middle C, the second space up on the bass clef staff. In G position, LH 5 moves down to G, the bottom line of the staff. Figure 9-1 shows you the proper placement for C position.

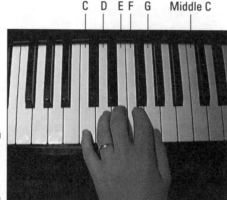

Figure 9-1: West side glory.

Change your life by switching hands

If you aren't left-handed by nature, start using Lefty to perform everyday tasks you normally perform with your right hand. For example, use your left hand to perform any of these day-to-day tasks:

♪ Open doors

♪ Flip channels on the TV remote

♪ Steer your automobile (just be careful)

♪ Hand people money (especially me, if we happen to meet)

♪ Brush your teeth

♪ Open tightly-sealed pickle jars (good luck)

By *consciously* switching hands for a couple of weeks, you *subconsciously* make your left hand stronger, more versatile, and more independent.

Getting used to the new neighborhood

For a quick (and stimulating) drill, Figure 9-2 helps limber up the left-hand fingers in C position. Sing or say out loud the name of each note as you play it. Seeing, playing, saying, and hearing all at once go a long way in helping you remember the notes on the staff.

Figure 9-2:
How the
West was
won.

Figure 9-3 features a similar workout, but in G position. Again, remember to sing each note out loud. Never mind what those around you think of your rantings and ravings — they're just jealous that you can play the piano.

Figure 9-3:
There's
gold in them
thar keys.

Playing More than Drills with Your Left Hand

You have several options with your left hand: You can play scales, melodies, simple one-note harmonies, chords, or just plain cool-sounding accompaniment patterns. That's not just a sales pitch — they really are cool-sounding. I show you single-note harmonies and chords in Chapters 10 and 11; in this section, I concentrate on scales, melodies, and patterns.

South-paw scales

I know scales aren't the most exciting things to play, but please be patient. By playing left-hand scales you unwittingly master the following music essentials:

♪ Reading the bass clef

♪ Playing with the correct fingering

♪ Using nifty patterns and harmonies

♪ Realizing how much you miss playing with the right hand

Start with some major and minor scales by reading and playing along with Figure 9-4. (Chapter 8 tells you all about major and minor scales.) As with right-handed playing, remember to use the correct fingerings as indicated by the numbers above each note. How and when you cross your fingers is very important for obtaining a smooth sound and comfortable left-hand technique. Good luck.

Figure 9-4: Scaling up with your left hand.

Playing scale fragments is one of the most common ways to accompany a right-handed melody. The notes in Figure 9-5 are fragments of major, minor, and blues scales. This piano playing could start sounding pretty darn groovy after a while.

Figure 9-5: Fragments of a good thing still make a good thing.

Left-hand melodies

Sometimes it's nice to play a melody with your left hand. You may tire of playing with your right hand, want to hear the melody lower, want to add a little variety to the song, or have an itch that needs a good right-hand scratching.

Whatever the reason, I do have a hidden agenda here: Playing melodies with the left hand helps you get familiar with the bass clef notes while strengthening your left-hand coordination. Don't hold it against me for having a secret agenda.

Left-hand melodies are lots of fun, but remember to observe the correct fingerings as you play these classics, "Swing Low, Sweet Chariot" and "Little Brown Jug" (Tracks 36 and 37). Actually, I renamed the latter "Little Keyboard" to give you a little musical inspiration.

TRACK 36

Swing Low, Sweet Chariot

TRACK 37

Little Keyboard

Accompaniment patterns

Scales and melodies are fine material for the left hand, but this isn't Lefty's main purpose. Rather, your left hand begs to be playing *accompaniment patterns* while your right hand noodles around with a melody or some chords. One of the most user-friendly left-hand patterns is the *arpeggio.* (I show you other, jazzier accompaniment patterns in Chapter 14.)

Oh, no! More Italian? Yes, in addition to *pizza, rigatoni,* and *ciao,* the other Italian word that should be part of your everyday vocabulary is arpeggio. The word translates to "harp-like," which means absolutely nothing to piano players. However, after many years of bad translations, musicians have come to understand this word as meaning "a broken chord."

Well, nothing's really broken about an arpeggio — it works great. You simply play the notes of a chord one at a time, rather than all at once. (See Chapter 12 for more about chords.)

Three-note arpeggios

In my opinion, three-note arpeggios are the easiest and most versatile left-hand accompaniment pattern to play. A three-note arpeggio fits the hand really nicely, too. For example, place your left hand on the keys in C position with LH 5 on C, LH 2 on G above that, and LH 1 on middle C. Fits like a glove, right?

The three notes you use for three-note arpeggios are the root, fifth, and top notes of the appropriate scale. (Chapter 8 tells you more about scales.) Using the C major scale, for example, the arpeggio notes are C, G, and C. Now comes the versatile part: The pattern is the exact same in the C *minor* scale. So, you can apply the three-note arpeggio to major or minor harmonies by playing the root, fifth, and top notes of the scale, as shown in Figure 9-6.

Figure 9-6:
Major or minor, the notes of these arpeggios have the same pattern.

The easiest way to start playing three-note arpeggios is with a quarter-note rhythm. In 4/4 meter, you play in an "up and back" motion — root, fifth, top, fifth — so that every measure begins with the root note of each arpeggio. In 3/4 meter, you play upwards — root, fifth, top — only, again so that each measure begins with the root note.

Figure 9-7 demonstrates these three-note arpeggio patterns with a simple quarter note rhythm in both meters. The first eight measures are in 4/4, the last eight are in 3/4.

Figure 9-7:
Getting the hang of left-handed arpeggios.

To play a faster arpeggio in eighth notes, simply speed up the process. That is, you play a full set of root-fifth-top-fifth for every two beats, so that beats 1 and 3 of every measure start again on the root note of the arpeggio. A 3/4 meter with eighth-notes is slightly different. Beat 3 of each 3/4 measure gets only two notes of the arpeggio, preferably the top and fifth again.

Try this faster eighth-note arpeggio pattern with the example in Figure 9-8. Gently rock your left hand back and forth over the keys until you feel this pattern is second nature to you. Of course, this may require quite a few repetitions, but practice makes perfect.

Figure 9-8:
Playing
faster
arpeggios.

Four-note arpeggios

Another very popular and handy (pardon the pun) arpeggio is the four-note
version. For this arpeggio, you add the third note of the scale. The four-note
major arpeggio uses the root, third, fifth, and top notes of the scale. To form
a four-note minor arpeggio, you simply lower the third note a half step. For
example, the notes of a C major arpeggio are C, E, G, and C. To make a C
minor arpeggio, simply lower the third note E to E-flat, just like you do in the
C minor scale. (See Figure 9-9.)

Figure 9-9:
Four-note
arpeggios
based on C.

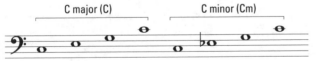

As with the three-note arpeggios, different meters allow you some rhythmic
options. Using quarter notes in 4/4 meter, you play up — root, third, fifth,
top — once in each measure. Each subsequent measure begins again with
the root note. For 3/4 meter, you play up in one measure — root, third, fifth —
and down in the next — top, fifth, third.

Take a gander at this rhythm in Figure 9-10. Call out the name of each note as you play. Hearing yourself helps you recognize the notes.

Figure 9-10: Getting up and back with four-note arpeggios.

With an eighth note rhythm, you can have lots of fun exploring different patterns for the four arpeggio notes. Just keep the correct four notes of each scale in mind — root, third, fifth, and top — and play two of them for every beat in the measure. Figure 9-11 gives you a few examples of different patterns.

Figure 9-11: Toying around with the four arpeggio notes.

Arpeggio, your friend in need

So, there you sit. It's late. The pianist finishes "My Funny Valentine" and heads off for an overdue coffee break. You decide to impress your friends and quickly steal up to the bench. The room is waiting. You open the songbook atop the piano and — egad! — all you see is a treble staff and chord symbols.

You're lost — doomed — Mud's the name! Relax.

What you see is probably a *fake book* (see Chapter 19 for more on fake books). This is a real songbook but with only the melody and chord symbols, allowing a working pianist to "fill in" the left hand as he or she feels is best suitable for the situation. Of course, you *aren't* a working pianist and *any* left hand would be suitable for this late night situation.

First, take a deep breath. Next, open your bag of tricks and pull out some arpeggios for the left hand that I tell you about in this chapter. Use the chord symbols — the little alphabet letters above the staff — to locate the name of the lowest note (or root note) of the arpeggio and play away. Pretty soon you'll have friends you never even knew.

Oh, yeah — don't forget to put the tip jar out.

Adding the Left Hand to the Right Hand

No matter how much you enjoy playing melodies with the right and left hands separately, the time comes when you have to get these two great friends together. Invite both hands to the keys and let them dance all night.

You have several things to keep in mind when you attempt to play songs with both hands:

♪ When playing music from the grand staff, read the notes vertically (top to bottom) before moving on horizontally (left to right).

♪ Play the song a couple of times with the right hand by itself. Then play the song a few times with the left hand only. When you're confident with the notes for each hand, you can try playing the song with both hands together.

♪ Play slowly at first and speed up the tempo as you become more comfortable with the songs.

♪ Be patient and calm.

♪ Ask listeners to leave for awhile and allow you a chance to practice. Invite them in for the concert after you feel good about your playing.

In the classic "Yankee Doodle" (Track 38), you can try reading from both clefs at once with a double-handed melody. Although the melodies look completely different on the different staves, they are actually the exact same — you play the same named keys with both hands.

TRACK 38

Yankee Doodle

"On Top of Old Smoky" (Track 39) gets you working a melody with the right hand and some arpeggios with the left hand. After you get the hang of it, your left hand starts rocking back and forth effortlessly on the arpeggiated patterns. If the bass clef gets too intimidating to read, lock your hand in position for an arpeggio and move LH 5 to each new root note. From each root note you can easily find the appropriate arpeggio notes and go to town . . . or to the top of Old Smoky.

TRACK 39

On Top of Old Smoky

Part IV
Living in Perfect Harmony

The 5th Wave   By Rich Tennant

"Normally, a cross-hand technique is used for reaching upper register notes. But what you're doing is fine, as long as it doesn't hurt."

In this part . . .

Ah, sweet harmony, the essence of life. The thing that brings the world together. To sing as one nation. To find the effervescent . . . oh, enough already.

Impress your friends with your newfound gift of "perfect pitch" by telling them the intervals used in lots of famous songs. Play a melody in different keys. Build huge chords of indescribable (until now) proportions. Part IV even shows you how to play songs on your telephone, among other, more useful skills.

Chapter 10

The Building Blocks of Harmony

● ●

In This Chapter

▶ Measuring the distance between two notes

▶ Recognizing notes by sound

▶ Constructing harmony

▶ Harmonizing up a melody

● ●

When you listen to music, the melody usually sticks out in your ears. Either that or the ultra-funky drumbeat. You are less aware of the other notes being played along with the melody to form the *harmony* of the music.

Without harmony, you would hear one single note at a time. On your piano, you can play more than one note at a time, giving it the coveted distinction of being an instrument capable of harmonizing. Sure, other instruments in a band or orchestra can play collectively to form harmony, but you can harmonize by yourself with a piano.

Playing many notes simultaneously is the essence of harmony. The notes you choose and how you arrange them around the melody determines the kind of harmony you produce, whether you use many notes or just one note with each hand. Go ahead and try it: Play two, three, four, even ten notes at once. Ah, sweet harmony . . . or a cluttered mess, depending on what notes you play.

Measuring Harmony on a Scale

The distance between any two musical notes is called an *interval*. You may think I'm just trying to make you swallow a music dictionary. Actually, you need to understand this term, the concept of intervals, and which notes make up each interval so that you can select the correct notes to build harmonies.

You measure an interval by the number of half steps and whole steps in between the two notes. (See Chapter 8 for more information on whole and half steps.) But because this method involves lots of counting, memorization, and complicated arithmetic, I have an easier solution: Use the major scale as a measuring tape. (Again, Chapter 8 tells you all about scales.)

Each major scale contains eight notes that you can use to name intervals. For example, Figure 10-1 shows the ever-popular C major scale. In the space below each note of the scale, I number the notes from 1 to 8. Don't I have nice handwriting?

Figure 10-1: Numbering notes on a scale.

You use these eight numbers to name every interval in a scale. You simply pick two notes and count the scale notes in between to find the name of the interval you are playing.

For example, if you play the first note of the scale (C) followed by the fifth note (G), you just played a *fifth* interval. If you count the scale notes in between C and G, you get five — C, D, E, F, G. From C to E (the *third* note) is a . . . *third* interval. Not much originality in these names, but is this easy or what?

But you don't have to start with the first note of the scale to make a fifth interval. Remember, this concept of intervals is all about distance. You can build a fifth interval on the note G with the fifth scale note up, D. It's easy to check yourself — just count the scale notes in between.

Notice that I count the number of scale notes, *not* the number of piano keys. If you count the piano keys (black and white) from G to D, for example, this simple number naming of intervals doesn't work. And I prefer not to devise some algebraic equation to make it work, thank you.

Figure 10-2 shows you the C major scale again, but this time I marked every interval in the scale.

Intervals

Figure 10-2: A family of intervals.

I use the C scale as an example because it's so easy, with no sharps or flats. However, this method of number-naming the intervals works for every single major scale. Simply write out the scale and number the notes from 1 to 8 — it works the same every time.

Interval shorthand

Like scales, intervals come in different varieties: *major, minor,* and *perfect.* Knowing these classifications helps you make appropriate harmonies for the music you play. For example, if you want to build a minor chord to harmonize with a melody, you must use a minor interval. (Chapter 12 tells you all about building chords.)

All intervals start out as either major or perfect. You can make a minor interval by lowering a major interval one half-step. The perfect intervals can't be made minor, because they're just too darn perfect as is.

In an eternal attempt to be lazy, er, efficient, most musicians use the following abbreviations, or shorthand, when discussing intervals:

♪ *M* for major intervals

♪ *m* for minor intervals

♪ *P* for perfect intervals

♪ Numbers for the size interval. For example, a fifth uses the number 5.

Therefore, when you see *P5,* you know I mean a perfect fifth. When you see *M2,* I mean a major second. When you see *m6,* I mean a minor sixth.

I would be remiss not to point out that intervals can be measured upwards or downwards. That is, when you play a C-G fifth interval, you can say that G is a fifth above C or that C is a fifth below G. So, when I say *descending* interval, I mean measured from the top note to the bottom note. Likewise, when I say *ascending,* I mean . . . oh, you can figure that out.

In the sections that follow, I explain each interval on the scale and give you an example of a famous tune that uses the interval. I encourage you, even beg you, to play each of the examples on your piano. Nothing trains a musician more than playing and hearing at the same time. Put these intervals in your head along with the corresponding famous tunes, and I guarantee that you won't forget them.

2nds

Have you ever sung a song called "Happy Birthday" to yourself or someone else at a birthday party? Okay, have you ever heard anyone sing "Happy Birthday" — perhaps six restaurant waiters more embarrassed than the person they're singing it to?

The first interval you sing in this celebratory song is a *major second interval,* or *M2*. Go ahead and sing it. "Hap-py Birth-" Stop! On "Birth" you jump up a major second interval. Using the C scale, a M2 is the distance from C to D.

Another song beginning with a M2 is "London Bridge," which you see in Figure 10-3. Every time you play the name of the bridge, you go up and back down a major second. Go ahead — try it on your piano.

Figure 10-3: Getting acquainted with major second intervals.

You create a *minor second,* or *m2,* simply by making the major second a half-step smaller. In other words, play C to D-flat. Play it again and again and again, faster, faster . . . look out — SHARK! Oh, sorry. I always hear a m2 as the famous interval used in the *Jaws* theme by composer John Williams. Figure 10-4 shows you an m2 on dry ground, this one from Rimsky-Korsakov's "Scheherazade." Play it yourself and hear how the interval sounds.

Figure 10-4: A minor second interval.

3rds

If a composer could copyright an interval, the copyright for the *major third (M3)* would belong to Ludwig van Beethoven. The first four notes of his legendary *Fifth Symphony* employ a M3. And if that isn't enough, Ludwig tried to own the *minor third (m3),* too, by using it in the next four notes of the theme. Play Figure 10-5, a snippet of the *Fifth Symphony,* and you will forever know thirds.

Figure 10-5:
Major and minor thirds together in the same piece.

You also hear the M3 interval frequently in spirituals. Figure 10-6 shows this interval in the songs "Kum-bah-yah" and "Swing Low, Sweet Chariot."

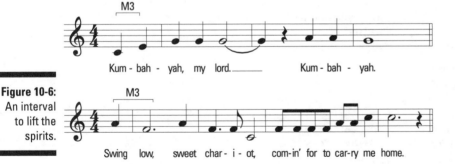

Figure 10-6:
An interval to lift the spirits.

For some reason even unknown to Beethoven, a m3 seems to attract children. As you see in Figure 10-7, the opening notes of the children's favorite "This Old Man" form a m3, which is smaller than a M3 by a half-step. Hip to the Pied Piper-effect of the m3, the creators of Barney adopted this tune for the Great Purple One's theme song.

Figure 10-7: A minor interval close to children's hearts.

4ths

The fourth interval gets the hyperbolic classification of being perfect. From C to F is a *perfect fourth (P4)*. Perhaps this is a good classification for this interval, because a P4 is perfect for just about any kind of emotion.

Composers use this interval to convey heroism, love, comedy, and even outer space in their melodies. I don't have the room, nor the copyright clearance, to show you the extended use of P4's in film music. So, how about a folk song?

Play and sing the opening notes of "I've Been Working On The Railroad" and you jostle back and forth on a P4 until the lyric "the" ruins the fun, as shown in Figure 10-8.

Figure 10-8: The perfect fourth interval in (loco)motion.

You can also hear a P4 at your best friend's wedding as the organist plays the attention-grabbing opening bars of "Here Comes the Bride," shown in Figure 10-9. See, I told you that composers use the P4 to write love music.

Figure 10-9: Conveying emotion with the perfect fourth interval.

5ths

Another perfect interval is the *perfect fifth (P5)*. Why is this one so perfect? Practically any song ever written has at least one P5 interval somewhere in it. And, hey, it fits the hand nicely: from C to G is C position. (Chapter 7 explains C position.)

As you play the first two notes of Figure 10-10, you may see stars. Or you may picture Bill Murray at a cocktail bar piano on *Saturday Night Live*, singing his parody of the song "Star Wars." Both "Twinkle, Twinkle Little Star" and the theme to "Star Wars" begin with a P5.

Figure 10-10:
A shining
star, the
perfect fifth
interval.

If you play a descending P5, from G to C, you may recognize the immortal classic "Feelings" and the theme from the *Flintstones* TV show. Speaking of classics and the Stone Age, Bach also used a P5 in the opening to his "Minuet," shown in Figure 10-11. Okay, Bach didn't live in the Stone Age, but it was a long time ago.

Figure 10-11:
A fifth
interval
descending
perfectly.

6ths and 7ths

A *major sixth (M6)* interval forms the opening interval of "My Bonnie Lies Over the Ocean," whatever the heck those lyrics mean. No, really, what does that mean? Anyway, "My Bon-" is the M6 interval, from C to A. If you play only from C to A-flat, you get a *minor sixth (m6);* Figure 10-12 shows you both sixths.

The *major seventh (M7)* and *minor seventh (m7)* are the last numbered intervals in the scale. Not many songwriters think of the seventh intervals as very melodic. Perhaps this is why no well-known songs use the M7 or m7 in a memorable way.

Figure 10-12: Bonnie's favorite intervals — the major and minor sixth intervals.

In any case, it's an important interval to know because the seventh interval helps form the third most popular chord in all music. (Chapter 12 tells you more about chords.) You can get to know these two interval sizes and judge for yourself how melodic they are after you play the notes in Figure 10-13.

Figure 10-13: Seventh (interval) heaven.

Octaves

You may think that the last interval in the scale would be called an eighth. You're partly right. For some reason, interval namers (another short-lived profession) grew tired of using numbers after the seventh and tried to liven things up with a fancy word. After about an hour of flipping through a thesaurus, they came up with the prefix *octa*, which means eight. (Think of the eight-legged octopus or the eight-sided octagon.) Bingo! An eighth interval is called an *octave (P8)*. The interval-namers were so proud of their accomplishment that they classified it as a perfect interval.

Figure 10-14 shows you a perfect octave, an interval made memorable by Judy Garland singing "Over the Rainbow" in *The Wizard of Oz*. In the opening lyrics, from "some" to "where" is an octave leap. Another easy way to remember this interval is that both notes have the same name.

Figure 10-14: Somewhere over the octave.

Building Harmony with Intervals

In the preceding section, you play each interval as single notes to see and hear the distance between each. But that's not harmony. You have to play the intervals together to get harmony.

Playing two notes together

Figure 10-15 shows each interval — perfect, major, and minor — from 2nds to an octave. Try playing the notes of each interval at the same time. Notice that the notes in each interval are stacked. When two notes appear stacked, or attached to the same stem, this means to play them at the same time. You know, in harmony.

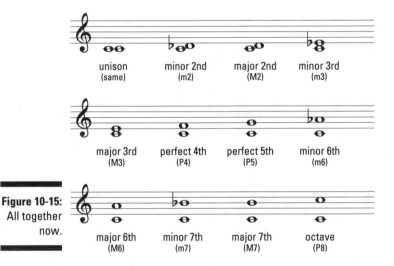

Figure 10-15: All together now.

Well, they sound just perfectly lovely. But how do you use these intervals for harmony? You can:

♪ Add intervals to the right hand under a melody line.

♪ Play intervals in the left hand while the right hand continues the melody.

♪ Do both.

Any way you choose, intervals can bring harmonic life to your music.

Adding intervals to the melody

Adding intervals to the melody really fills out the sound. For example, on Track 40, you can hear "America the Beautiful" played as a single-note melody, followed by the same melody played with right-hand intervals. Listen to the difference this harmony makes.

TRACK 40

America, the Beautiful

Try another song with right-hand intervals, this time with "Shenandoah" (renamed "Piano"), which can be heard on Track 41.

TRACK 41

Piano

It's not necessary for you to figure out how or when to add these intervals to a melody. The composer will do that for you and notate these intervals in the printed music you play. But you should understand that all of these intervals combine with the melody to make a very harmonic tune. Sure, you could just play the melody, or top note of each group of notes, but your audience will appreciate the extra effort of playing the intervals. Besides, why do you think you have so many fingers?

Of course, if you want to add intervals yourself, a sixth is the interval to choose. Take a simple melody like "Yankee Doodle" and add the sixth interval below each right-hand melody note. You can see how this is done in Figure 10-16.

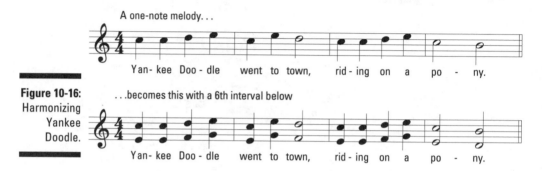

A one-note melody. . .

Yan- kee Doo - dle   went to town,   rid - ing on a   po - ny.

Figure 10-16: Harmonizing Yankee Doodle.

. . .becomes this with a 6th interval below

Yan- kee Doo - dle   went to town,   rid - ing on a   po - ny.

Find the sixth interval below the first melody note and freeze your hand in that position. Your pinky always plays the top note and your thumb always plays the bottom interval note. As you play up and down the melody, your hand lands on the correct sixth interval every time.

Encouraging lefty to join in

One of the easiest ways to add harmony to music is to play single notes with the left hand that form intervals with the right-hand melody notes. Often, you simply play one note with the left hand and hold it for several measures, adding harmony to several measures with just that one note.

You can see and hear the harmonizing power of single-note harmony in the song "Marianne." It may be helpful to play through the melody by itself, right hand only, along with Track 42 a couple of times. Then try the left-hand part only. When you're relaxed and confident, put both hands together.

TRACK 42

Marianne

"I'm Called Little Buttercup" (Track 43) is bit more difficult because the left hand plays notes of various lengths. Just hang in there and be patient, practicing each hand separately until you feel comfortable with the notes.

TRACK 43

I'm Called Little Buttercup

Bass note harmonies aren't always single notes. Try playing fifth intervals with your left hand in a song made famous by Elvis Presley (Track 44). Of course, Elvis used different lyrics — something about loving him tender. If you get lost as you play, just slow down and try each hand separately until you feel like putting them together again.

TRACK 44

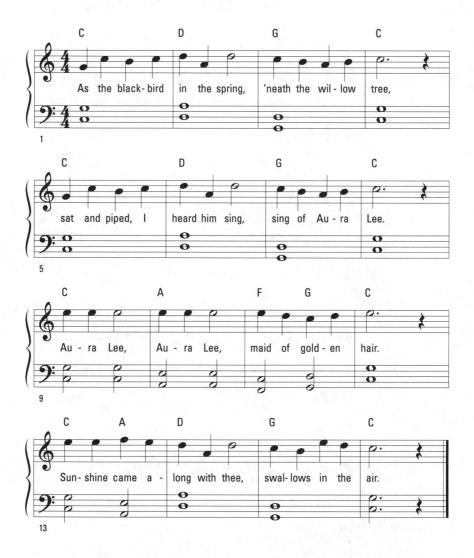

Your left hand isn't limited to single notes or fifth intervals. The composer may give you thirds, sixths, octaves, or anything else he or she desires. You can give your left hand a real workout with the next song, "Auld Lang Syne" (Track 45), which mixes up several types of intervals in the left hand. And I'm not embarrassed to say it again: Practice each hand separately before putting the two together.

14

Chapter 11

Understanding Keys

● ●

In This Chapter

▶ Finding a home for your music

▶ Introducing key signatures

▶ Naturalizing some notes

● ●

Keys allow you to drive a car, open doors, read maps, and even roller skate. Keys may be frustrating when you misplace them several times a week, but they're still handy and essential tools in life — and in music.

In this chapter, I tell you about musical keys. I'm not talking about the black and white keys you press when you play a keyboard. This is a completely, utterly, totally, wholly different type of key. And it won't unlock your car either.

Home Sweet Home

A *key* is a set of notes that corresponds to a certain scale. (Chapter 8 tells you all about scales.) Keys (scales) provide a foundation of compatible notes which composers can use to construct melodies and harmonies.

A musical key is a song's home. The key tells you several things about a song: which sharps and flats will be used in the song (see Chapter 2 to understand sharps and flats), which scale the song is based on (see Chapter 8 for more on scales), and much more.

When a song is *in the key of C,* it means that the song is primarily based on the C major scale, using mostly (or only) notes from that scale for the song's melody and harmony. Throughout the song, your ears get comfortable with notes from the C major scale. If the composer throws in a slew of other notes from another scale (like F-sharp), it's a bit unsettling to your ears. When the song returns to notes from the C major scale, your ears feel at home again.

The real definition of a song's key is not, of course, a song's home. As some music snobs quickly point out, a song's key is its *tonal center,* meaning the *tones* of a scale that the melody and harmony of the song are *centered* around. But, please. That's just about as interesting as watching paint dry.

A whole ring of keys

Music uses many different keys, which are named after the many different notes on your keyboard. In other words, you have a musical key for the notes A, B, C, D, E, F, and G, plus all the sharps and flats.

Like the various homes in your neighborhood, each key has its own unique character, look, feel, and sound. A composer uses a particular key to give his or her music the right sound and feeling. How so? Each musical key has a slightly different overall sound to it.

I can expound on the differences between each of the keys for probably another 30 pages, but you would bypass such a snoozerama quicker than you can say "spare me." The best way to show you the difference keys can make to music is to have you listen to the same song written in two different keys. Listen to, or play, "Good Night, Ladies" (Track 46), which is in the key of C.

 TRACK 46

Good Night, Ladies (in the key of C)

You can also play "Good Night, Ladies" in the key of F (Track 47). Although the melody and harmony of the song are exactly the same, the sound and character are subtly changed simply by changing keys.

TRACK 47

These songs are the same; only the names of the notes and chords have been changed . . . to protect the innocent (I couldn't resist!).

Composers and performers find keys very, very helpful. Keys allow musical selections to be modified to fit different performers. For example, if a composer writes a song in the key of G, for example, and the melody is too high for a particular singer to sing, the song can be changed to a lower key (like F or E) to accommodate the singer's voice. The composer likes this, because the overall song isn't affected, only the highness or lowness of the melody. Changing the musical key of a song is called *transposing,* a frequent occurrence in music.

Leaving and returning to the "home" key

No matter what a home looks or sounds like, its basic purpose is the same as every other house: to have a place to cool your heels and relax. The same applies to keys.

Melodies and harmonies in a song often venture outside of the song's basic key. Particularly in jazz music, performers realize that exploring notes and chords outside of the original key lifts the music and gives it a fresh sound. Composers as far back as you can imagine used various keys to carry the music to new and unfamiliar places. Hey, an all-expenses-paid vacation for the ears! After such an "out of key" experience, you feel a sense of "coming home" when the song returns to the original key.

To get a better grasp on this concept of musical travel, listen to Track 48, Figure 11-1, which begins in the key of A and travels around to other keys for a few measures. Just by listening (without cheating and looking at the notes), see if you can tell when the song returns home to its original key.

Did you hear it? In measure 9, the music begins to venture outside of the original home key of C. In measure 13, the song returns safely to the key of C. I hope you weren't too "tense" during measures 9 through 12.

Figure 11-1: Destination unknown . . . leaving and returning home.

Using Keys to Play Music

As a performer, recognizing and reading keys is an invaluable skill, more so than just how high or low a song sounds. Understanding keys helps you play better because the key of a song tells you a little more about the music under your fingers — more specifically, which notes to play or not to play.

For example, if you play a melody in the key of G, you mostly play notes from the G major scale. Your knowledge of scales (see Chapter 8) reminds you that G contains the note F-sharp. Thus, you play all the Fs in the song as F-sharp.

Those crafty composers invented a way to remind you which sharps and flats to play within a particular key. To conserve ink, composers employ a little tool called a *key signature*. Placed just after the clef on every line of music, a key signature allows the composer to:

♪ Stop writing all those little tic-tac-toe symbols next to every sharp in the song.

♪ Stop writing flats next to every flat in the song.

♪ Instantly tell the performer (that's you!) what key the song is in.

Sure, you may already have framed pictures of sharps and flats on your living room wall because you like the looks of them so much. But as the music becomes more and more complex, please believe me that you do not want to see these symbols cluttering the music. Instead, you too will want to use the ink-saving key signature tool thingamajig.

Reading key signatures

Figure 11-2 shows you two key signatures: one for the key of G and one for the key of F. The first shows a sharp symbol on the top line of the staff. This tells you to play every F as F-sharp. The G major scale contains one sharp, so this must be the key of G. The second key signature uses a flat on the middle line of the staff, telling you to play every B as B-flat. This must be the key of F, because the F major scale has one flat, B-flat.

Key of G:

Figure 11-2: Key of F:
Sign on
the line.

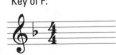

You may think that only Fs on the top line are altered by the sharp in the key signature. Nope! The key signature applies to every F, not just the one on the top line. This, of course, is another time- and ink-saving decision. Otherwise a G key signature would look like the one in Figure 11-3.

Figure 11-3:
All right,
already . . .
F-sharp!

The only time the same note is marked with a sharp or flat twice in a key signature is when you have two staves. In this case, you get one key signature on the treble staff and one on the bass staff, as shown in Figure 11-4.

Figure 11-4:
Signing with
both hands.

Try playing an entire song with a key signature. It's no more difficult than playing a song without one. You just have to remember (with a little help from your friendly key signature) which notes to sharp or flat throughout. Track 49 features a familiar tune, called "Worried Man Blues," in the key of G. Play along when you're ready and remember that all Fs are actually F-sharp.

TRACK 49

Worried Man Blues (in the key of G)

Try the same song, now written in the key of D, which you can hear on Track 50. Notice the key signature and remember to play Fs as F-sharp and Cs as C-sharp. Have fun and good luck!

Finding keys the E-Z way

A key signature tells you instantly which key the song is in. You may be thinking, "Well, if I have to count all the sharps or flats and then figure out which scale they're in, that's not going to be very instantaneous!" Think again. You don't have to do anything of the sort. Without counting, without playing — without even thinking about it really — you can simply glance at the key signature and know immediately which key the song is in.

Key signatures with sharps

To read a key signature that contains sharps, follow these steps:

1. **Locate the last sharp (farthest to the right) on either the treble or bass clef.**

2. **Move up one half-step to find the name of the key the song is played in.**

For example, if you have two sharps, F-sharp and C-sharp, the last one is C-sharp. Up a half-step from C-sharp is D. The song is in the key of D.

Figure 11-5 shows you key signatures for all sharp keys. See how quickly you can name the key for each of these.

Figure 11-5:
Sharp keys.

G   D   A   E   B   F♯   C♯

Note that keys with lots of sharps use a slight bit of brain power. For example, on your piano keyboard the key one half-step up from E is F. This is also (technically) called E-sharp. So, if the sixth sharp in the key signature is E-sharp (which is the same as F-natural), you raise it one half-step to determine the correct key, which is F-sharp.

Key signatures with flats

To read a key signature that contains flats, just locate the next-to-the-last flat (second from the right) in the key signature. That's the name of the key you're in. For example, if you have three flats in a key signature — B-flat, E-flat, and A-flat — the next to the last one is E-flat. The song is in the key of E-flat. Figure 11-6 shows all of the flat keys.

Figure 11-6:
Flat keys.

F   B♭   E♭   A♭   D♭   G♭   C♭

There is one key that has a signature you must memorize — the key of F. Because it has only one flat (B-flat), there is no such thing as a "next-to-the-last" flat for you to read. So, you must remember that one flat in the key signature means that a song is in the key of F. I have no easy way for you to remember this, and I am terribly sorry.

Whoops! Taking back the key signature

Occasionally a composer adds some variety to a song by throwing in a note from outside the key, such as an F-natural in the key of G. These notes from outside the key are called *accidentals.*

Personally, the term *accidental* makes me laugh. If the note is really an accident, the composer would surely have corrected it by now. In any case, the note indicated is the correct note (not an accident) and you should play it as it's written.

Composers use a *natural sign,* shown in measures 1 and 3 of Figure 11-7, to indicate when you should play a note from outside the key. For example, in the key of G, all Fs are F-sharp. So, if a composer "accidentally" wants you to play F-natural, you see a natural sign next to the F. The natural sign over-rules the sharp in the key signature, but only for one measure or until you see another F-sharp, whichever comes first.

Figure 11-7: Not all Fs are sharp.

Many songs use accidentals to add freshness to the melody. If you've ever seen a baseball game, an Olympic gold medal ceremony, or a station sign-off on TV, you know "The Star-Spangled Banner" (Track 51). But you probably don't know that the melody contains several accidentals. Do you know that the composer is Francis Scott *Key?* How appropriate.

The Star-Spangled Banner

Accidentals aren't always natural notes. Because the key of C has no sharps or flats, the notes F-sharp, B-flat, or any other black key on the keyboard are deemed accidentals in the key of C. Thus, you see a sharp or flat symbol next to these accidental notes.

Give yourself a hand

Want an easy way to find the key signature for the most common keys? All you need are five fingers and a short memory.

The most common keys you play in are C, F, G, D, A, E, and B. The first two are a piece of cake to remember: C has no sharps or flats, and F has only B-flat. For the other five common keys (which happen to all have sharps), memorize the order G-D-A-E-B with a simple mnemonic of your choice:

♪ **G**ood **D**iamonds **A**re **E**xpensive (to) **B**uy

♪ **G**lass **D**oors **A**re **E**asily **B**roken

♪ **G**rand **D**ivas **A**ren't **E**ver **B**ashful

Next, count out the keys in order on the fingers of one hand until you get to the key you need. For the key of A, count G, D, A. How many fingers are you holding up? Three. The key of A has three sharps.

The sharps in a key signature always appear in ascending 5ths, starting with F-sharp. Thus, the three sharps in the key of A are F-sharp, C-sharp, and G-sharp.

Chapter 12

Filling Out Your Sound with Chords

● ●

In This Chapter

▶ Building chords

▶ Reading chord symbols

▶ Flipping the notes around

● ●

A quick glance through this chapter may have you thinking, "Why do I need to know how to build chords?" I have one answer you may like: to impress your friends. Wait, here's another: to play like a pro.

Playing melodies is nice and all, but harmony is the key to making your music sound fuller, better, cooler, and just downright great. Playing chords with your left hand is perhaps the easiest way to harmonize a melody. Playing chords with your right hand, too, is a great way to accompany a singer, guitarist, or even a circus performer.

This chapter shows you step-by-step how to build chords and use them to accompany any melody.

Pulling the Chords

Three or more notes played at the same time form a *chord*. These notes can be played by one hand or both hands. Chords have but one simple purpose in life: to provide harmony. (Chapter 10 tells you all about harmony.)

To understand the power of harmony, listen to "Red River Valley" on Track 52 of the CD. The first time, the song is played as melody only, without any harmony. The second time, you hear the melody and harmony. Doesn't that sound much better?

You may have encountered chords already in a number of situations, including the following:

♪ You see several musical notes stacked on top of each other on a printed sheet of music.

♪ You notice strange symbols above the treble clef staff that make no sense when you read them: F#m7(-5), Csus4(add9).

♪ You hear a band or orchestra play.

♪ You honk a car horn.

Yes, the sound of a car horn is a chord, albeit a hideous-sounding chord. So are the sounds of a barbershop quartet, a church choir, and a sidewalk accordion player (monkey with tip jar is optional). Chances are, though, that you probably won't use car horns or barbers to accompany your melodies — piano chords are much more practical.

Why the phone company hates me

Want to annoy the heck out of your friends? Call them up and play some songs with the touch-tone buttons on your phone. It's not exactly playing chords, but it's a whole lot of fun.

The following figure gives you the notations for three well-known songs. Under the notes are the phone numbers to press. Have fun!

A word of caution: Don't just pick up the phone and start playing the songs. You may end up dialing China, the police, or (even worse) your in-laws.

And you can stop wondering . . . 9-1-1 isn't a song, so don't "play" it.

The Anatomy of a Chord

Chords begin as very simple little creatures. Like melodies, chords are also based on scales. (Chapter 8 gives you the skinny on scales.) To make a chord, you select a note, any note, and put other scale notes on top of it.

Generally, the lowest note of a chord is called the *root note*. (Think of this like trees — the roots are on the bottom.) The root note also gives the chord its name. For example, a chord with A as its root note is an A chord.

The notes you use on top of the root note give the chord its *type*, which I explain later in this chapter.

Most chords begin as *triads*, or three *(tri)* notes added *(ad)* together. Okay, that's not the actual breakdown of the word *triad*, but it may help you remember what triad means.

A triad consists of a root note and two other notes — a 3rd interval and a 5th interval. (Chapter 10 tells you about all the fun and games involved in intervals.) Figure 12-1 shows you a typical triad played on the white keys C-E-G. C is the root note, E is a 3rd interval from C, and G is a 5th interval from C.

Figure 12-1:
C, a simple
triad.

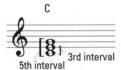

By altering this C triad in any of the following ways, you build new chords:

♪ Raising or lowering notes of the triad by a half step or whole step.

♪ Adding notes to the triad.

♪ Both of the above.

♪ None of the above (some triads are perfectly good chords just as they are).

For example, you could use other intervals from the C major scale to change the C triad and make new chords all day long. Figure 12-2 shows you four different ways to change the C triad and make four new chords. Play each of these chords to hear how they sound. I've marked the note intervals in each chord. (Again, Chapter 10 explains these intervals and abbreviations.)

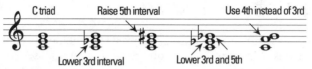

Figure 12-2: Making chords from the C triad.

And, of course, the C triad by itself is a perfectly good chord as is. In fact, it is a *C major chord,* explained in the next section.

Major Chords

Major chords are perhaps the most frequently used, most familiar, and easiest chords to play. Many triads are also major chords.

You make major chords with the notes and intervals of a major scale. (Chapter 8 provides a field guide to major scales.) You build a major chord by starting out with a root note and then adding other notes from the desired chord's scale. For example, suppose you want to build a G major chord. Play the root note G and add the third and fifth notes from the G major scale on top of the root note — or the 3rd and 5th intervals.

Major chords are so common that musicians treat them as almost the norm; major chords are named with just the name of the root. (Figure 12-3 shows you four such major chords.) Similarly, musicians rarely say "major," except for those musicians in the army. Instead, they just say the name of the chord.

Figure 12-3: Major chords.

Use fingers 1, 3, and 5 to play major chords. If you're playing left-hand chords, start with LH5 on the root note. For right-hand chords, play the root note with RH1.

Play a few of these major monsters with your left hand in the song "Down by the Station" (Track 53). You can play the melody with your right hand or just play the chords with your left hand while the piano player on the CD (that's me!) plays the melody.

TRACK 53

Down by the Station

Minor Chords

The second most popular chord is the *minor chord*. Like the major chord, a minor chord is composed of three notes: a root note, a 3rd interval, and a 5th interval. Minor chords get the suffix *m,* or sometimes *min*. Get it? An abbreviation for "minor."

Don't be fooled by the name "minor." These chords are no smaller or any less important than major chords. They simply sound different. Many purists would banish me from their kingdom for saying this, but I like to think of major chords as sounding "happy" and minor chords as sounding "sad." (I also use this analogy when discussing scales in Chapter 8.)

You can make a minor chord two different ways:

♪ Play a major chord and lower the second note, or 3rd interval, by one half step. For example, a C major chord has the notes C-E-G. To play a C minor chord, lower the E to E-flat.

♪ Play the root note and add the third and fifth notes of the minor scale on top. For example, play A as the root note and add the third note (C) and fifth note (E) of the A minor scale on top.

Figure 12-4 shows you several minor chords with the root notes and intervals marked. Please feel free to play them and hear how they sound. Compare these chords to their major counterparts in Figure 12-3 of the previous section.

Figure 12-4:
Minor,
but not
insignificant,
chords.

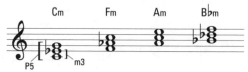

Just like playing major chords, use fingers 1, 3, and 5 for minor chords. For left-hand minor chords, play the root note with LH5; for right-hand chords, play the root note with RH1.

Try playing a song that has both major and minor chords mixed together. Composer Edward MacDowell's little gem "To a Wild Rose," heard on Track 54, is one such example. This mixture of major and minor chords isn't weird by any means. Many songs use a combination of these chord types. The subtle difference in the two chords' sounds gives the music an interesting harmony.

Exploring Other Types of Chords

Major and minor chords are great, and by far the most popular chords, but other types of chords get equal opportunity to shine in music. These "other" chords are formed by altering the notes of a major or minor chord or by adding notes to a major or minor chord.

Augmented and diminished chords

Major and minor chords differ from each other only in the 3rd interval. But the top note, the 5th interval, is the same for both types of chords. By altering the 5th interval of a major or minor chord, you can create two new chord types.

An *augmented chord* contains a root note, a major third (M3) interval, and an *augmented fifth* interval, which is a perfect fifth (P5) raised one half step. Think of this as simply a major chord with the top note raised one half-step. Figure 12-5 shows several augmented chords.

Figure 12-5: Augmented chords.

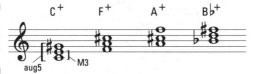

The suffixes used for augmented chords include +, *aug,* and *#5.* I like the last suffix because it actually tells you what to do to change the chord — to sharp the fifth.

A *diminished chord* contains a root note, a minor third (m3) interval, and a *diminished fifth* (dim5) interval, which is a perfect fifth interval lowered one half-step. Figure 12-6 gives you a selection of diminished chords.

Figure 12-6: Diminished, but not defeated, chords.

Notice the two suffixes used to signal a diminished chord: *dim* and °. Is it hot in here, or does one of those symbols look like a degree sign?

For some reason, I find it easiest to use fingers 1, 2, and 4 for augmented and diminished chords played with the right hand. For the left hand, I find it comfortable to use 5, 3, and 1 just like with major and minor chords.

Fire up the keyboard (please, not literally) and take these new chords out for a spin. The song "Rags and Riches" (Track 55) is a good example of how augmented and diminished chords subtly affect a song's harmony. In some ways, your ears expect major or minor chords, but what a treat they get instead.

Adding suspense to your chords

Another popular type of three-note chord, although it's technically not a triad, is the *suspended chord.* Talk about leaving you hanging! The very name means "hanging," and the sound of a suspended chord always leaves you waiting for the next notes or chords.

The two types of suspended chords are the *suspended second* and *suspended fourth.* Because of their hip abbreviated suffixes, these chords are often referred to as the *sus2* and *sus4* chords. Furthermore, the sus4 is so popular that musicians often just call it the *sus* chord. So, when the bandleader says to play "a sus chord on beat 1," that probably means to play a suspended fourth. But I recommend asking for clarification.

A sus2 chord is made up of a root note, a major second (M2) interval, and a perfect fifth (P5) interval. A sus4 chord has a root note, a perfect fourth (P4), and a P5 interval. Figure 12-7 shows you some of these suspenseful chords.

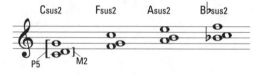

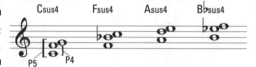

Figure 12-7:
Sus chords.

What's being suspended, exactly? Nothing, really; you're still playing three notes in the chord. But notice in Figure 12-7 that these two types of chords differ from major and minor chords by only one note. That is, the middle note of a major chord is a major third interval; the middle note of a minor chord is a minor third interval. When you play a suspended chord, it sounds so close to a major or minor chord that your ear misses hearing the more common 3rd interval in the middle, so it sounds like you're suspending the 3rd interval. Actually, you're just playing a cool new chord.

Fingering suspended chords is pretty easy. For the right hand, use fingers 1, 2, and 5 for sus2 chords; use fingers 1, 4, and 5 for sus4 chords. For left-hand sus2 chords, use fingers 5, 4, and 1; use fingers 5, 2, and 1 for left-hand sus4 chords.

Not always, but most of the time, the *resolution chord* that follows a sus-pended chord is the major or minor chord that your ear was longing to hear. It's called a *resolution chord* because it resolves the conflict your ear is having with you for not playing its favorite major or minor chords. Play along with Figure 12-8, Track 56, and listen to how the chord that follows each sus chord sounds resolved.

Figure 12-8:
A little
suspension
tension.

More Four the Money

Adding a fourth note to a triad fills out the sound of a chord even more. Composers often use chords of four notes or more to create musical tension. Hearing this tension, or unresolved sound, the ear begs for resolution, usually found in a major or minor chord that follows. (The previous section also discusses resolved chords.) At the very least, these chords make you want to keep listening. To a composer, that's always a good thing.

Many people consider the 7th interval an ugly-sounding interval. But the 7th interval isn't ugly when it's added to a chord. In fact, the result is perhaps the third most popular chord in Western music. I certainly like it.

Each of the four types of three-note chords I introduce earlier in this chapter — major, minor, augmented, diminished — is capable of becoming a *seventh chord,* if it tries really hard and eats all of its spinach. But seriously, folks, simply attaching a 7th interval, or the seventh note of the scale, on top of any chord makes that chord a seventh chord.

Your basic seventh chord uses the *minor seventh* interval. This is the seventh note up the scale from the chord's root, but lowered one half step. For example, if the root note is C, the seventh note up the scale is B. Lower this note by one half step and you get a minor seventh interval, B-flat.

The four-note chords shown in Figure 12-9 are all seventh chords. Careful with the suffix: It's a highly-complicated Arabic numeral *7*.

Figure 12-9:
Nothing
plain about
these
seventh
chords.

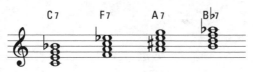

The suffixes used by seventh chords are placed *after* the triad type's suffix. For example, if you add an m7 to a diminished chord, the suffix *7* would come after *dim,* giving you *dim7* as the full chord type suffix.

To play seventh chords, use fingers 1, 2, 3, and 5. My apologies to finger 4 for not allowing it to take part in these chords. For right-hand seventh chords, play the root note with RH1 and the top note (the 7th) with RH5. With the left hand, the root note is played with LH5, while LH1 plays the top note.

You find all kinds of seventh chords in all kinds of music, from classical to pop. Johannes Brahms' famous "Lullaby" (Track 57) is an example of how seventh chords can create a little harmonic variety. Just don't let it lull you to sleep.

TRACK 57

Lullaby

Reading Chord Symbols

When you encounter sheet music or songbooks with just melodies and lyrics printed in them, you usually also get little letters and symbols above the staff, as shown in Figure 12-10. These are called *chord symbols,* which are abbreviations for the names of the chords to play with the melody. And this is precisely why I explain how to build chords — so that you can make a G diminished chord, for example, when you see the symbol for one, *Gdim.*

Figure 12-10: Reading chord symbols above the staff.

A chord's symbol tells you two things about that chord: *root* and *type.* As with scales, the root note gives the chord its name. The root of a C chord is the note C.

Any suffix following the chord name represents the chord's type. In previous sections of this chapter, I explain suffixes like *m* for minor and *7* for seventh chords. Major chords have no suffix, just the letter name.

Try playing the song "Bingo" (Track 58), which shows only melody, lyrics, and chord symbols. Your right hand plays the melody as written; your left hand plays the chords named by the symbols above the staff. It helps to figure out the chords first and play through them a couple of times before adding the melody.

 TRACK 58

Bingo

The chord name, or chord symbol, is your set of blueprints for what type of chord to construct and how to do it. For any chord types you may come across in your musical life (and plenty of chords are out there), you can build the chord by placing the appropriate intervals or scale notes on top of the root note. For example, *C6* means play a C major chord and add the 6th interval (A); *Cm6* means to play a C minor chord and add the 6th interval.

You may encounter many ominous-looking chord symbols in the songs you play. Table 12-1 is a list of the most common and user-friendly chord symbols and what they mean.

Table 12-1	Chord Suffixes
Chord type	*Chord suffixes*
Major	No suffix
Minor	m, min
Augmented	+, aug, (♯5)
Diminished	dim, °
Suspended second	sus2
Suspended fourth	sus, sus4
Flatted fifth	♭5, -5
Sixth	6
Minor sixth	m6
Seventh	7
Major seventh	maj7, M7, 7
Minor seventh	m7, min7
Diminished seventh	dim7, °7
Seventh, sharped fifth	7♯5, +7
Seventh, flatted fifth	7♭5, 7(-5)
Minor seventh, flatted fifth	m7♭5, m7(-5)
Add ninth	(add9)

In addition to knowing the names and symbols of the many chord types, keep Table 12-2 handy as your recipe box for making these various kinds of chords. The numbers represent your scale note ingredients. In other words, the numbers 1-3-5-7, for example, mean to play the root, third, fifth, and seventh scale notes. If you see a flat or sharp sign, it tells you to lower or raise that scale note by a half step. Be sure to save these recipes for generations to come. (I've chosen the root note C for all of the chord types in Table 12-2. But don't be deceived — you can apply these recipes to any darn root note you like.)

Table 12-2	Chord Recipes	
Chord Symbol	*Chord Type*	*Scale Note Recipe*
C	Major	1-3-5
Cm	Minor	1-♭3-5
C+	Augmented	1-3-♯5
Cdim	Diminished	1-♭3-♭5
Csus2	Suspended second	1-2-5
C(add2), C(add9)	Add second (or ninth)	1-2-3-5
Cm(add2), Cm(add9)	Minor, add second	1-2-♭3-5
Csus	Suspended fourth	1-4-5
C♭5	Flat fifth	1-3-♭5
C6	Sixth	1-3-5-6
Cm6	Minor sixth	1-♭3-5-6
C7	Seventh	1-3-5-♭7
Cmaj7	Major seventh	1-3-5-7
Cm7	Minor seventh	1-♭3-5-♭7
Cdim7	Diminished seventh	1-♭3-♭5-6
C7sus	Seventh, suspended fourth	1-4-5-♭7
Cm(maj7)	Minor, major seventh	1-♭3-5-7
C7♯5	Seventh, sharp fifth	1-3-♯5-♭7
C7♭5	Seventh, flat fifth	1-3-♭5-♭7
Cm7♭5	Minor seventh, flat fifth	1-♭3-♭5-♭7
Cmaj7♭5	Major seventh, flat fifth	1-3-♭5-7

Figure 12-11 shows you exactly how to make a chord from the recipe shown in Table 12-2. I've applied the number recipe of 1-3-#5-7 to three different root notes — C, F, G — to illustrate how chord building works with different root notes and thus different scale notes. By the way, the resulting chord is called a *Cmaj7#5,* because you add the seventh interval and sharp (raise one half step) the fifth interval.

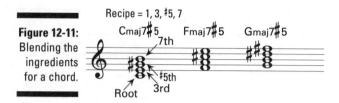

Figure 12-11:
Blending the
ingredients
for a chord.

Standing on Your Head

A chord's root is usually the bottom note of the chord, but not always. Thanks to certain civil liberties and inalienable rights, you're free to rearrange the notes of a chord any way you like without damaging the chord's type. This rearrangement, or repositioning, of the notes in a chord is called a *chord inversion*.

How many inversions are possible for a chord? It depends on the number of notes contained in the chord. If you have a three-note chord, you can make three inversions. If you have a four-note chord, you can make four inversions. Simple enough?

Putting inversions to work

Why would you want to rearrange a perfectly good chord? Play the left-hand chords in Figure 12-12 and notice how much your left hand moves around the keyboard.

Figure 12-12:
It's in your
roots.

Playing the chords in Figure 12-12 at a fast tempo becomes tiring and sloppy-sounding. The solution is to use chord inversions. Play Figure 12-13 and notice how your left hand moves around much, much less. You are playing the same chords, but without moving your left hand up and down the keyboard.

Making a song easier to play is just one of the various reasons you may choose to use chord inversions. Using inversions may be helpful for any of the following reasons:

♪ **Hand position:** Avoid moving your hands up and down the keyboard from one root note to the next.

♪ **Top note:** Most of the time, you hear the top note of the chord above the rest of the notes. You may want to bring out the melody by playing chords with melody notes on top.

♪ **Chord boredom:** Yep. Root position chords get boring if used too frequently. Add some variety to a song with inversions.

♪ **The composer said so:** Enough said.

Figure 12-13:
Less effort, sounds great.

Flipping the notes fantastic

The most common chord positions are *root position, first inversion,* and *second inversion.* Root position is just like it sounds: The root goes on the bottom, as shown in Figure 12-14.

Figure 12-14:
Grabbing chords by the roots.

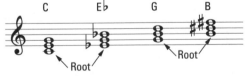

For the first inversion, you put the root on top, one octave higher than its original root position. The 3rd interval note is now on bottom. See Figure 12-15 for an example of a first inversion.

Figure 12-15:
Exposing
your roots.

Second inversion puts the 3rd interval note on top (or one octave higher than its original position), so that the 5th interval note is on the bottom and the root note is now the middle note of the chord. Figure 12-16 shows you some 2nd inversion chords.

Figure 12-16:
Roots in the
middle.

Use the exact same process for four-note chords. The difference is that another inversion is possible: the *third inversion*. It's easy enough to guess what you do: Put the top note, or fourth note, on the bottom, an octave lower than its original position. Figure 12-17 is an illustration of a third inversion, using seventh chords as an example.

Figure 12-17:
Third
inversions
of seventh
chords.

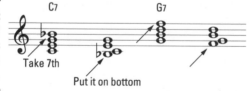

Experiment with these inversions on various types of chords. That way, when you're playing from a fake book, you'll know which inversions of which chords work best for you. (Chapter 19 explains what fake books are.)

Part V
Technique Counts for Everything

The 5th Wave   By Rich Tennant

The Liberace School of Classical Piano

That's very good, Martin. Except after the focosamente section you're forgetting to look out at the audience and give them a wink and a smile.

In this part . . .

In my opinion, this part is by far the coolest part in the book. I show you how to dress up your music so that people believe you if you tell them that you've been playing the piano for years.

Even if you *have* played piano for years, you can benefit from Part V. Sure, you may zip past the things you already know, like articulations and dynamics in Chapter 13, but the tricks in Chapter 14, or the styles in Chapter 15? You get left-hand patterns, intros and outros, key changes, and chord substitutions. It's indispensable material!

Well, indispensable except for the fact that it's printed on paper, which can be burned, torn, or thrown away. But you wouldn't do that, would you? Would you?

Chapter 13

Dressing Up Your Music

. . . .

In This Chapter

▶ Adding the perfect touches

▶ Making your notes fancier

. . . .

"When [the great pianist] Paderewski . . . played Beethoven, you could have written another sonata with the notes that showered from his hands, and any little second-rate piano-teacher could find plenty to criticize. But what feeling!"

— Composer Ottorino Respighi

Playing the right notes and rhythms of a song is important, but *how* you play is even more important. Playing music with feeling, technique, and passion makes a performance worth listening to. Dressing up the music and making it your own takes more than just playing the notes. And throwing in a few special effects doesn't hurt, either.

Dazzling effects and techniques in your music keep the audience listening, sometimes even on the edges of their seats. With a little practice, all of these effects are easy. And when you add them to the right spots in the music, your playing comes alive and you sound like a real pro.

Articulate the Positive

Don't think I'm reprimanding you when I tell you to "articulate" when you play. I'm simply referring to the way you play each note. The various ways to play a note are called *articulations*, often referred to as *attacks*. But I think "attack" implies a little more force than is necessary, so I use the less-combative word.

Articulation symbols

Articulations come in all shapes. Each one is represented by a symbol that tells you how to play the note: hard, long, short, and so on. You can change the entire sound and style of a song with the use of a few articulations. (Chapter 15 introduces you to many different musical styles and shows you which styles use which articulations.)

Table 13-1 shows you the symbols that composers use to indicate the various articulations.

Table 13-1		Musical Articulations
Symbol	**Name**	**How to Play the Note**
.	Staccato	Short
—	Tenuto	Long
>	Accent	Hard
∧	Accent (Housetop)	Harder
≥	Accent with staccato	Hard and short
≥	Accent with tenuto	Hard and long
tr	Trill	Alternating notes
↘	Gliss	Slide across the keys
♪	Grace note	Quickly before the "real" note
⌒.	Fermata	Hold

To add these articulations to music, the composer just places the appropriate symbol right underneath or right above the note.

The power of articulation

If you play music without articulations, you can forget about pleasing your audience. Listening to music without articulations is like suffering through a speech given in a monotone voice. Boring.

To understand the importance of articulation, listen to the song "Camptown Races" on Track 59 of the CD as you follow along with the printed music. The first time, you hear the song played without any articulations. But the second time, I play the music with all the articulations. (Measure 5 contains a trill, which you can read about later in this chapter.)

Camptown Races

Choose the articulations that interest you and apply them to your music. I'm sure Mozart and Co. wouldn't appreciate me telling you this, but forget what the composer says: Pencil in your own articulations and play the music your own way. It's not like you're changing the melody, just the style. Of course, following the composer's articulations is always your best solution for achieving the sound and style the composer intended — if that is your goal.

Will You Say Grace?

The term *grace note* sounds pretty fancy, but grace notes are actually a very uncomplicated effect that can make your music sound more complex. A grace note is a note that you play just slightly before a "real" note. In my opinion, it should be renamed a *graze* note because your finger just grazes the grace note before playing the real note.

Grace notes can be written in a number of different ways. Figure 13-1 shows you the most common types of grace notes. A single grace note looks like an eighth note with a slash through it. Think of the slash as meaning "cancel the rhythmic value." Multiple grace notes look like very small sixteenth notes. You play these very quickly, too, with a "rolling-into-the-note" kind of sound.

Figure 13-1:
Amazing
grace
notes, how
sweet the
sound.

A grace note does not have to be in close proximity to the full note that follows. Heck, a grace note could be all the way at the other end of the keyboard. The effect of a grace note is not derived by closeness but by how it gives the full note a little lift.

To hear some grace notes in action, listen to Track 60 as you follow along with the music to the rousing classic "Pop! Goes the Weasel," which is just bursting with grace notes. Practice the song slowly at first until your fingers sort of feel where to go . . . gracefully.

TRACK 60

Pop! Goes the Weasel

Grace notes are a common feature of blues, jazz, country, and classical piano music styles, which you can read more about in Chapter 15. Heck, you can use grace notes anywhere you like. The best grace notes are those that are a half-step or a whole step away from the full melodic note, but feel free to try ones that are even farther apart. Beginning a song's melody with a grace note is an excellent idea, especially if the song is in the jazz or blues style.

Just Trillin'

If you've ever heard the sound of a piccolo twittering high above the band in a John Phillip Sousa march, you've heard the effect of a *trill*. What sounds like a very elaborate trick for the piccolo player is actually a very simple procedure of alternating between two notes in rapid succession. The same holds true for trills in piano music.

What do they sound like? You mean the piccolo metaphor wasn't good enough for you? A trill sounds like a bunch of 32nd or 64th notes, as shown in Figure 13-2. (For more on 32nd and 64th notes, flip to Chapter 5.)

To conserve ink and to avoid having to write all those darn beams, composers use a shorthand symbol for trills: They write a *tr* above the trilled note. You know, "tr" as in the first two letters of the word "trill." Sometimes, music isn't so complicated.

Figure 13-2:
What a trill
sounds like.

Generally speaking, a note is trilled upward to the next closest scale tone. However, sometimes a composer wants a downward trill or even a half-step trill. If this is the case, the specific note to be used in the trill can be written several ways, as shown in Figure 13-3.

As you can see in Figure 13-3, a neurotic and overly productive composer has several ways to make absolutely sure that you trill to the right note. In addition to the *tr* symbol, the composer can write a sharp or flat sign, which tells you to trill to the note's sharp or to the note's flat. Another way of notating the trill is to write the specific trilled note as a small stemless notehead in parentheses next to the original note.

Figure 13-3:
Simon says,
"Trill this
note."

To err is human, to deceive is divine

Articulations and special effects, such as grace notes, trills, and glissandos, can really help you dress up your sound. In addition, they can help you cover up mistakes and wrong notes.

Whenever you play a wrong note, follow the mistake with a grace note, trill, or glissando.

For example, if you meant to hit a G, but you hit F-sharp, just make the F-sharp into a grace note and slide into the correct G note. You'll fool the audience nearly every time.

So, enough talk about trills — you should try playing some yourself. Listen to Jeremiah Clarke's famous "Trumpet Voluntary" on Track 61 to get an idea of how it should sound. Then try it yourself. Each trill is on the note D, played with RH2 (your right-hand index finger), and trills upward to E (the next highest scale tone), played with RH3. Alternate very rapidly between these two notes while counting the number of beats required for the trill, a dotted quarter note.

TRACK 61

Trumpet Voluntary

Don't wait for the composer to give you a trill — add 'em yourself. I feel confident that you can write *tr* above a note without much trouble. Half notes and whole notes are the best note lengths to trill because they are longer and allow you more time to get those fingers fluttering. Experiment with half-step and whole-step trills in different directions. Trills add a certain classical finesse to your playing style. (Chapter 15 tells you all about the classical style of music.)

Don't Miss the Gliss

A *glissando* (also known as a *gliss* in this lazy music industry) is a fast slide across several keys on the keyboard. There's nothing quite like starting and ending a song with this effect. I guarantee that it will dazzle any audience you care to play for.

To do a gliss, put your thumb on a high C note and drag your thumb down across the keys very quickly all the way to the bottom of the keyboard. Cool, huh?

Figure 13-4 shows you how this effect is notated, generally with a wavy line and the abbreviation "gliss" going from the note in the direction of the gliss. That is, if you see a wavy line going up from C, play the note C and slide up the keyboard. Sometimes the specific ending note is shown at the other end of the wavy line. Other times, it's up to you to decide where to stop.

Figure 13-4:
Gliss me,
gliss me,
now you
gotta
kiss me.

(Slide quickly from F to F)

(Slide quickly from C to C)   (Slide from C to your choice)

When the composer specifies both the beginning *and* ending of the gliss, all I can advise is practice, practice, practice. Starting on a specific note is easy, but stopping on the right note is like trying to stop a car on a dime.

Depending on the direction of the gliss and the hand you use, different fingers do the job. Figures 13-5 through 13-8 show you the correct hand positions for each of these glisses:

♪ **Downward with right hand:** Gliss with your thumb (RH1) as shown in Figure 13-5.

♪ **Upward with right hand:** Gliss with your middle finger (RH3) and perhaps a little help from RH4, as shown in Figure 13-6.

♪ **Downward with left hand:** Gliss with your middle finger (LH3) and perhaps a little help from LH4, as shown in Figure 13-7.

♪ **Upward with left hand:** Gliss with your thumb (LH1), as shown in Figure 13-8.

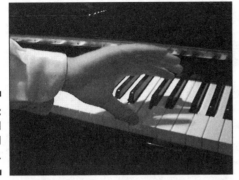

Figure 13-5:
Downward
right-hand
gliss.

Figure 13-6:
Upward
right-hand
gliss.

Figure 13-7:
Downward
left-hand
gliss.

Take away the gliss from rock 'n' roll and you might as well give artists like
Jerry Lee Lewis or Dr. John a copy of *Job Hunting For Dummies*. (Chapter 18
tells you more about these artists.) The effect of a glissando is altogether
powerful, energetic, and just plain rocking! Play a Jerry-sounding song along
with Track 62 to experience this sound sensation.

Figure 13-8:
Upward
left-hand
gliss.

To Gliss Is Bliss

After several times raking your fingers across the keys, you may begin to curse my name when your fingers start hurting. It's not my fault! You're using the wrong part of your finger to gliss: Use your *fingernail*. Of course, many hard-nosed perfectionists say to use the cuticle to avoid the sound of your fingernail clicking against the keys. But I say, "That hurts!" Besides, the volume from a glissando is more than enough to cover the sound of your nail clicking. And above all, don't play a gliss with your fingertips. Not only can this cause a blister (ouch!), but the squeaking sound is worse than scraping a chalkboard! You'll thank me for this someday.

Trembling Tremolos

A trill occurs when you flutter your fingers very quickly between two notes that are close together, either a half step or whole step apart. (I explain trills earlier in the chapter.) So, what do you call fluttering between two notes that are farther apart? Well, you call it whatever you want, but the world of music calls it a *tremolo*.

To play a tremolo, pick an interval, any interval larger than a whole step, and alternate playing the two notes as quickly as possible. (Chapter 10 tells you all about intervals.) Like a trill, this sounds as if you're playing a bunch of 32nd or 64th notes. But unlike the notation for a trill, which just puts the letters "tr" above one note, the notation for a tremolo actually shows you both notes that your fingers rumble between. (See Figure 13-9.)

Figure 13-9:
Too many
notes?

In Figure 13-9, you see that the two notes of a tremolo are shown with the same note length. At first glance, this notation looks like too many beats are in each measure, but the three diagonal lines between the notes signal you that this is a tremolo. These two notes share the note length. Therefore, you only count the beats of the first note.

Tremolos of any size sound great played by either hand. Probably the most popular left-hand tremolo is the octave tremolo. Stretch your hand over a C octave and let this interval rumble in a familiar melody. After one listen to Track 63, you may know this as the theme to the movie *2001: A Space Odyssey.*

TRACK 63

Also Sprach Zarathustra

You can also play tremolo chords. All you do is break the chord into two parts: a bottom note and the remaining top notes. Tremolo these notes by alternating between the top and bottom notes as quickly as possible. Tremolo chords may look intimidating, but if you can play the chord, you can play the tremolo. (Chapter 12 acquaints you with chords.)

Figure 13-10 gives you a chance to play a few tremolo chords. For the first measure of Figure 13-10, put your hand in position for a G major chord and rock between the top notes (B and D) and the bottom note (G) very quickly. Move to the next measure and do the same with a 2nd inversion C chord, and so on, and so on. (See Chapter 12 for more information on inversions.)

Working under the hood

In the 20th century, many composers and pianists became bored with the normal sounds of a piano. No longer satisfied by the effects of trills, glissandi, and tremolos, these brave (and misunderstood) pioneers started tinkering around under the piano lid.

Try it yourself. Open your piano lid and pluck the strings with your fingernail. Now try a gliss across all of the strings while holding down the sustain pedal. The sound is mysterious and a bit creepy.

Composers like Henry Cowell and John Cage didn't stop there. Oh, no! They began writing pieces that incorporated these sounds, asking the player to pluck certain notes on the inside of the piano. And you think playing the black and white keys is hard!

Pushing the limits even further, a new phenomenon called "prepared piano" became quite popular (and still is) with modern composers. A myriad of new sounds were created by inserting various objects between the piano strings — screws, yarn, pillows, spouses, and so on.

I don't advise trying prepared piano at home: Hardware between the strings can damage your expensive piano; spouses between the strings can damage your expensive marriage. If you really want to experience these sounds the right way, check out the following recordings:

♪ **Henry Cowell,** *The Banshee:* Among other things, you hear strumming or plucking of the piano strings.

♪ **George Antheil,** *"Airplane" Sonata:* A number of strange piano effects are evident in this eclectic piece.

♪ **Arvo Pärt,** *Tabula rasa:* The piano part is prepared with screws between the strings.

♪ **Dave Grusin,** *"The Firm" Soundtrack:* This piece uses all types of things, including a violin bow playing across the strings.

Figure 13-10:
Shivering
chords.

Tremolo chords come in handy when playing rock 'n' roll, especially as part of a band. A tremolo turns the otherwise dull task of playing straight chords into a sizzling rhythmic romp. I don't know exactly what a "sizzling rhythmic romp" is, but it sure sounds fun!

Dynamically Speaking

How loud you should play depends 5 percent on what the composer wants and 95 percent on how close your neighbors live. The composer usually requests that certain notes be played at certain volumes. Your neighbor usually requests that all notes be played in a sound-proofed box. These varying degrees of volume give the music a different dynamic. And that's exactly what volume levels are called in music: *dynamics*.

As with TVs, car stereos, and crying babies, the world of volume has a wide range: from very soft to very loud. Composers are quick to realize this and tell performers exactly where in the volume spectrum to play. Of course, to make things a bit fancier, all dynamics in music are Italian words.

Speaking Italian in volumes

When you talk about volume, you say something is loud or soft. This kind of description is always a good starting point. From there you can explain *how* loud or *how* soft. Music uses the same principle: You start with two little Italian words, *piano* (soft) and *forte* (loud), to describe the volume of notes.

Wait! Piano? Stop scratching your head; you look like a monkey. In Chapter 1, you find out that your instrument, formally known as the *pianoforte,* derives its name from the ability to play soft and loud. Why the name's been short-ened to "soft" probably has something to do with cranky landlords.

Anyway, by writing *piano* or *forte* under the music, a composer tells you to play certain notes soft or loud. Many years and ink wells later, abbreviations for these words are now the norm. Therefore, soft and loud are simply marked as *p* and *f*. But not plain-Jane letters. Never! Music employs some fancy, stylized letters.

When you see a dynamic marking, whatever the requested volume may be, you continue to play at this volume level until you see a new dynamic marking. Or, of course, until your sibling yells, "I can't hear the TV!"

You can see and hear loud and soft in composer Alexander Borodin's "Polovtsian Dance" (Track 64). Please play along.

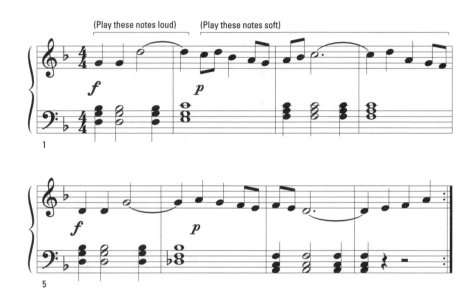

Widening the range

If soft and loud were the only volume levels available, home stereos would just have two volume buttons, not a turning knob. But, as you know, anywhere you turn the volume knob gives you a variety of volume levels: "kind of soft," "not very loud," you name it. Rather than keep track of some more highly descriptive but multi-syllable Italian words, you need only remember one abbreviation for the in-between volumes: *m*, which stands for *mezzo* (or *medium*). Attach this word before piano or forte, and you get two more "shades" of volume.

And for extreme volumes like "very soft" and "insanely loud," just throw a few more *p*'s or *f*'s together. The more you have, the more you play. That is, *pp* means "very soft" (no jokes, please). The written word isn't *piano-piano*, however. Instead, you use the Italian suffix *-issimo*, loosely translated as "very," and you end up with *pianissimo*. The symbol *ff* would be "very loud," or *fortissimo*.

Gather all of these words, abbreviations, and suffixes together and you get the list of dynamic ranges shown in Table 13-2.

Table 13-2	Dynamic Markings	
Abbreviation	*Name*	*How the Note Sounds*
ppp	Pianississimo	Almost inaudible
pp	Pianissimo	Very quiet
p	Piano	Soft
mp	Mezzo piano	Not too soft
mf	Mezzo forte	Kinda loud
f	Forte	Loud
ff	Fortissimo	Very loud
fff	Fortississimo	Ridiculously loud

Bird beaks: Gradual shifts in volume

Two dynamic symbols that you encounter quite often are those that tell you
to gradually play louder or gradually play softer. To me, these symbols look
like bird beaks. A bird gets louder as it opens its beak; softer as it closes its
beak. So, with this marvelous Audubon analogy, check out Figure 13-11 and
see if you can tell what the chicken scratchings mean.

To gradually play louder is a *crescendo;* to gradually play softer is a *diminuendo.* Composers opposed to using the bird beak symbols in their music
write out these long Italian words or use abbreviations like *cresc.* and *dim.*
But you and I know that they're just avoiding drawing diagonal lines.

Figure 13-11:
Open up
and say
"Tweet!"

Whether they appear as a word, abbreviation, or symbol, these instructions are almost always preceded and followed by dynamic markings that tell you to play from volume A gradually to volume B. Maybe the composer wants you to gradually go from very soft *(pp)* to very loud *(ff)*, or perhaps the music indicates a subtle change from mezzo piano *(mp)* to mezzo forte *(mf)*. Whatever the case, it's up to you to decide exactly how to play these volume changes.

Sometimes the composer asks you to play louder and then softer, sort of an up-and-down effect. Many musicians and beauticians call this marking (shown in Figure 13-12) a *hairpin* because of how it looks. But I must admit that after umpteen years of reading music, I *still* can't see the resemblance. Maybe you can.

Figure 13-12:
Get loud,
get soft.

Why even bother with volume? Why not just play everything really loudly so everyone can hear? This approach works fairly well for some heavy metal guitar anthems, but with piano music the subtle degrees of volume show off your ability to display emotion in your playing. Sure, you may not make anyone cry with a crescendo, but at least the mood is enhanced by your efforts. I'm tearing up just thinking about it.

Chapter 14

Great Grooves

In This Chapter
▶ Accompanying your right hand with patterns for your left hand
▶ Beginning and ending a masterpiece
▶ Wowing your friends

*W*ant to make even a simple song like "Row, Row, Row Your Boat" into a showstopper? This is the chapter for you. After reading this chapter, you can apply a handful of tricks and techniques to just about any song you encounter in your piano career. Whether it's a good intro or finale, a cool accompaniment pattern, or just a nice little riff thrown in, the tricks I show you in this chapter help you spice up your music.

If, after you read this chapter, you still feel like you need even more playing tools and tips, I have a suggestion for you: Write to IDG Books Worldwide and urge them to publish *MORE Piano For Dummies*. I'll be, er, you'll be glad you did.

Great Left-Hand Accompaniment Patterns

One of the most important tools to put in your bag of tricks is a good supply of left-hand accompaniment patterns. Any time you're faced with playing straight chords, or even playing melodies from a fake book, you're left to your own resources to supply an interesting-sounding bass line. (See Chapter 19 for more on fake books.)

Fret not. Look no further. Put away the antacid tablets. I'm here to help. This section gives you nine excellent and professional-sounding left-hand patterns that you can apply to just about any song you come across. Each of these patterns is versatile and user-friendly. Plus, I present each pattern in the two most common meters, 4/4 and 3/4.

It's important to practice these patterns again and again to master the right notes and the way each pattern feels under your fingers. After a while, though, you can ignore the printed music and just try to feel the pattern: the distance between the intervals, the shape of the chord, the rhythm, and so on. This way, you can easily apply the pattern to any key, any chord, and any scale.

Fixed and broken chords

The easiest left-hand accompaniment is playing chords, whether you play them as straight chords or arpeggios. (Read Chapter 12 for more on chords; Chapter 9 tells you more about arpeggios.)

Start with the basic chords and find inversions that work well for you without requiring your left hand to move all over the keyboard. (Chapter 12 tells you all about inversions.) Also, you should experiment with various rhythmic patterns. For example, try playing quarter-note chords instead of whole-note chords. Or try a dotted quarter–eighth note pattern.

In Figure 14-1(Track 65), the left hand plays a simple chord progression but with several different rhythmic patterns. Play along and decide which rhythmic pattern works, sounds, and feels best to you.

Figure 14-1:
A left-hand pattern of varied rhythm chords.

You can break up the chord monotony a little with a constant arpeggiated pattern in the left hand. For every chord symbol in Figure 14-2 (Track 66), use the 1st, 5th, and octave notes of the chord's scale to form an up-and-down pattern throughout the song. This pattern can work for fast or slow songs.

Figure 14-2: Arpeggios are great-sounding and easy patterns.

Chord picking

Left-hand "chord picking" is a style best suited to country music (which you can read more about in Chapter 15). But even if you aren't a fan of this genre, you can apply this pattern to just about any song you like.

Chapter 12 tells you that most chords are made up of a root note, a third interval, and a fifth interval. You need to know these three elements to be a successful chord picker.

To play this pattern, break a chord into two units: the root note and two top notes. Play the root note on beat 1 and the top two notes on beat 2. To make it sound even more impressive, do something a little different on beat 3: Play the top note of the chord by itself but one octave lower, as you see in Figure 14-3, which shows you four measures of this pattern with four different chords.

Figure 14-3:
Getting
ready to
pick.

You can try playing this pattern in "Picking and Grinning" (Track 67). After you get the feel of this bouncy rhythmic pattern, you won't even need to look at your hands. Your pinky will find the two alternating bass notes because they're always the same distance from the root note. Good luck!

Octave hammering

Here's an easy, but perhaps tiring, left-hander. This groove is really fun and easy if your right hand is just playing chords. But if you're playing a melody or something other than chords with your right hand, this pattern probably won't sound right.

To hammer out some octaves, you simply fix your left hand in a wide-spread "octave" position and jump around the keyboard playing the appropriate chord's root note. You can play the octaves at any speed that sounds good to you — try whole notes, half notes, even eighth notes, depending on the character of the song.

Picking and Grinning

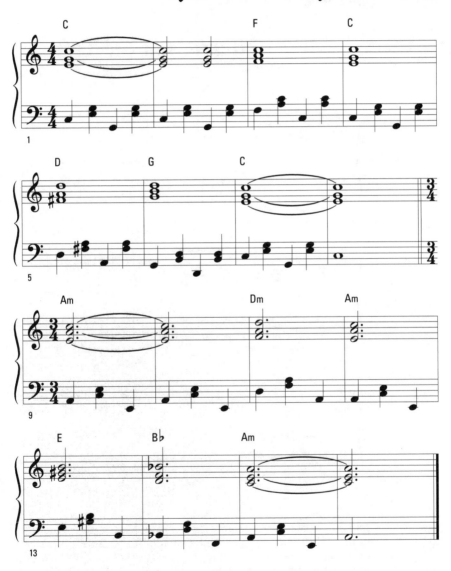

"Octaves in the Left" (Track 68) lets you try your hand at hammering out some octaves.

TRACK 68

Octaves in the Left

As you become more familiar with harmony, try playing left-hand octaves built on different notes and intervals of the appropriate chord or scale. For example, the octaves in "Jumping Octaves" (Track 69) move from the root note to the 3rd interval note to the 5th interval note for each right-hand chord.

TRACK 69

Bouncy intervals

In addition to slamming octaves, a nice rock 'n' roll–sounding bass pattern may use notes from intervals of various sizes. (Chapter 10 explains intervals in great detail.)

You can create a great bass pattern using the octave, the 5th, and the 6th interval notes. Try this rockin' accompaniment along with "Rockin' Intervals" (Track 70). After a few times through, your hands will know what to do.

TRACK 70

Rockin' Intervals

The great Chuck Berry made the locomotive-sounding pattern shown in "Berry-Style Blues" (Track 71) very popular on the guitar. It was only a matter of time before some trail-blazing pianist adapted this guitar sound to the piano. All you have to do is alternate between playing a 5th and a 6th on every beat.

Track 71

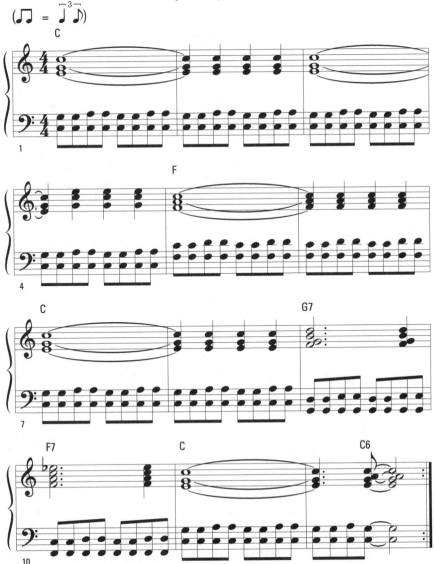

Berry-Style Blues

Melodic bass lines

Some left-hand patterns are so widely used that they are better known than the melodies they accompany. "Bum-Ba-Di-Da" (Track 72) is one such pattern that was made famous by Roy Rogers in his show-closing song "Happy Trails." All you need are three notes from each chord's scale: the root, 5th, and 6th. Play them back and forth, over and over. Have fun and happy trails.

 TRACK 72

Bum-Ba-Di-Da

Another melodic left-hand pattern played by every pianist from novice to pro is the "boogie-woogie" bass line. It doesn't even need a melody. This bass line uses notes from a major scale, but the seventh note of the scale is lowered a half-step (also called a *flatted 7th*) to give you that bluesy sound.

For each new chord in "Boogie-Woogie Bass Line" (Track 73), you play the following scale notes up the keys and then back down: root, 3rd, 5th, 6th, flatted 7th. Get down, boogie-oogie-oogie.

▶ TRACK 73

Great Intros and Outros

A good pianist should always be able to begin and end a piece in an interesting way. You can join the ranks of good pianists by filing away some stock intros and outros in your head, ones you can apply to any piece of music at any given time. An intro or outro is your time to shine, so milk it for all it's worth.

In my humble opinion, few things are more fun than playing a great intro or outro. Heck, some of them sound great alone, without a song attached.

Most of the intros and outros in this section are geared toward popular music. When it comes to classical music, the composer usually gives you an appropriate beginning and ending. Of course, if you really want to fire up Chopin's "Minute Waltz," consider adding one of these intros.

Applying intros and outros to songs

You can add any of the intros and outros in the next two sections of this book to virtually any piece of music. Just follow these steps to apply the intros and outros you select for your song:

1. **Check the song's style.**

   Each of these intros and outros has a different style or sound. Consider the style of the song you are playing and choose an intro that works best with it. For example, a rock 'n' roll intro may not sound very good attached to a soft country ballad. But, then again, anything is possible in music. (Chapter 15 introduces you to many musical styles.)

2. **Check the song's key.**

   All of the intros and outros you find in this book are written in the key of C. If the song you want to play is also in the key of C, then you're ready. If not, adjust the notes and chords of each intro and outro to correspond with the song's key by using the helpful hints shown with each intro and outro.

3. **Check the song's first chord.**

   All of the intros I show you transition easily into the first chords or notes of a song, provided that the song begins with a chord that is built on the first tone of the scale. (Chapter 12 explains these types of chords.) For example, if the song you are playing is in the key of C and begins with a C major chord, any of the intros I show you work perfectly. If not, use the hints provided with each intro to adjust the chord accordingly.

4. **Check the song's last chord.**

   Like intros, you can tack all of the outros I give you onto the end of a song if the song ends with a chord that is built on the first tone of the scale (and most songs do). For example, if the song you are playing is in the key of C and ends with a C major chord, you'll have no problem with one of these outros. If not, you'll need to adjust the outro to the appropriate key.

Adjusting the intros and outros into a different key is a lot of work. If you're just starting out with the piano, do yourself a favor and apply these intros and outros to songs in the key of C. This book includes many such songs.

The big entrance

When the singer needs a good intro, who's going to play it? The drummer? I think not! You are. And it can't be any old intro; it's gotta be good. The audience has a tendency to talk between songs, so it's your job to shut 'em up and announce the start of the new song. You have a few options:

♪ Play the first four chords of the song. *(Ho hum!)*

♪ Play a scale or two. *(Yawn!)*

♪ Stand up and say, "Ladies and gentleman, please quiet down. Here comes a song." *(Nerd!)*

♪ Play a few bars of show-stopping, original material that really gets things hopping and leaves them begging for more. *(That's the ticket!)*

The "Get Ready, Here We Go" intro

The intro you see in Figure 14-4 (Track 74) is bound to grab the audience's attention. It's been used in just about every style of music, from vaudeville to ragtime to Broadway. After you hear it, you'll never forget it. After you play it, you'll be hooked. Just keep playing the measures between the repeat signs until you're ready to continue to the melody. (Chapter 5 talks about repeat signs and what they do.)

Figure 14-4: The "Get Ready, Here We Go" intro.

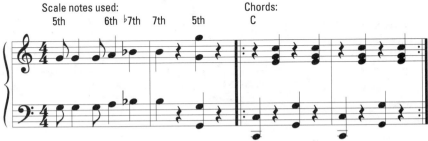

The "Rockin' Jam" intro

You can knock some socks off with a rock 'n' roll intro like the one in Figure 14-5 (Track 75). The triplets are tricky, but you can play this one fast or slow. A slower-tempo version works well with a blues song, while a fast version is good for . . . well, a fast rockin' song. (This intro contains grace notes, which you can read about in Chapter 13.)

Figure 14-5: The "Rockin' Jam" intro.

The "Sweet Ballad" intro

If a slow ballad is more your speed, the intro in Figure 14-6 (Track 76) works well. You can skip the opening sixteenth-note arpeggio if you want. It may be a little difficult, but it sure does add emotion.

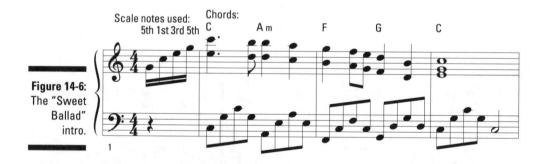

Figure 14-6: The "Sweet Ballad" intro.

The "Killing Time" intro

Sometimes you need to repeat an intro over and over. Perhaps you've forgotten the melody. Perhaps you're waiting for divine inspiration. Or maybe you're waiting for the singer to get off the phone, adjust the hair, and decide to join you. Whatever the case, you can easily repeat an intro like the one in Figure 14-7 (Track 77) until the time comes. Simply play the first four measures over and over until you're finally ready. Then you can move on to measure 5 and play away.

Figure 14-7:
The "Killing Time" intro.

The "Saloon Salutations" intro

When you're just tinkering around in a piano lounge, perhaps all you need is a few bars of honky-tonk style piano, like the ones I show you in Figure 14-8 (Track 78). Notice how effective the grace notes (measure 1) and tremolos (measure 2) are in this intro. (Chapter 13 tells you more about grace notes and tremolos.)

Figure 14-8:
The "Saloon Salutations" intro.

Exit, stage left

Time for the big finish. The band is holding the final chord. The singer has ended the last lyric. It's up to you to drop the curtain. Quick! Grab a handful of these outros and you're sure to receive an encore request.

The "I Loved You, You Left Me" outro

The "I Loved You, You Left Me" outro shown in Figure 14-9 (Track 79) is a simple but effective ending, perhaps even a tear-jerker when played with the right emotion. You certainly wouldn't want to use this as an end to a rocking song like "Burning Down the House," but the right ballad would benefit greatly from it.

Figure 14-9: The "I Loved You, You Left Me" outro.

The "Let's Load Up the Bus" outro

After a classic rock hand-jam, something like the "Let's Load Up the Bus" outro, Figure 14-10 (Track 80), finishes the song with the appropriate amount of flair. The triplets should be played as smoothly as possible, so please feel free to slow down the tempo until you conquer the correct fingering. And make sure to really punch that last chord! (Chapter 4 gives you tips on playing the triplets you find in this outro.)

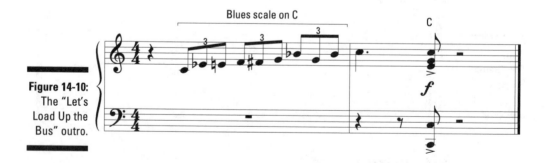

Figure 14-10: The "Let's Load Up the Bus" outro.

The "Last Call" outro

The triplets in the "Last Call" outro, Figure 14-11 (Track 81), give this outro a distinctive feel that works best with a blues or jazz piece. It has the sound of winding down to a halt.

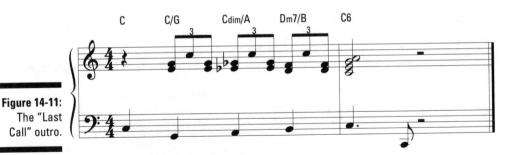

Figure 14-11:
The "Last
Call" outro.

During the "Last Call" outro, you play the notes of chords C, Cdim, Dm7, and C again. You can easily transpose and attach this outro to a song in any key by applying the correct chord types and breaking them up. For example, in the key of G, the chords would be G, Gdim, Am7, G. (Chapter 12 explains how to build all of these chords.)

The "Shave and a Haircut" outro

Everyone knows it. Everyone loves it. Very few know how to notate it. How could I possibly not include the ever-famous "Shave and a Haircut" outro? Figure 14-12 (Track 82) shows you this all-time classic in all its glory. Chords would be meaningless in this one, so I've placed the name of each scale note above the staff. With this information, you can buy a shave and a haircut in the key of your choice.

Figure 14-12:
The "Shave
and a
Haircut"
outro.

Great Riffs to Impress Your Friends

A *riff* is a little musical ditty that can be played as part of a song's accompaniment or just played by itself. Riffs aren't really recognizable melodies, they're just . . . um . . . riffs. Players usually throw out riffs casually as a sort of decoration on the overall song, as filler in between songs, or just to impress anyone who happens to be listening.

For each of the following riffs, it's important to observe the tempo, articulations, dynamics, and effects. Even the easiest of these riffs comes across as more difficult when you add in all the trimmings. To get a good handle on them, play the hands separately a few times before putting them together.

After you master these really easy but really impressive-sounding riffs, you may never spend another Friday night alone. Your friends will want to hear more and more, again and again. Go ahead, charge admission!

The "Bernstein Would've Been Proud" riff

After a nice classical piano piece, play a riff like the "Bernstein Would've Been Proud" riff, Figure 14-13 (Track 83), to get the audience to quiet down again for the next piece. Of course, if the audience is still applauding your first piece, you can just sit there and smile proudly.

Figure 14-13:
The "Bernstein Would've Been Proud" riff.

The "Love Me Like You Used To" riff

You're alone with your date, and you see a piano. Here's your chance to impress your one true love with your piano-playing proficiency (try saying that quickly four times!). Play the "Love Me Like You Used To" riff, Figure 14-14 (Track 84), and when your swooning one asks what song you're playing, just say, "Oh, something I made up."

Figure 14-14: The "Love Me Like You Used To" riff.

The "Classic Boogie" riff

ON THE CD

Play the Boogie riff in Figure 14-15 (Track 85) and no one will believe that you just started to play the piano. This is a bass riff, played by the left hand, but the triplet chords are equally important to the overall sound. You can insert this riff in the middle of a song, in between two different sets of lyrics, or while you're waiting for the guitarist to stop running around the stage.

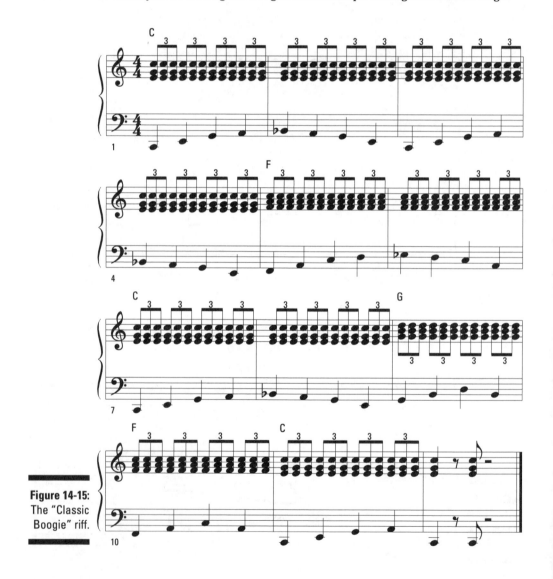

Figure 14-15:
The "Classic Boogie" riff.

The "Hank the Honky-Tonk" riff

The "Hank the Honky-Tonk" riff, Figure 14-16 (Track 86), is easy on the fingers but even easier on the ears. If you're playing with a band, you can use this riff for your stand-out solo. If you're playing without a band, just throw it in during a break and act like you're goofing around on the keys. Either way is sure to be a crowd pleaser.

Figure 14-16: The "Hank the Honky-Tonk" riff.

The "Chopsticks" riff

"Chopsticks" (Figure 14-17, Track 87) isn't all that impressive, but every pianist should know how to play it. It's so easy and has become such a joke for pianists to play that someone somewhere will request it from you. Just make sure you ask for a big fat tip.

Figure 14-17:
The
"Chopsticks"
riff.

Chapter 15

Perusing the Aisle of Style

· ·

In This Chapter

▶ Adding style to your songs

▶ Finding yourself between a rock and a hard jazz

▶ Combining techniques

▶ Impersonating Mozart, Jerry Lee Lewis, and the gang

· ·

During a recent shopping spree, I noticed five separate CDs containing the classic song "Star Dust," each recorded by a different artist — Willie Nelson, Hoagy Carmichael, Louis Armstrong, Bing Crosby, and John Coltrane. Each artist took the same song and recorded it in his own way, making the song sound almost entirely different in each recording. This just goes to show you that there are literally hundreds of different ways to interpret a piece of music, each way offering its own sound and feel, which is known as *style*.

This chapter introduces you to many different styles and explains what each style has to offer. Then I show you how to apply each of those styles to a well-known song. When you get the different styles under your skin, try applying them to your favorite songs. Hey, maybe you can be the first artist to record "Star Dust" as a cha-cha.

Classically Trained

It's difficult to say that *classical* is a style of music. But there, I said it, and it wasn't so difficult.

Many people think of classical music as old, intellectual, sometimes boring music written by a bunch of dead guys who wore wigs. This may be true (except for the "boring" part), but the sound and feel of classical music is unique. You, too, can apply the sound and feel of classical music to your songs, even ones written in this century.

Here's a list of the musical tools you need in order to add that classical sound to your music:

♪ **Trills:** See Chapter 13.

♪ **Arpeggios:** See Chapters 9 and 14.

♪ **Scales:** See Chapter 8.

♪ **Octaves:** See Chapter 10.

♪ **A wig to look like Mozart:** Borrow one from Aunt Rhoda.

Sweet Suite

Figure 15-1 is an excerpt from a classical piano piece by Mozart called "Sonata in C." Notice the use of arpeggios in the left hand and the trills scattered throughout in the right hand. Then, after introducing the cute little melody, what does he give us? Scales!

Figure 15-1: Part of Mozart's "Sonata in C."

Using this same approach, you can make "This Old Man" (Track 88) sound like a piece by Mozart. Play the song slowly, softly, and as smoothly as possible. You may find yourself being appointed court composer . . . hopefully not of the County Court, though.

TRACK 88

This Old Man Wore a Wig

This old man wore a wig, and he thought it'd make him big in the world of class-i-cal mus-ic, but it on-ly made his head itch, so he made a switch. Ah, _____ now he wears a tux.

Rhapsodic intervention

Not all classical music is soft and sweet. Composers like Liszt and Grieg wrote some very dramatic and loud piano music. The opening bars of Grieg's monumental *Piano Concerto* begin with loud, descending octaves as shown in Figure 15-2. (This piece also contains dynamics, which you can read about in Chapter 13.)

(8va means to play these notes one octave higher than written)

Figure 15-2:
Part of
Grieg's
Piano
Concerto.

You can also achieve this sound with the popular song "Dixie" (Track 89). Get both hands locked in the octave position and fire away. I doubt Maestro Grieg even knew where Dixie was!

TRACK **89**

Dixie a la Grieg

Rockin' around the Keys

Hop in your time capsule and travel to a time when Elvis was still king, The Beatles didn't have solo careers, and avocado green was a popular appliance color. *Rock 'n' roll* burst onto the music scene in the 1950s and 1960s with a pair of swinging hips and masses of screaming groupies.

Rocking ingredients

Pull out your bag o' tricks and find the following musical ingredients to make any song rock:

- ♪ **Bouncy intervals:** See Chapter 14.
- ♪ **Glissandos:** See Chapter 13.
- ♪ **Chords:** See Chapter 12.
- ♪ **Lots and lots of pyrotechnics:** You will need these for your elaborate stage show. Visit a fireworks stand.

Slamming and jamming

Jerry Lee Lewis practically invented the classic rock piano sound. For this style, all you need is an opening glissando, fast chords, and lots of energy. You may also find the "Bouncy Intervals" section in Chapter 14 helpful. Figure 15-3 is a good example of this fast-paced, chord-slamming style.

Add a flair of the rock style to the popular song "Mary Had a Little Lamb" (Track 90). Play it with attitude and enough volume, and even Jerry Lee Lewis would be proud. Notice the glissando that ends the piece — this finish will leave them breathless.

Figure 15-3:
Shake,
rattle, and
rock.

TRACK 90

Jerry Had a Little Lamb

Singing the Blues

The *blues* is a style of music all its own. Heck, it even has its own scale (which you can read about in Chapter 8). In this section, you won't apply the blues style to an existing song. Instead, I take you a step farther — I show you how to create your own blues music from scratch. That's right: You can be a composer.

You can play fast blues, slow blues, happy blues, and sad blues. Whether your dog left you or your boss done you wrong, playing the blues is as easy as counting to 12.

Clues for the blues

Two important elements in blues music are form and rhythm. When you have these down, add a few more essential musicalities, like grace notes and minor chords. Then you can sing the blues with any of your songs:

♪ **12-bar form:** See the next section, "12-bar ditties."

♪ **Shuffle rhythm:** See Chapter 6.

♪ **Major and minor chords:** See Chapter 12.

♪ **Grace notes:** See Chapter 13.

♪ **Sad story to tell:** Oh, just make something up.

12-bar ditties

Most blues music utilizes a widely recognized form called *12-bar form,* aptly named because each musical "phrase" of the song is 12 measures (bars) long. The same 12-bar chord sequence repeats over and over, usually with different lyrics and perhaps a slightly different melody, until you genuinely feel sorry for the storyteller.

Melody notes, rhythms, and lyrics may differ from one 12-bar phrase to the next, but the chords usually stay the same. The chords most often used in the 12-bar form are the following:

♪ Chords with the first scale note as their root note, called a **I** chord.

♪ Chords with the fourth scale note as their root note, called a **IV** chord.

♪ Chords with the fifth scale note as their root note, called a **V** chord.

These chords appear in the same order and for the same number of measures every time the 12-bar phrase is repeated.

Just follow these easy instructions, playing with either hand or both hands, and you can play your own blues. When you have the chord progression memorized, you can try playing these chords with the left hand while your right hand plays a simple melody, riff, or blues scale:

1. **Play a I chord for four measures.**

2. **Play a IV chord for two measures.**

3. **Play a I chord for two measures.**

4. **Play a V chord for one measure.**

5. **Play a IV chord for one measure.**

6. **Play a I chord for two measures.**

7. **Repeat Steps 1 through 6 until you have your audience singing with you.**

Figure 15-4 shows an example of 12-bar blues, using chords only. They may be just chords, but try to play with conviction and an ever-present realization of how much you owe on your taxes — that'll make you blue.

Figure 15-4:
The 12-bar blues.

Changing it up

All blues players realize that the same chords over and over can become quite dull, so they substitute other chords within the 12-bar form. For example, try a IV chord in measure 2 and make the last V chord a V7, as shown in Figure 15-5.

Figure 15-5:
Revising
the 12-bar
blues.

Minor chords sound kind of sad and help enhance the feeling of being blue. Try the blues chord sequence, as shown in Figure 15-6 (Track 91), but make all the chords minor this time to enhance the right emotion. Remember that the only difference between a major and minor chord is the 3rd interval. (Chapter 12 tells you everything you ever wanted to know about chords, both major and minor.)

Figure 15-6: A blues progression.

You're a Little Bit Country

Before there was rock 'n' roll, there was *country*. This style often sounds relaxed, lyrical, simpler, more grass roots-ish. But it ain't afraid to rock, roll, and rumble. Artists like Garth Brooks, Shania Twain, and others put all kinds of musical influences in their country music, including elements of rock, blues, and even jazz. Influences aside, though, the folks in Nashville still call it country.

Country-style cooking

To enhance your musical dish with the tastes of country, add some of these stylistic flavorings:

- ♪ **Intervals:** See Chapter 10.
- ♪ **Grace notes:** See Chapter 13.
- ♪ **Tremolos:** See Chapter 13.
- ♪ **Chord picking:** See Chapter 14.
- ♪ **Ten-gallon hat and pair of boots:** Purchase these from a local Western store.

Finger-pickin' good

Figure 15-7 shows a nice, relaxed-sounding slice of the country music style. The right-hand intervals are unique in that the melody notes are actually on the bottom while the top notes stay the same. Grace notes and tremolos peppered throughout also give this example that "saloon" feel.

The left-hand accompaniment pattern is challenging, so practice each hand separately until you can safely and surely put them together. After this inspiring tune, you may find yourself adding a saddlebag to your piano bench.

Figure 15-7:
Good old
country
music.

Give "Michael, Row the Boat Ashore" (Track 92) an unmistakable country sound in much the same way you played the previous example. Plenty of grace notes and tremolos throughout, accompanied by the left-hand chord picking, makes it sound like Michael's riding the trails.

If you have an electronic keyboard, try to call up a sound similar to an out-of-tune piano. Then try "Michael" again and hear just how honky-tonk it sounds. If you have a piano and it happens to be out of tune, no adjustment is necessary!

Pop! Goes the Piano

Arguably, every song on the radio is a *popular* song, because few radio stations play songs that listeners don't like. Country, rock, rap, Latin, and any other style of music are popular with one audience or another. But most people know the term *pop* (short for "popular") to be the category for Top 40 songs and superstar ballads by such artists as Mariah Carey, Celine Dion, Elton John, Sting, and a multitude of others. Pop is also a term for soda beverages, but that's a different book entirely.

Pop music can be rhythmic, romantic, nostalgic, funky, sad, and about 13 other adjectives. In this section, you can concentrate on one style of pop music: the smooth-sounding pop ballad.

The dictionary defines a *ballad* as "a slow, sentimental popular song." A fitting definition for your musical purposes, but to my amazement it neglects to mention that a ballad can also make your dates swoon. It's a pity Mr. Webster didn't realize a ballad's full potential.

Popular picks

What you need to play this style of pop music is a small arsenal of musical ornamentations, including the following:

- ♪ **Right-hand intervals:** See Chapter 10.
- ♪ **Dotted quarters:** See Chapter 6.
- ♪ **Dimmer switch:** Essential for setting the right mood.

Topping the charts

To add a little pop romance to any song, take a simple melody and add the ever-so-sweet 6th interval below each right-hand melodic note. (Chapter 10 sheds light on intervals.) The new melodic line should now look like the one in Figure 15-8. For some reason, unknown to many a trusted and frustrated musicologist, the 6th interval adds an element of romance to a melody.

This trick may look difficult, but it's not. All you do is find the 6th interval below the first melody note and freeze your hand in that position. Your pinkie always plays the top note and your thumb always plays the bottom interval note. As you play up and down the melody, your hand will land on the correct interval every time.

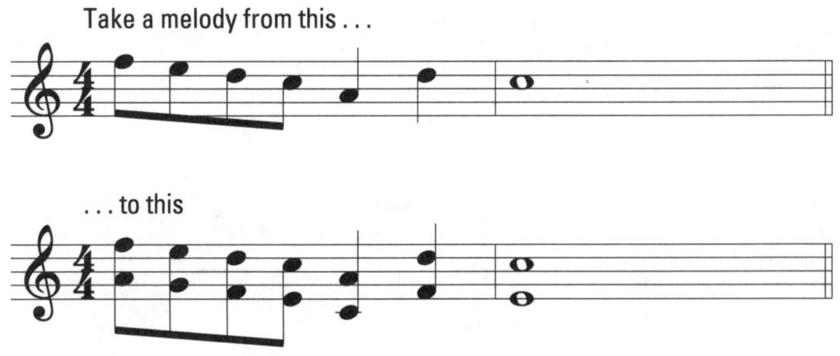

Take a melody from this . . .

. . . to this

Figure 15-8:
Romancing
the tone.

Try this new harmonic trick with the song "Go Tell Aunty Rhody You Love Her" (Track 93) and make it into a pop-style ballad. By the way, now would be an opportune time to use that dimmer switch I recommended earlier.

TRACK 93

Go Tell Aunty Rhody You Love Her

Soul Searching

Talk about a broad category of music! *Soul* can incorporate anything from *R&B* (a hip abbreviation for "rhythm and blues") to *gospel* to *rap*. Such soulful styles are made popular by artists like Stevie Wonder, Aretha Franklin, and Otis Redding. And in my opinion, it's great for dancing, although I don't recommend sashaying too much while sitting at the piano.

Saving your soul

Danceable music requires danceable rhythms, so have the following rhythmic concepts in your repertoire before strutting over to the keys:

♪ **Dotted eighth–sixteenth pattern:** See Chapter 6.

♪ **Right-hand intervals:** See Chapter 10.

♪ **Syncopation:** Again, see Chapter 6.

♪ **Disco ball:** Rent from your local party supply outlet.

Motown sounds

In the 1960s, Motown Records had a stable of artists specializing in the R&B sound. So popular were these artists that their style became known as the *Motown sound*. But don't think the 1960s are gone. You can add the Motown sound to any of your favorite songs.

Using a left-hand pattern with a syncopated rhythm, play Figure 15-9. Pretty soon you'll be hearing The Temptations doo-wopping right along with you.

You can make "Home on the Range" (Track 94) sound like a Motown hit by playing a similar left-hand accompaniment pattern against the melody. A bit of advice, though: Take the song slowly at first and with each hand separately.

Funky sounds going round

Soul and R&B styles often incorporate elements of *funk*. You know, like James Brown or George Clinton. Heavy syncopation coupled with dotted eighth-sixteenth rhythmic patterns provide the funky feel for this funky sound. Play Figure 15-10 with a little attitude.

TRACK 94

Home on the Motown Range

Figure 15-10:
Check out
the funk.

Take that attitude and those syncopations and add them to a favorite song like "For He's a Jolly Good Fellow" (Track 95). Never did a children's song sound so funky!

TRACK 95

For He's a Funky Good Fellow

All That Jazz

If there's one particular music style that embraces unusual chords, it's gotta be *jazz*. Celebrated by many as America's greatest art form, jazz is king of interesting chord harmonies, changing rhythms, and improvisation. Legendary jazz pianists like Bill Evans, Art Tatum, Bud Powell, and many others have taken these elements and added them to classic songs to make them a little more jazzy. You, too, can do this after reading this section.

Jazzing it up

All of the legendary jazz pianists use tried-and-true musical tricks from time to time to freshen things up. Borrow these tricks yourself:

♪ **Chord substitutions:** See the "Substituting chords" section later in this chapter.

♪ **Swing rhythm:** See Chapter 6.

♪ **Syncopation:** See Chapter 6.

♪ **Knowledge of scales:** See Chapter 8.

♪ **Knowledge of chords:** See Chapter 12.

♪ **Nickname like Duke, Bird, or Satchmo:** May I suggest "Cool Cat"?

It's up to you

It's time to be creative. Improvisation is perhaps the most important element of jazz music. It can be *literal improvisation,* where you (the performer) make up your own rhythms and riffs, or *implied improvisation,* where the music just sounds improvised the way it's originally written.

The easiest way to improvise is by changing the rhythm. Take a straight quarter-note melody like "Yankee Doodle" (Track 96) and change the rhythm every two measures. As you can hear, the melody is virtually the same, but you've just made it your own with subtle shifts in the beat.

TRACK 96

Yankee Doodle Went to a Jazz Club

Yan-kee Dude went to a jazz club.

Substituting chords

Figure 15-11 is the well-known children's song "Merrily We Roll Along." As you play it, notice the simple chord progression of C-G7-C.

Figure 15-11:
Merrily we
roll along.

Mer- ri - ly we | roll a- long, al - | though the chords are | dull.

Few jazz compositions use the standard major and minor chords throughout. In fact, few jazz pianists play the original chords that are written in a song. Instead, they break the rules and substitute new chords to liven up an otherwise simple melody.

Even "Merrily We Roll Along" (Track 97) can sound not-so-childish with the use of *chord substitution*. The idea is to find a more interesting chord progression from I to V7 to I. Try the following options:

♪ **Use major scale tones for chord roots:** Move up the scale from C to G-7, building triads on each successive scale note, as in Figure 15-12.

♪ **Use black and white keys for new chord roots:** Move up in half-steps, building triads on each new root note, as in Figure 15-13.

♪ **Move up in 4ths:** Change to an Em7 chord in measure two and then move up a 4th interval and build an m7 chord on each new root note, as shown in Figure 15-14.

♪ **Hire a saxophonist to play with you:** That always sounds jazzy.

Figure 15-12:
"Merrily
We Roll
Along 1."

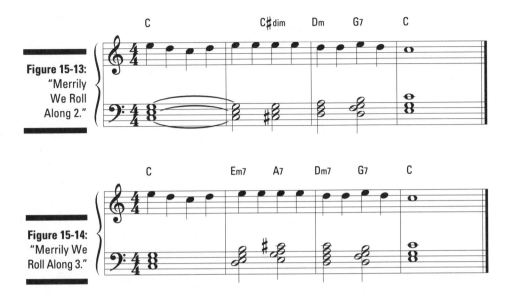

Figure 15-13: "Merrily We Roll Along 2."

Figure 15-14: "Merrily We Roll Along 3."

Or just do it like the pros do it: Listen to the melody and make up your own chords to go with it. You can find plenty of chord books at your local music store. These books give you hundreds of different-sized chords, which you can use to your substituting satisfaction.

Part VI
So Many Toys, So Little Time

The 5th Wave   By Rich Tennant

"These are your custom sound buttons. There's an 'oink-oink' here and a 'gobble-gobble' there, here a 'quack', there a 'moo'.,"

In this part . . .

Now you find out about all those cool musical toys on the market, what they do, where to find them, and how to take care of them through the years.

You get tips on how to buy a keyboard, how to ask the right questions at the store, and how to keep from getting a raw deal. You get addresses, phone numbers, and Web sites for many of the manufacturers. You get all kinds of stuff. All you need is an open mind and an open wallet. The kind salesperson can take care of the rest for you.

Chapter 16

Finding the Perfect Keyboard

● ●

In This Chapter

▶ Choosing between acoustic and electric keyboards

▶ Shopping around

▶ Asking the right questions before you buy

▶ Accessorizing your keyboard

● ●

Gramma's old upright piano may satisfy your urges to play the keyboard for a while. However, at some point you may experience the undeniable urge to purchase or rent a piano or keyboard of your own. Probably right around the time that Gramma gets tired of hearing you play "Yankee Doodle" for the hundredth time.

When the urge to acquire a piano strikes, don't pull out that checkbook immediately. If you want to invest the money, then spend the time to research, shop around, and choose exactly the kind of keyboard you want.

This chapter gives you some important tips on buying or renting the keyboard that's right for you. Like a good pair of shoes or a nice felt fedora, the one you choose should fit you just right.

To Hum or Not to Hum: Electric or Acoustic?

The first thing you need to decide before selecting a keyboard is whether you want an acoustic or an electric one. (See Chapter 1 for an explanation of these two types of keyboards.)

Don't just flip a coin. Choose your type of keyboard carefully, much like you would choose between lemon or piña colada air freshener in your car. Heck, you're going to be driving it for a while; it should smell right. Make a list of pros and cons to help you decide which type of keyboard is best for you.

In the following two sections, I help you get started with a small list of pros and cons for both acoustic and electric keyboards. But please personalize the lists, adding your own perceptions, factors, and concerns. It's *your* keyboard. Base your buying or renting decision on the pros and cons that *you* come up with.

Buying acoustic

Pianos, harpsichords, and pipe organs are acoustic keyboards. (See Chapter 1 for more information on the differences between acoustic and electric keyboards.)

Psalteries, virginals, clavichords, and harmoniums are also acoustic keyboards. However, you don't need a list of pros and cons for buying one of these very rare instruments. If you find one and can't live without it, terrific! Go ahead and purchase it.

Knowing the right time to buy

Before stepping inside a store, answer the following questions as truthfully as possible:

1. How much can you spend?

   a) None

   b) Less than $1,000

   c) $1,000 to $5,000

   d) More than $10,000

2. Where do you live?

   a) At home with parents

   b) College dorm or small apartment

   c) House

   d) Castle

3. How much space do you have?

   a) None

   b) Space for one small beanbag chair

   c) Space for an extra couch

   d) Space for the Chicago Bulls to camp out

4. How long have you been playing piano?

   a) One day

   b) Less than a year

   c) 1 to 5 years

   d) More than 5 years

If you answered mostly a's and b's, consider saving your money for a while and keep playing Gramma's upright. Or ask your local music stores about the possibility of renting a keyboard. If you answered mostly c's and d's, then grab your checkbook or credit card and start looking for your dream instrument.

Pros

I consider the following characteristics to be real selling points for an acoustic keyboard:

- ♪ **Sound quality:** No matter how good a synthesizer is, it just can't exactly match the sound of a grand piano (or even your standard upright piano).

- ♪ **Value:** Believe it or not, some acoustic keyboards actually appreciate in value over the years if kept in good condition. So, think of your purchase as an investment.

- ♪ **Aesthetics:** There's nothing like sitting at and playing an acoustic keyboard. It feels real, it looks great, and you can imagine that you're sitting on a concert stage in front of thousands.

Cons

I would be remiss not to point out the following, which I consider to be detractions in the case for buying or renting an acoustic piano:

- ♪ **Cost:** Plain and simple, new acoustic keyboards are more expensive than new electric ones.

- ♪ **Size:** Just think how that pipe organ would look next to the living room fireplace. And if you relocate, guess what? You have to pay movers to move the piano, harpsichord, or organ for you.

- ♪ **Maintenance:** Annual or semi-annual tuning at a cost of around $50 to $75 per hour ain't cheap, but it's essential. (Chapter 17 tells you more about maintaining your acoustic keyboard.)

Buying electric

You can rent some electric keyboards, but not all. Synthesizers and samplers are mostly for sale only, although you may find some used ones in good condition. On the other hand, plenty of stores offer a rental option on the larger electric pianos or electronic organs.

I came up with a pretty balanced list of reasons why buying a synthesizer, sampler, electric piano, or electronic organ can be a good and a bad choice.

Pros

Electric keyboards have the following positive points going for them:

- ♪ **Cost:** Unless you're talking about the very high-end models of synthesizers and electric pianos, most electric keyboards are affordable and much less expensive than acoustic keyboards.

♪ **Size:** Wherever you live, I bet you can find a spot for your electric keyboard. Plus, you can move it yourself should the need arise — for example, if you go on tour with your band, The Dummies.

♪ **Versatility:** Most electric keyboards come loaded with different sounds, so you can be a one-person band (The Dummy) or play a pipe organ without buying the enormous acoustic version.

♪ **Maintenance:** Electric keyboards require no tuning and no tweaking — you just plug and play. You need to keep your keyboard dusted monthly, but that won't cost you anything. (Check out more of my tips for maintaining your electric keyboard in Chapter 17.)

♪ **Headphones:** If you have grouchy neighbors or sleepy baby siblings, the option of headphones is an important one. You can turn off the sound to the outside world and still hear yourself practicing long into the wee night hours.

Cons

Yes, even electric keyboards have a few negative characteristics, like the following, which you should consider before purchasing one:

♪ **Complexity:** Knobs and levers can break, circuitry can go haywire, and any number of other things can go wrong over the years. Because of the sophisticated gadgetry in most electric keyboards, they tend to run amuck more often than your average acoustic keyboard.

♪ **Power:** You must have electricity, or at least a whole bunch of D-size batteries, in order to play your electric keyboard.

♪ **Sound quality:** Some sounds are out-of-this-world fantastic. But some sound exactly like an electric keyboard trying to mimic an acoustic instrument.

♪ **Volume variation:** Many electric keyboards are not *touch-sensitive*. That is, whether you play the key hard or soft, you hear the same volume. Only the volume knob can control the volume on some models.

♪ **Obsolescence:** Like most electronic devices and computers, today's keyboards probably won't be tomorrow's desire. You, too, will want to upgrade to the latest and greatest. And, no, very few synths retain their value.

♪ **Addiction:** If you buy one, pretty soon you'll want another, and another, and another. The common mantra among electric keyboard players is "I need more gear!"

Picking the Perfect Piano

If you decide that an acoustic piano suits your needs best, use this section to help you select the right model piano for you. I even list a few of my own personal favorites; any of these pianos are good for the beginning player.

Taking location into account

Most older pianos were produced with a particular climate in mind. The wood used to make them was weathered for the finished product's climate. Japan, for example, has a wetter climate than many locations in the United States. Therefore, the wood in many pianos manufactured for use in Japan has been dried out more than the wood used to make pianos for use in the United States. If you live in the United States and you buy a piano made for use in Japan, you may face some serious problems with the wood parts of your piano drying out.

Why does dryness matter? Perhaps the most important element of a piano is its *soundboard,* which is the very thick and very heavy piece of wood that you find under the strings. If the soundboard ever cracks or breaks . . . well, want to play guitar?

For example, if you purchase an older piano that was made for use in Japan, chances are that prior to manufacture, the wood was dried out too much to survive a hot, dry summer, say in Mississippi. Maybe not this year or next, but one of these days: crack! There goes the soundboard; there goes your investment.

If it's a brand-spanking-new piano you want, this issue of locale doesn't matter much. New pianos are made with a more global philosophy. But it doesn't hurt to discuss this with your sales representatives, anyway, just to show them that you've really taken the time to get to know the issues.

Getting all the pedals you deserve

Some underhanded dealers claim that they can save you money by offering you a piano with no middle pedal. (For more on piano pedals, see Chapter 3.) Baloney! Hey, you may never use the middle pedal, but just in case Evgeny Kissin comes over for lunch, you need to have one. (Chapter 18 tells you more about Evgeny Kissin.)

Getting a middle pedal is not like adding a sunroof to a new car. Three piano pedals shouldn't be an optional, added, "special" package. If you want three pedals, ask to see piano models with three pedals. And it shouldn't cost you more or less. Three pedals are part of the overall purchase.

But after this little speech, I must point out that many upright pianos don't have a middle pedal. So, if the piano you want is an upright with only two pedals, it's probably perfectly fine. Just ask about the third pedal to be on the safe side.

If you're buying an older piano, lack of a third pedal sometimes indicates that the piano was made outside the U.S. To understand why this may not be a good thing, read the previous section.

Finding good buys (and avoiding the shams)

If you shop around and find a certain piano for a ridiculously low price — far lower than the same model anywhere else in town — it's either used, broken, or a Memorial Day sale to really remember.

Be smart about a deal that seems too good to be true. If most stores offer a certain model for $20,000 and suddenly you're staring at the same model at PianoMax for $5,000, something's wrong. The soundboard may be cracked, it may be missing strings, who knows? To be sure, call a professional to look the piano over. A reputable piano technician can usually spot the faults. (See Chapter 17 for more information on finding piano technicians.)

Of course, if you've found your dream piano at a garage sale, the low, low price is not necessarily an indication of anything wrong. It's a *garage sale!* While you're at it, pick me up the garden hose and old socket wrench set.

If kept in good condition, there's nothing wrong with a used piano. Just make sure to hire a technician to check it out first, testing that the soundboard is in good condition and the tuning sounds pretty good. Any scratches on the outside? Any sun-faded spots? Well, what do you expect for half price? Cosmetic dings won't affect the sound quality, so the value of your piano's outer beauty is up to you to decide. It's the inner beauty that counts.

Demo models are also good buys. Stores frequently loan pianos to local universities or concert halls for use by students, competitions, and guest artists. Even if used only one time, the piano can no longer be sold as "new." Of course, pianos don't have odometers, but most dealers will be honest about this point.

If you've heard one, you haven't heard them all

So you want a particular brand of grand piano. Think it's as easy as that? Think again. Not only do different brands sound completely different, the sound of two pianos made by the *same company* can sound different. This is why you must, must, must go to the store and put your hands and ears on every piano you consider. Play every darn key, and at all volumes.

You think I'm exaggerating? I've played many pianos that sounded beautiful except for one key. If you are playing "Camptown Races" in the key of G, you may never notice that silent low D-flat key. But I bet that a few days after you get the piano home you'll notice.

Play and listen to those keys again and again. Trust your instincts. Only you know what you like to hear. Some people don't like the sound of a Steinway; some don't like a Baldwin. Everyone has their own tastes.

Give yourself the upper hand in your final negotiation at the piano store: Find two or three pianos that you like and repeat "Oh, Susannah" over and over on each of them. Sure, you're comparing the sound of each, but you're also driving the sales team insane, hopefully to the point of a 50-percent discount just to get you to leave the store!

Looking at some specific brands

In alphabetical order, the following are some of my favorite brands of pianos from around the world. Contact these companies directly and ask where to find their pianos in your area. Trust me, they won't mind your call at all:

♪ **Baldwin Piano & Organ Company:** 422 Wards Corner Road, Loveland, OH, 45140. Phone: (513) 576-4500; fax (513) 576-4546. E-mail: baldwin@bpao.com; Web site: www.pianovelle.com. Their brands include Baldwin, Wurlitzer, Chickering, and Concertmaster.

♪ **L. Bösendorfer Klavier:** 1010 Wien, Bosendorferstrasse 12, Vienna, 1010 Austria. Phone: (431) 504-6651; fax (431) 504-6651-39. E-mail: mail@bosendorfer.com; Web site: www.bosendorfer.com. They carry all Bösendorfer models.

♪ **Kawai America Corporation:** 2055 East University Drive, Compton, CA, 90220. Phone: (310) 631-1771; fax (310) 604-6913. E-mail: jdeleski@kawaius.com; Web site: www.kawaius.com. They offer every Kawai you can find under the sun.

♪ **Music Systems Research:** 4111 North Freeway Boulevard, Sacramento, CA, 95834. Phone: (916) 567-9999; fax (916) 567-1941. E-mail: sales@pianodisc.com; Web site: www.pianodisc.com. They carry Knabe, Mason & Hamlin, and Knabe with PianoDisc.

♪ **Samick Music Corporation:** 18521 Railroad Street, City of Industry, CA, 91748. Phone: (626) 964-4700; fax (626) 965-5224. They offer the brands Samick and Kohler & Campbell.

♪ **Schimmel Piano Company:** 251 Memorial Road, Lititz, PA, 17543. Phone: (717) 627-0684; fax (717) 626-0657. They carry any Schimmel piano you could ever need.

♪ **Steinway & Sons:** 1 Steinway Place, Long Island City, NY, 11105. Phone: (800) 366-1853. Web site: www.steinway.com. They offer Steinway pianos.

♪ **Yamaha Corporation of America:** 6600 Orangethorpe Avenue, Buena Park, CA, 90620. Phone: (714) 522-9011; fax (800) 926-2429. Web site: www.yamaha.com. Contact them for any type of Yamaha piano.

♪ **Young Chang America Incorporated:** 13336 Alondra Boulevard, Cerritos, CA, 90703. Phone: (562) 926-3200; fax (562) 404-0748. E-mail: admin@yca.ccmail.compuserve.com; Web site: www.youngchang.com. They carry Young Chang and Kurzweil pianos.

It's fun to ask the manufacturer which artists play which of their pianos. Any company will be proud to give you a list of famous performers who endorse their products. You may find it personally important to play the same piano that Billy Joel plays, for example.

Selecting an Electric Keyboard that Lasts

After much deliberation, and for whatever reasons, you decide to buy an electric keyboard over an acoustic one. Your job is done? Not so fast, pal. Now you must decide what *type* of electric keyboard you want. Break it down into three categories (you can read more about the characteristics of all these instruments in Chapter 1):

♪ Electric pianos and organs

♪ Synthesizers and samplers

♪ Other

Don't think you've necessarily gone the cheaper route by selecting an electric keyboard as your instrument of choice. These can be quite expensive, sometimes more than an acoustic piano. But oh, the versatility! Instead of being limited to the sound of a piano, you can have literally hundreds or even thousands of different sounds at your fingertips.

The number of sounds you can have depends on the type of keyboard you select and the amount of memory it has. Yes, just like computers, electric keyboards have memory, storage space, and performance limitations. Some you can add memory and sounds to, but some are what they are and no more.

Avoiding obsolescence

As with computers, keyboards are updated and become outdated as quickly as they reach the stores. But unlike some unfriendly and money-hungry computer and software developers, keyboard manufacturers are constantly trying to make products that won't become obsolete by creating keyboards that can be upgraded or added to as technology grows.

Ask the manufacturer or a salesperson these questions to minimize the possibility that your keyboard won't be thrown out the window when the next big thing comes along:

♪ **Can I add memory?** Adding memory to keyboards is quite common these days. More memory means the ability to accommodate new sounds, software, and hardware at a later date. Also ask what the memory limitations are. If you don't understand the terminology, ask the salesperson to explain it to you in non-technical terms.

♪ **Is it SCSI (pronounced "scuzzy") compatible?** This means that you can connect your keyboard to an external computer hard drive or CD-ROM drive. These external devices can store extra sounds or other software that may benefit your keyboard.

♪ **Is the unit upgradeable?** When the manufacturer comes out with the next model, you want to be able to simply upgrade your model, not throw it out.

♪ **Can I purchase extra sound cards or libraries?** Many synthesizers and samplers have vast libraries of sounds. Whether they're developed by the original manufacturer or other sound developers, you can add extra sound cards and libraries to make old keyboards sound new again.

♪ **Is the company still making this model or series?** If not, it's already headed toward the land of obsolescence. But if it meets all the other criteria on this list and you can get it for a cheaper price, just add memory, upgrades, and sounds over the years.

Don't be embarrassed to ask the preceding questions. If the salesperson looks at you funny, and you're sure it's not your haircut, then call the manufacturer directly (using the information listed in the section "Looking at some specific brands") and ask them.

Knowing the features you want

Decide what features are important to you and make a list before you even start shopping. This can be different for each user, each performer. For example, I don't tour with a band, so I have no need for a feature allowing me "quick live performance flexibility." If you play concerts, however, this may be an important feature.

As technology expands, more and more keyboards are beginning to feature all kinds of nice little bells and whistles. Here are some of the features you can expect to find:

♪ **Multi-note polyphony:** The bigger the number, the more notes you can play at once. Try to get at least 32-note polyphony. Sure, you don't have 32 fingers, but if you use MIDI (which I tell you about later in this chapter), 32-note polyphony comes in handy. Some current models even have 128-note polyphony. Now *that's* excellent.

♪ **Multi-timbral:** This means you can play more than one sound at the same time. For example, you can play sounds like a piano, a violin, a banjo, and a bagpipe together on "Danny Boy." Wow, please send me a tape of that!

♪ **MIDI capable:** You can read more about MIDI later in this chapter.

♪ **Pitch bend and modulation:** Fun little effects to make your sounds say "wah wah" and "woob woob."

♪ **SCSI compatible:** See the previous section for an explanation of SCSI, or just trust me — you want it.

♪ **Sound editing:** Do you want to change the sounds — make the piano sound brighter, the horns sound brassier, the goose calls goosier? If so, make sure you have this feature.

♪ **Weighted keys:** Makes it feel more like a piano feels when you play.

♪ **Hammer-action keys:** Yeah, right! What are the keys hammering? The circuitry inside? Just don't pay extra for this load of salesmanship.

♪ **Internal sequencing:** Want to record what you play without using a tape deck or computer? You need a sequencer, which you can read more about later in this chapter.

♪ **Internal effects:** Allows you to add cool little sound effects without buying extra effects devices.

♪ **Other mumbo-jumbo:** Flash ROM, DSP Plug-Ins, BIAS Peak, sub-oscillators, vocoders, modeling filters, arpeggiators. All of this is very cool, but what does it have to do with you playing music? Not much. It's simply saying that your model is on the cutting edge of current keyboard features.

Looking at some specific brands

Here's my list of recommended brands and models for electric pianos and organs. If you're having trouble finding any of these brands in your city, contact the company directly. They'll be more than happy to help sell you a piano or organ:

- ♪ **Kawai America Corporation:** 2055 East University Drive, Compton, CA, 90220. Phone: (310) 631-1771; fax (310) 604-6913. Web site: www.kawaius.com. Recommended models: MP9000 and ConcertArtist.

- ♪ **Roland Corporation US:** 7200 Dominion Circle, Los Angeles, CA, 90040-3696. Phone: (213) 685-5141; fax (213) 721-4875. Web site: www.rolandus.com. Recommended model: The EP Series.

- ♪ **Yamaha Corporation of America:** 6600 Orangethorpe Avenue, Buena Park, CA, 90620. Phone: (714) 522-9011; fax (800) 926-2429. Web site: www.yamaha.com. Recommended models: Clavinova and YPP series.

The following list points you toward some quality manufacturers of synthesizers and samplers. (For more information on samplers and other models, read the sidebar "Sample this!" in this chapter.) For most companies I list, I give recommended models. This is not an exhaustive list of models by any means. Each company makes lots of different-priced, various-featured models. Notice I didn't say "inexpensive," though:

- ♪ **Akai Musical Instrument Corporation:** 1316 East Lancaster Avenue, Fort Worth, TX, 76102. Phone (817) 336-5114; fax (817) 870-1271. E-mail: akaisusa@ix.netcom.com; Web site: www.akai.com. Recommended model: S series sampler.

- ♪ **Alesis Studio Electronics:** 1633 26th Street, Santa Monica, CA, 90404. Phone: (310) 558-4530; fax (310) 836-9192. E-mail: alecopr@alesis1.usa.com; Web site: www.alesis.com. Recommended model: QS series synth.

- ♪ **Casio Incorporated:** 570 Mount Pleasant Avenue, Dover, NJ, 07801. Phone: (973) 361-5400; fax (973) 361-3819.

- ♪ **E-Mu Systems Incorporated:** 1600 Green Hills Road, Suite 101, Scotts Valley, CA, 95067. Phone: (408) 438-1921; fax (408) 438-7584. E-mail: mail@emu.com; Web site: www.emu.com. Recommended models: E-Synth, ESI series sampler Proformance piano module.

- ♪ **Ensoniq Corporation:** 155 Great Valley Parkway, Malvern, PA, 19355. Phone: (610) 647-3930; fax (610) 647-8908. E-mail: music-support@ensoniq.com; Web site: www.ensoniq.com. Recommended model: ZR-76 workstation.

- ♪ **Generalmusic Corporation:** 1164 Tower Lane, Bensenville, IL, 60106. Phone: (630) 766-8230; fax (630) 766-8281. E-mail: gmail@generalmusicus.com; Web site: www.generalmusic.com. Recommended models: Pro series, SK series, RealPiano module.

♪ **Kawai America Corporation:** 2055 East University Drive, Compton, CA, 90220. Phone: (310) 631-1771; fax (310) 604-6913. E-mail: jdeleski@kawaius.com; Web site: www.kawaius.com. Recommended model: K5000 workstation.

♪ **Korg USA Incorporated:** 316 South Service Road, Melville, NY, 11747. Phone: (516) 333-9100; fax (516) 333-9108. Web site: www.korg.com. Recommended models: N series, Trinity series synths.

♪ **Kurzweil Music Systems:** 13336 Alondra Boulevard, Cerritos, CA, 90703. Phone: (562) 926-3200; fax (562) 404-0748. E-mail: kurzweil@aol.com; Web site: www.youngchang.com/kurzweil. Recommended models: K2500 synths and samplers, PC88 controller.

♪ **Roland Corporation US:** 7200 Dominion Circle, Los Angeles, CA, 90040-3696. Phone: (213) 685-5141; fax (213) 721-4875. Web site: www.rolandus.com. Recommended models: A series, JV series, JP-8000, XP series synths and samplers.

♪ **Technics Musical Instruments:** One Panasonic Way, 1C8, Secaucus, NJ, 07094. Phone: (201) 392-6140; fax (201) 348-7484.

♪ **Yamaha Corporation of America:** 6600 Orangethorpe Avenue, Buena Park, CA, 90620. Phone: (714) 522-9011. Web site: www.yamaha.com. Recommended models: EX series synth, A3000 sampler.

Other electric keyboards

Nothing's wrong with a no-frills keyboard from your local toy or electronics store. Many of these have several different sounds and a built-in rhythm section and are very affordable. You probably can't do all kinds of funky little tricks or engineer a hit CD on it, but it will allow you to do the thing that made you buy this book: play the piano.

Before You Drive It Off the Lot: Sealing the Deal at the Store

If you've ever bought a car, you know that looking at and test driving different models is almost as much fun as taking one home. Buying a keyboard should be a similar experience.

If you've never bought a car, or even driven one, don't worry. I tell you everything you need to know about being a savvy keyboard shopper.

Take it for a spin

No matter what kind of music store you walk into, the pianos and keyboards are there for you to try out. Go ahead — touch it, play it. Push the buttons and turn the volume up and down. If it's a piano, have a seat and play a while. You don't have to leave your driver's license, and you don't have to let the salesperson ride with you. It's just you and the keyboard . . . and perhaps a dozen other customers standing around listening.

If the salesperson or manager of the store asks you not to touch or play "the merchandise," abruptly ask them to remind you where the door is and the quickest route to a store that _would_ like to make a sale today. Either they will show you the door or you'll be given a much more comfortable chair and encouraged to resume playing. Either way, you win.

Keep in mind that many electric keyboards on display are routed through processors, effects, and other digital enhancements to make them sound better. Don't be fooled by this extra gear. Kindly ask the salesperson to turn off all effects so that you can hear the keyboard as-is. Otherwise, you may be disappointed with the way it sounds after you get it home — unless, of course, you also buy all the effects processors.

Notice the following about each piano or keyboard you try:

 ♪ Is the overall sound full or wimpy, bright or dull?

 ♪ Do long notes actually last as long as you play them?

 ♪ On an acoustic piano, do the top five keys sound good, not metallic? Do the lower five keys sound good, not thick and sloppy?

 ♪ Do you get a quick response when you play the keys? Is it too sensitive or not sensitive enough?

 ♪ Do your fingers have enough room on the keys?

If you like the sound and feel of one particular piano or keyboard, take a good look at it. Do you like the size, color, and overall look? Can you be happy looking at it taking up half of your living room for the next 25 years?

Can you make out any noticeable dents or scratches that would signal you that this is a used piano? Used pianos can be great buys, but not if they're selling at new prices.

Love it and leave it

You found it. It's the perfect keyboard for you. You love it. This is the one. Now leave the store quickly with a tip of your hat and a polite "I'll think about it" to the sales manager over by the water jug.

You are in trouble if you sit down and negotiate the first time you walk into the store. You are too emotionally attached to think clearly. You think I'm kidding, but this is love — true love. Your keyboard is your baby.

Before negotiating a price, leave the store and spend the next few hours or days searching for that identical piano at a lower price. When you are 100 percent sure that you (a) can't find it cheaper, and (b) can't live without it, head back to Piano Depot (or wherever you found it) and start negotiating.

Never pay the sticker price

Many people think that the art of negotiating a price is reserved for car buying and movie star contracts. On the contrary, the wonderful world of instruments and accessories is open for price haggling.

The sticker price is merely a starting point. If the price for that baby grand piano you want is $15,000, you could find yourself taking it home (in a very big truck) for as low as $10,000.

Generally, you can hope to get anywhere from 10 to 15 percent off the sticker price. The closer you pay to their asking price, the more apt they are to throw in freebies like delivery to your home — which can sometimes cost as much as $300 — or a free year of tuning, piano cleaner, or fuzzy dice.

Don't be impolite about making a deal, though. Start negotiating a price with the salesperson *only* after you're pretty darn sure you're going to buy it. If you're not going to buy the instrument, don't waste the salesperson's time by trying to reduce the price just so you know how much they're willing to move.

Comparing prices is one thing, but using price quotes from two or three different stores is manipulative and unfair, and you probably won't win. Hypothetical scenario: Piano Superstore quotes you $5,000 on a piano. You go to Pianos 'R' Us and say, "Can you beat that?" They say $4,000. You return to Piano Superstore and say, "I can get the same thing at Pianos 'R' Us for $4,000. Can you beat that?" Guess what they'll tell you? "Then go buy it from Pianos 'R' Us." Okay, it's not a hypothetical story. It really happened . . . but I can't imagine to whom!

Go in the store with an *absolute maximum* dollar amount in your head. When you're sure about a particular model, sit down with the salesperson in one of the store's nice air-conditioned offices and ask the salesperson what's the best they can do on that model piano. If you get an answer equal to or less than the maximum figure you're holding in your head, then shake hands and write the check.

If you're nowhere close, then stand up and say, "Well, thank you very much. You have my number if you change your mind." Hey, there are more piano stores and more piano models in this world. You have only a certain amount you can spend.

A piano store is a store like any other, complete with sales at key times during the year. For some reason, Memorial Day is always a big piano-buying time. Okay wait, that makes sense: It's starting to get hot, so to stay out of the sun, you buy a piano for your living room!

Getting the Most Out of Your Gadgets

Your new keyboard is wonderful, exactly what you wanted. But now you want to know about these other cool toys you've heard about. This section explains several other types of musical devices that can hook up to your new keyboard and that help you go even further in your pursuit of a musical career.

The world of MIDI

Yes, even musicians use four-letter words, but not just the ones shouted when you play the wrong notes in Beethoven's "Moonlight Sonata." The four capital letters I'm talking about — MIDI — stand for *Musical Instrument Digital Interface.* Wait, don't turn the page! It's not nearly as boring as it sounds. In fact, MIDI (pronounced "mid-ee") can change your musical life.

In a nutshell, MIDI allows you to connect several keyboards and play them all at once. Say you have three keyboards. You select the first one to be the *controller* and set it to sound like a piano. You connect the other two keyboards to the controller and set each of them to different sounds, perhaps a flute and a tuba. As you play the controller, the other two keyboards are sent MIDI *messages* (binary codes) telling them which notes to play, how long, how hard, and so on. But it sounds like three players are playing three separate instruments, instead of just you on a piano.

But that's not all MIDI can do. You can buy MIDI-recorded CDs and hear the songs played with the sounds of your own keyboard. You may remember player pianos from many years ago — this is the electronic version of those player pianos, without all those big fussy rolls of paper with holes punched in them. These relatively new types of MIDI software and recordings have become quite popular teaching aids, because you can follow along note for note as your keyboard plays the songs.

Are you feeling left out of the MIDI world because you bought an acoustic piano? No problem. You can now have your acoustic piano retrofitted with a MIDI box and various other wires. Use your grand piano as a MIDI controller, or load disks and CD-ROMs and hear your baby grand play songs for you and your dinner guests. It's quite expensive to do, but maybe the result is worth it to you. Most piano dealers can give you more information and, of course, a cost estimate if this interests you.

Sequencing and recording

Sooner or later, you'll probably want to record your virtuosic playing for the world to hear. Well, at least for your friends and family to hear. Electronic keyboards offer you a host of options that help you record your sound. You can choose to record on tape, on disk, or on your computer.

Putting it in sequence with MIDI

If you use MIDI, you can record exactly what you play without ever using a single cassette tape. The MIDI messages you send from your keyboard as you play can be stored in a computer or *sequencer*. Later, all you do is push "play" on the sequencer and hear note for note, volume for volume, exactly what you played.

But that's not all! Most sequencers have several different tracks. So, you can record yourself playing the melody of a song with a piano sound on Track 1, followed by the drum part on Track 2, and then the guitar part strumming away on Track 3. But you never used any instrument other than your keyboard and its sounds.

Push "play" and the sequencer plays all three tracks at once, which sounds like a four-member band. Want more? Just add some violins on Track 4 of the sequencer. Perhaps the sound of rain on Track 5. Pretty soon you've got the entire London Philharmonic playing on Tracks 6 through 16.

Recording the old fashioned way

If MIDI isn't your bag, baby, you can still record your performance on cassette tape, digital audio tape, or hard disk. Several pieces of equipment are available, each unique in what it can offer the aspiring recording artist. You must decide between *analog* and *digital recording.*

Technical explanations aside, analog is the old-fashioned way of using magnetic cassette tapes to record audio; digital is the new and improved means of converting audio into a binary code to be stored on tape or computer disk. Both work fine, but digital is often easier to work with, especially when editing your performance.

After you decide on your brand of recording, buy the equipment you find easiest to use:

♪ **Multi-track tape recording:** These units can record up to eight separate audio tracks on an ordinary (analog) cassette tape, digital audio tape, or minidisc. The recording can then be edited, mixed, and enhanced to your liking. Recommended models: Alesis ADAT, Fostex X series, Tascam 488 Portastudio.

♪ **Hard disk recording:** Record separate tracks of audio digitally and save it on a hard disk, floppy disk, or removable storage cartridge just like you would save a computer program or document. This can be done on an individual unit or on your home computer with the appropriate hardware and software. Edit, mix, and enhance to your heart's content. Recommended models: Akai DPS12, Fostex DMT, Roland VS-880, Tascam 564 Digital Portastudio.

After you start investing in recording equipment, two things happen: (1) you spend far less time practicing music, and (2) your bank account shrinks. For now, it's nice to know these recording options exist, but consider playing music for a while before diving into a new career as a recording engineer.

Fried keys, anyone?

Always, always, always, always use a *surge protector* for any and all electronic music equipment you use. You can find these at electronics, office supply, or home supply stores. Plug the protector into the wall and plug *all* of your equipment into the protector. If lightning strikes, or the power goes out, or you accidentally flip the breaker switch while dancing a tango, your expensive music equipment could be fried without a surge protector.

And don't go cheap on me either. The most expensive surge protectors are less than $40, and some have guarantees to repay you thousands of dollars if they should ever fail to protect your equipment.

Sample this!

Synthesizers aren't the only kinds of electric keyboards with knobs, sliders, buttons, and other gizmos to make whacky sounds. As you shop around, you're bound to hear terms like *sampler, tone module,* and *workstation* rolling off the salesperson's tongue. Don't be baffled — I'll explain.

♪ **Samplers:** Unlike synthesizers, samplers don't mimic another sound. Rather, they *sample* (or record) the sound. For example, you can sample the note A from a violin and then have your sampler assign that sound to each key on your keyboard, raising or lowering the pitch of the note for the appropriate key. You can play all the notes on a violin without ever lifting a bow. And because it's a recording and not a mere imitation, a good sampler can sound almost exactly like the instrument or sound it sampled. Heck, sample the sounds of your dishwasher and play "Moon River" if you want to!

♪ **Tone modules:** Simply put, these are very inexpensive little boxes that have lots of great sounds but no keys. That's right —

you have to hook the box up to a *controller* (another keyboard or computer) to play the sounds, but it's a very inexpensive way to get a lot of very cool sounds.

♪ **Workstations:** This fancy name implies that you can do all your musical work right there on your keyboard without adding any other equipment. And you know something? The implication is correct. You can sample sounds with the internal sampler, change the sounds with the internal synthesizer, record and edit your music on the internal sequencer, and perform lots of other time-consuming but fun musical endeavors. They may be expensive, but workstations definitely give you the most bang for the buck.

Don't be fooled at the store. You can easily mistake a synth and a sampler. Most of these models look identical, and some don't actually say which they are on the outside. Do the manufacturers expect you to decode the ambiguous model numbers — ESI-4000, A-3000 — to know what the unit is? Just ask the salesperson if you have any doubt.

Chapter 17

Raising Your Keyboard

. . . .

In This Chapter

▶ Finding the right home for your keyboard

▶ Cleaning your keyboard

▶ Realizing you can't fix it yourself

▶ Taking the pain out of moving day

. . . .

As with any baby, it's important to be the best parent you can be to your keyboard. Consider this chapter to be your "Bringing Up Baby" manual. Don't worry . . . no diaper changing is necessary.

A Good Place to Live

Whether you bought an acoustic or electric keyboard, the first thing to do when you get your new baby home is to find a spot for it to live. This spot doesn't have to be a permanent resting place — keyboards adapt well to future changes in their lives. But some spots are better than others in terms of keeping your keyboard humming along and in good health for the duration of its life. Your ideal spot has all of the following characteristics:

♪ **No direct sunlight:** Even through a window, over-exposure to sunlight can damage your keyboard over time. The wood can warp or dry out, affecting both the sound and overall appearance. A faded keyboard doesn't sell well (if necessary) down the road.

♪ **Controlled climate:** Don't expose your keyboard to violent temperature swings. For example, don't leave it on a porch that gets really hot in the summer and dreadfully cold in the winter. To avoid fickle weather changes, try to place your keyboard near an interior wall rather than an exterior wall.

♪ **Good ventilation:** For acoustic pianos, good ventilation reduces the buildup of excess moisture. For electric keyboards, ventilation keeps the "engine" cooled when the power is on. You don't have to put your keyboard right under an air conditioning unit or right over a heating duct. Just make sure that the room has good airflow through it.

♪ **Safety:** Don't set your expensive keyboard under a bookshelf or suspended refrigerator that may soon fall. All the king's horses and all the king's men can't put your Humpty . . .

Of course, you also want your keyboard in a spot that encourages you to play. Try to find a place for your instrument that also has the following characteristics:

♪ **Elbow room:** When you feel cramped or uncomfortable, you are more likely to avoid practicing. Lack of practice leads to poor playing, so give yourself ample space for stretching out when you play.

♪ **Convenience:** Don't confine your keyboard to an area that's hard to reach. When inspiration hits, you want the keys close at hand. And speaking of convenience, make sure your room has plenty of electrical outlets. Using miles and miles of extension cords is expensive, irritating, and just plain ugly.

♪ **Lighting:** Until you're in a dark, smoke-filled bar, in front of hundreds of adoring fans, always play with good lighting. Not only is it easier to see the non-colorful black and white keys, but reading music is next to impossible in the dark. You can set a lamp on or near your keyboard, but I don't advise the clip-on kind — they can damage the keyboard's finish.

♪ **Neighbors:** Consider how the location of your piano or keyboard might impact your relationship with your neighbors. For example, don't put your keyboard in the room right over your downstairs neighbor's bedroom. All those late-night practice sessions will soon be history.

Making It Shine

Keep your baby clean. You don't need to give the instrument a Saturday night bath every week, but make sure to keep your keyboard free of dust and dirt as much as possible.

And don't be afraid to be mean about keeping your instrument clean — insist that no one (not even you) eats or drinks around your keyboard. A spilled drink in the back seat of your car is one thing; a spilled drink on your keyboard can be fatal (for the keyboard, that is). And do you really want to clean out old cracker crumbs from between the keys once a month?

In addition to keeping food and drink away from your keyboard, don't allow dust to build up on your instrument. Dust buildup in electric keyboards may eventually short out the circuitry or cause the keys or buttons to stick. Either of these results is bad news. Dust buildup in acoustic pianos is not as critical, but constant sneezing can be a drawback while playing.

The two most important cleaning tools to have near your instrument are a feather duster and a small, medium-bristle paint brush. Yes, you read that correctly. Use the feather duster for an overall dusting, followed by a "get in all the grooves and between the keys" detailing with the paintbrush at least once a month. Simply press down each key and clean both sides before moving to the next one. If you're in a hurry, just jam the brush in between the keys and give it a better, more thorough cleaning later.

Be careful what cleaning solvents you use on your keyboard's finish. For most keyboards (electric or acoustic), I recommend a cloth that is slightly damp with plain soap and water. Don't be embarrassed to ask the dealer what cleaning products are advised and exactly how to use them. The finish on many grand pianos can be ruined by normal furniture polish.

When using a liquid solution on the finish, whether soap and water or window cleaner (sometimes recommended, but ask first!), use an old T-shirt or newspaper instead of a paper towel. Newspaper won't leave those little white fuzzballs as you clean. Get enough of those fuzzballs and you may as well not have dusted!

Don't spray liquid cleaners directly on your instrument. Spray first onto your newspaper or cloth and then wipe the instrument. Continue again and again until the instrument is clean.

Secret revealed: Special Piano Cleaner

Your dealer may suggest you buy a "special cleaner" packaged in a very handy and attractive bottle. Having just written a very large check, you jump at the chance to protect your investment, never mind the added cost.

You get home and decipher the scientific ingredient names on the label, only to discover that you just purchased some expensive soap and water. Save your money; make your own using the following tools:

♪ An empty spray bottle

♪ A marker

♪ Liquid soap

♪ Water

Rinse out the spray bottle until it's free of residue from any previous products. Use your marker to write "Special Piano Cleaner" or "Baby Shampoo" on the outside. Add four or five squirts of soap to the bottle. Fill the plastic bottle with clean water. Shake well.

Calling Dr. Help for a Check-up

Playing the keyboard is one thing. Knowing how to repair and maintain one is another. You should leave such matters to a qualified professional, a person I like to call Dr. Help. You have enough to worry about with playing, reading music, and touring around the world.

This section gives you tips on hiring piano tuners, piano technicians, keyboard technical support people, and others who can help you maintain and prolong your instrument's life.

Tuning acoustic keyboards

Okay, so your friend can tune his own guitar, as can your friends with violins, clarinets, and kazoos. But keep in mind how much larger your piano is, how many parts are inside, and how much more you probably paid for it. Swallow your pride, pick up the phone, and call a piano technician when it's time to tune your piano.

Piano technicians are skilled professionals with years of education and experience. And this kind of doctor still makes house calls. It may look like they're just playing separate keys and tightening screws, but you won't even know where to begin if you try to do it yourself.

Don't think that you'll suddenly hear your piano go out of tune one day. Loss of intonation is a gradual process that takes place over a long period of time. Your tuning will be much overdue if you actually say to yourself, "Wow! My piano's out of tune."

Schedule a tuning each year, preferably twice a year. Generally, the visit will take two to three hours and cost you between $50 and $100, which is well worth the cost! Plus, once you have a technician, he or she will probably contact *you* each year, so you don't even have to remember to schedule an appointment to have your piano tuned.

Too many years of tuning neglect results in a piano that's permanently out of tune. Ever heard an old honky-tonk saloon piano? Sure, the sound is sort of fun, but not when it's coming from your $30,000 nine-foot grand piano.

You can get recommendations for a good piano technician from friends, teachers, music stores, and music schools. Don't just select at random from the telephone book. A bad technician can ruin a piano.

In addition to tuning, I highly recommend asking the technician to have a look "under the hood" and make sure everything else is functioning properly. Ask the technician to check the following items:

♪ Do the pedals work?

♪ Are the legs secure?

♪ Is the soundboard cracked?

Keeping electric keyboards happy

You don't need to tune your electric keyboard. However, it does need attention, though probably not once a year. If you keep your keyboard clean and dust-free, chances are you won't need to call Dr. Help for quite some time.

Electric keyboards have lots of little buttons, digital displays, knobs, sliders, and other gadgets. Over time, through constant pushing and pulling, these gizmos experience normal wear and tear. If a button appears to be stuck, don't, I repeat *don't*, try to fix it yourself with one of your own tools.

Call a professional — perhaps the dealer who sold you the instrument originally. For a minimal fee, the dealer can assess the damage (if any) and fix it for you. If your warranty is still good — usually only for one year — repairs may cost you absolutely nothing.

Never, ever, under any circumstances, subpoena, or act of desperation should you unscrew or open the top of your keyboard. Sure, it looks really cool inside with all the computer chips and circuit boards. Sure, you think you know what you're doing and want to save a buck. But you will (a) void your warranty automatically, and (b) more than likely damage your keyboard irreparably.

Technical support lines

Each and every time you buy a new keyboard, fill out and send in the registration card that comes with it. Don't be afraid that you'll be put on some mailing list or give away the combination to the family lockbox. You are simply telling the manufacturer, "Just letting you know that I bought your really cool product. Here's my name and here's where I live." That's all.

Then, day or night, any time you have a problem, you can call the manufacturer's *technical support line* and speak with a knowledgeable professional (maybe even someone who designed your keyboard) about the specific problem you are having and how to rectify it.

The call to technical support is usually free. All you have to do is fill out that pesky little card and mail it. Oh, and if you're still too lazy to fill it out, most manufacturers allow you to register online via the Internet or direct modem connection.

To find the technical support line for your instrument, call the manufacturer directly, or see the sample list of manufacturer phone numbers in Chapter 16.

To the Emergency Room

Unfortunately, some problems can arise for your keyboard that require some serious time, effort, and money to fix. If you experience any of the following problems, you should get at least two separate estimates from two separate people before deciding whether or not to salvage your instrument:

♪ **The soundboard on your acoustic piano cracks or breaks.** The soundboard is the large, polished board lying under the strings. The soundboard can break during a move, if performed by unqualified movers. It can also be caused by constant changes in humidity, causing the wood to swell and contract. You probably won't notice a broken soundboard on your own. Have the piano technician can check out the soundboard for you.

♪ **You hear only a thump when you press an acoustic piano key.** Either the hammer, damper, or both are not functioning properly. You may have to replace the mechanism for that one key or replace the entire set of keys and hammers. Hope for the first option. Of course, it could just be a broken string, which can be fixed for under $20.

♪ **Your electric keyboard will not power on.** First, make sure you paid last month's electric bill. Unless you have a battery-operated keyboard with old batteries, your keyboard should always power on when plugged in correctly. If not, it may be dead.

♪ **Your LCD display shows nothing legible.** If the words and program names on the front panel display are suddenly a bunch of letters that you recognize only from your recent alien abduction, the brains of your board may be fried.

♪ **You spill a beverage all over your electric keyboard.** Oh, dear! You probably just shorted out the entire board. Few, if any, of your buttons and keys are going to work. This is why no drinks are allowed in recording studios. If you spilled on an acoustic keyboard, quickly get a towel and start sopping it up. The wood, strings, hammers, and even keys may be damaged, but at least there isn't anything electrical to bug out.

A few mishaps that seem terrible actually aren't that bad, including pedals falling off, strings breaking, headphone jacks snapping off inside the unit, and even keys sticking. True, these are big headaches, but they aren't serious problems. Just leave the problem alone and call a professional.

Making Moving Day Worry-Free

If you own or rent an acoustic piano, moving from one residence to another is always going to be more expensive. You must hire a qualified piano mover to transfer your baby to its new home.

Don't be cheap about hiring a mover. Inexperienced movers can ruin — let me say that again, please — *ruin* your piano.

I have three words of advice when it comes to moving your piano:

> ♪ Don't ever try to move the piano by yourself or with friends.
>
> ♪ Always ask the moving company if they are qualified piano movers.
>
> ♪ Don't watch when they move it.

Please allow me to clarify the last piece of advice. You should definitely be present to watch the movers and make sure they are taking extreme care when moving your precious baby. But I'm warning you that you're guaranteed to grimace when you see them flip that piano over on its side. You just know it's going to crash on the floor.

Piano moving involves its own specialized equipment: a *piano board*. This long flat board has lots of padding and several handles, or handholds. The movers lay the piano on its side on this board and strap the piano and piano board to the dolly. The piano board holds your baby securely and cushions any jarring bumps. If your movers show up without a piano board, then I strongly advise you to bid them farewell and call new movers.

Your local piano dealer can recommend several good moving companies who specialize in piano moving. The good ones actually receive endorsements from piano manufacturers.

Part VII
The Part of Tens

Yeah-barrel-house boogie-woogie!! Go Stuart, go! Make that harpsichord growl!!

In this part . . .

Nothing tough about this part at all. Part VII is the light reading part of this book. You can read up on some legendary performers, find things to do after you finish this book (like reading it again!), and receive my complimentary (actually, you paid for them) Teacher-Tracking Tips.

Whatever you do, find a cozy spot to sit back and relax while you read this part. Get away from the hum of your keyboard or the dust on your piano for awhile. You deserve it; you've been working (playing!) way too hard.

Chapter 18

Ten Types of Performers and Their Recordings

● ●

In This Chapter

▶ Performers who define musical styles
▶ Great performances preserved in great recordings

● ●

*P*ersonally, I don't like to categorize music. Regardless of the category, you like a song, or the performer of that song, simply because you like it — not because of what style or genre it fits into. Put simply, you don't need a cowboy hat to enjoy a Garth Brooks CD. But visit any record store, supermarket, or even your own sock drawer, and you realize that categorization is an unavoidable part of life. So, please allow me to introduce you to some legendary keyboardists and their recordings, separated for you by . . . category.

Old Masters

Many of the composers of classical music were also keyboard players — some of them better known for their playing ability than the music they wrote. Whether they used a piano, harpsichord, or pipe organ, these old masters managed to find a set of black and white keys to suit their styles.

Johann Sebastian Bach

Regarded by many as the forefather of Western music — not to mention that he was the actual father of many musicians — this German musician (1685–1750) learned to play the violin under the tutelage of his father. After his parents died, Bach moved in with his big brother, who taught him to play the organ. At the age of 18, Bach got a job as a church organist. This job didn't last long — the church said he improvised too much. He took a job at another church in Weimar, where he had to compose a new piece for the choir and organ every month. Thankfully, this church did not discourage his improvisations, thus giving the world the masterpieces it now knows and loves.

Ludwig van Beethoven

One of the greatest composers that ever lived, German-born Beethoven (1770–1827) was also a great pianist. His piano-playing and original piano pieces were in high demand throughout his career. Unlike many other composers, he became a celebrity during his lifetime. He would change the rules and shock the public, but people still lined up to buy his next piano sonata. Although Beethoven was opposed to naming his sonatas, his publisher insisted that he do so. Names like "Moonlight" and "Appassionata" sold sheet music by the bundle.

Tragically, Beethoven began to lose his hearing as he got older. He would often lay his ear on the piano lid as he played, just to feel the vibrations of the strings. By the end of his life he was completely deaf, unable to hear the crowds cheering. And, oh, how they did cheer!

Franz Liszt

This Hungarian pianist's father taught him piano and began to exploit his talents when he was only 9. Young Liszt (1811–1886) toured constantly and never even took the time to receive a formal education.

A reputation for theatrical and awe-inspiring concerts produced a huge demand for his music and an enormous fan club (not to mention a nice-sized ego). He's rumored to have once played so hard he broke a piano string. "Lisztomania" became a cultural phenomenon, and although no Liszt action figures survive, he did leave the world a bizarre relic: A plaster cast of his hands was made upon his death.

Sergei Rachmaninoff

This Russian-born musician enjoyed huge success as a composer, conductor, and solo pianist. He also had huge hands. Rachmaninoff (1873–1943) built his own solo repertoire, writing intricate, very difficult compositions.

Shine on, if you can

Countless piano pieces have been called too difficult to play. Perhaps the most infamous of these is Rachmaninoff's *Piano Concerto No. 3.* As portrayed in the Oscar-winning film *Shine,* this piece (and an overbearing father) was said to be the catalyst for Australian pianist David Helfgott's complete collapse and subsequent mental disorder.

As the story goes, Helfgott practiced the piece incessantly, even when a keyboard was not close by (like in the shower). He not only mastered its difficult passages but memorized them! Although the old adage says "practice makes perfect," the moral of this story is that too much practice makes problems — Helfgott was so consumed by the piece that he had a complete nervous breakdown.

Later in life, after the success of the biographical movie, Helfgott commenced a worldwide tour, but his once extraordinary talents had been severely damaged.

Among these was the famous *Prelude in C-sharp minor,* which was an enormous hit. Long before the movie *Casablanca,* audiences would cheer, "Play it again, Sergei!" when he played this prelude. He later referred to this popular piece as the "It" prelude. Even today, his *Piano Concerto No. 3* is regarded as perhaps the most difficult piano concerto ever written. (See the sidebar "Shine on, if you can.")

Mastering the old

Although the old masters weren't able to leave behind any gold records of their own, their music has been recorded extensively by this century's greatest pianists:

- ♪ **Johann Sebastian Bach:** *Harpsichord Concertos,* Igor Kipnis (CBS); *Toccata and Fugue and Other Organ Works,* E. Power Biggs (CBS).

- ♪ **Ludwig van Beethoven:** *Piano Sonata No. 14 ("Moonlight"),* Emil Gilels (DG); *Piano Concerto No. 5 ("Emperor"),* Wilhelm Kempff with Ferdinand Leitner and the Berlin Philharmonic (DG); *Sonatas,* Artur Schnabel (Pearl - UK).

- ♪ **Franz Liszt:** *19 Hungarian Rhapsodies,* Mischa Dichter (Philips); *Piano Concerto No. 1,* Claudio Arrau with Eugene Ormandy and the Philadelphia Orchestra (CBS).

- ♪ **Sergei Rachmaninoff:** *Prelude in C-sharp minor,* Vladimir Ashkenazy (London); *Piano Concerto No. 3,* Rachmaninoff with Eugene Ormandy and the Philadelphia Orchestra (RCA).

Virtuosos

Without the skill of an accomplished virtuoso, much of the difficult music written for piano would simply be notes on paper. Years of discipline, training, practice, and maybe a good physical therapist helped these performers make their fingers do funny things that other piano players only wish they could.

Martha Argerich

Early in her career, Argerich (born in Argentina in 1941) won many important competitions, including the 1965 Chopin Competition in Warsaw. Her incredible and unmatched technique makes her one of the most brilliant pianists of the 20th century. But she's also very temperamental, often canceling concerts without warning. Although she records a wide range of solo, chamber, and orchestral music, she focuses primarily on concertos in public appearances.

Vladimir Horowitz

A piano genius, Russian-born Horowitz (1903–1989) had an on-again, off-again career. His annual tours received great acclaim, but he stopped playing publicly from 1936 to 1939. Then in 1953, after a successful Carnegie Hall concert, he stopped playing concerts but continued to record. In 1965, again at Carnegie Hall, he made a "spectacular comeback," as one critic wrote, and returned to public performing. Despite many personal and physical problems, Horowitz had an uncanny way of reinventing his career each time he dropped out. Either that, or he had a really good agent!

Evgeny Kissin

Youthful Evgeny Kissin (born in Russia in 1971) is arguably the most exciting pianist on the classical music scene today. He began playing at the age of 6 and recorded two Chopin concerti at the age of 12. He toured throughout his teens, having little time for softball or movies. His U.S. debut was in 1990 with the New York Philharmonic, followed quickly by a debut at Carnegie Hall. A young but accomplished virtuoso, he practically eats the difficult piano repertoire for breakfast. The world must wait and see what he'll have for lunch.

Jugglers and acrobats

So you think it's challenging to play the piano with both hands while trying to read the music while using your feet to control sustain and volume while seated in front of an audience of 500 or more? Try doing all that while also conducting a full orchestra!

Such conductor-pianist hyphenates as Leonard Bernstein, Daniel Barenboim, Christoph Eschenbach, and Vladimir

Ashkenazy adeptly juggle playing the lead and leading the orchestra . . . without ever missing a beat or even getting up from their piano benches.

So, next time you're frustrated with the job at hand, be thankful you've only got yourself to worry about, and not 90 other pent-up musicians.

Wanda Landowska

Born in Poland, Landowska (1879–1959) began playing at the age of 4. After studying in Berlin and Paris, she became interested in the harpsichord and gave concerts called "musique ancienne" (ancient music) all over the world. She began to teach harpsichord classes in 1913. She gave the first modern performances on harpsichord of many Bach masterpieces. One of these performances resulted in a recording of Bach's "The Well-Tempered Clavier," which Landowska described as her "last will and testament."

Arthur Rubinstein

Many piano connoisseurs consider Polish-born Rubinstein (1887–1982) to be the greatest pianist of the 20th century. After studying in Berlin, he moved to France to pursue his career as a solo concert pianist. His wide range of styles was amazing, from Mozart to Stravinsky and everyone in between. He is particularly well-known for his brilliant Chopin interpretations. In his two volumes of memoirs, his adventurous stories of wine, women, and song convey to the world what a true cosmopolitan Rubinstein was.

Virtuous listening

Hear just how able these skilled virtuosos' fingers can be on the following recordings:

♪ **Martha Argerich:** *Martha Argerich Collection* (DG).

♪ **Vladimir Horowitz:** Scriabin, *Preludes* (BMG); *Private Collection Vol. 2* (BMG).

♪ **Evgeny Kissin:** Chopin, *Piano Concertos*, with Dimitri Kitaenko & Moscow Philharmonic (RCA).

♪ **Wanda Landowska:** Bach, "The Well-Tempered Clavier" (BMG).

♪ **Arthur Rubinstein:** Chopin, *7 Polonaises* (BMG); Chopin, *The Nocturnes* (BMG).

Child Prodigies

Imagine cleaning house one day and hearing beautiful music pouring out of the living room. You think to yourself, "Hmm. I forgot to turn off the radio." As you head toward the living room, you are shocked to find your five-year-old child seated happily at the piano. The following child prodigies also made a parent drop the mop at some point in their lives.

Josef Hofmann

Josef Hofmann (1876–1957), born in Poland, debuted at the age of 6, and began touring Europe at 9. After his U.S. debut in 1887, he became so busy touring that, at one point, he played 52 concerts in only 10 weeks. Concerned, a friend of the family donated $50,000 so the young boy could take time to receive formal training and not return to public performance until he was 18. The time away served him well: Even the great Rachmaninoff once called Hofmann the "greatest living pianist."

Wolfgang Amadeus Mozart

Perhaps the most famous child prodigy, this young Austrian (1756–1791) turned to his father for lessons. At the age of 5, Mozart began composing, not just piano pieces, but full-scale symphonic works. He had an amazing memory and infallible ear for music, which allowed him to play entire sonatas perfectly after only one listening. His father proudly paraded his son's talents in front of nobility all across Europe with a "road show" that lasted 14 years. Mozart's piano concertos are regarded today as some of the most important pieces in the keyboard repertoire.

Stevie Wonder

Steveland Judkins Moore (born blind in Michigan in 1950) was instantly drawn to playing piano, harmonica, organ, and drums. Where his eyes failed him, his ears made up the difference and then some. At the age of 10, Berry Gordy signed him to Motown Records. At the age of 21, he began producing, arranging, and performing all of his own material, emerging as the first (and youngest) Motown artist to have complete artistic control. His style ranges from R&B and gospel to pop and rock. He was inducted into the Rock and Roll Hall of Fame in 1989.

Kids, gather 'round

Inspire your kids and others with a sampling of these young prodigies' magnificent creations:

♪ **Josef Hofmann:** *Complete Josef Hofmann, Vol. 3* (VAI).

♪ **Wolfgang Amadeus Mozart:** *Piano Concertos No. 20 & 21*, Mitsuko Uchida with Jeffrey Tate and the English Chamber Orchestra (Philips); *4 Piano Sonatas*, Alicia de Larrocha (London).

♪ **Stevie Wonder:** *Looking Back* (Motown); *Songs in the Key of Life* (Motown).

Hip Cats

Jazz comes in many flavors: bebop, New Orleans, big band, ragtime, and just plain cool. Jazz has attracted performers who took piano music to places it had never gone before in terms of skill, harmony, and rhythm. A sample list of these hip cats includes the following musicians.

Dave Brubeck

During breaks from studying classical music with his mother, Dave Brubeck (born in California in 1920) jetted off to form local jazz bands. In 1949, he formed a trio which soon became a quartet after saxophonist Paul Desmond joined. The quartet recorded many albums and stayed together until 1967. Their historic album *Time Out* was the first jazz album to experiment with compound meter (see the sidebar "What time is it, anyway?"), giving birth to the first jazz single, "Take Five," to sell a million copies.

What time is it, anyway?

Meter is a theoretical way to measure time in music. (See Chapter 5 for more on meter.) The most common meter, or time signature, is appropriately called common time, and it consists of four beats per measure. In music shorthand, this is referred to as 4/4 meter.

Jazz music was always rich in harmonic complexity, melodic improvisation, virtuoso playing, and free-swinging rhythms. But not until the Dave Brubeck Quartet's experimental album *Time Out* did jazz begin to explore musical meters other than common time (4/4) or waltz tempo (3/4).

After a tour abroad, Brubeck was entranced by a Turkish rhythm in the remote meter of 9/8. Inspired, he and his band set out to make a jazz album that would experiment specifically with meter. The result was a surprise hit and a hit single — yes, there is such a thing in jazz — and an even bigger surprise. The single, "Take Five," was set to a previously undanceable 5/4 meter.

Since then, there has been only one other huge hit in 5/4: Lalo Schifrin's theme to the TV show *Mission Impossible*. Even today, meters other than 4/4, 3/4, and 6/8 are rarely heard in popular songs.

Bill Evans

Born in New York, Evans (1929–1980) played piano through college and the army. Undeterred by Uncle Sam, he recorded his first album in 1956, joined the legendary trumpet player Miles Davis in 1958, and formed a trio in 1960. Evans's most controversial recording was the album *Conversations with Myself,* in which he mixed two or three recordings of his own piano playing together for one combined sound. Jazz purists were horrified! But time quickly proved that Evans's unconventional mind would soon pave a whole new way for jazz composition and recording.

Herbie Hancock

Hancock (born in Illinois in 1940) studied piano from the age of 7. Four years later he played the first movement of a Mozart concerto with the Chicago Symphony. After recording for Blue Note Records and playing with Miles Davis, he formed a new kind of jazz quartet that used several keyboards and synthesizers. Hancock was more commercially-minded than some of his contemporaries, producing the song "Rockit" that rocketed up the pop charts and winning an Oscar for his score to the motion picture *'Round Midnight.* He has recently returned to less-commercial, more jazz-oriented projects.

Thelonious Monk

He may not have chanted in a Gregorian monastery, but this Monk from North Carolina left an indelible mark on the history of American music. Monk (1917–1982) worked as a house pianist at a popular club, Minton's Playhouse, and introduced a new form of jazz called *bop,* which was more complex, less traditional-sounding, but oh so cool to hear. His first recording came in 1944 and was followed by a series of his own compositions for Blue Note Records. Initially his records were not big sellers, but his controversial and unorthodox style of playing and composing was finally accepted as genius. Hey, hindsight is always 20/20, right? The film *Straight, No Chaser* chronicles Monk's life.

Art Tatum

Mostly self-taught, Ohio-born Tatum (1909–1956) was a first-class musician. He began losing his sight at an early age, becoming completely blind in one eye and partly blind in the other. Vision impairment didn't inhibit his career; he recorded, toured, and frequently broadcast on the radio. Bringing new meaning to the words *two-hand piano,* his unique and amazing style caused listeners to think they were hearing two pianists, when in fact it was Art alone. He formed a trio in 1943 but returned to recording as a soloist a few years later. His style is noted for its stride and swing rhythms combined with sophisticated harmonies. Among his many fans was Russian classical pianist Vladimir Horowitz.

Jazz up your collection

Whether in a smoke-filled bar or smoke-filled recording studio, these giants loved to play. Hear them strut their stuff in these landmark recordings:

- ♪ **Dave Brubeck:** *Time Out* (CBS); *Time Further Out* (CBS).

- ♪ **Bill Evans:** *Conversations with Myself* (Verve); *Re: Person I Knew* (OJC).

- ♪ **Herbie Hancock:** *Headhunters* (CBS); *Best of Herbie Hancock* (Blue Note Records); *'Round Midnight Soundtrack* (CBS).

- ♪ **Thelonious Monk:** *Thelonious Monk Trio* (OJC); *Big Band and Quartet in Concert* (Columbia); *Straight, No Chaser* (Columbia).

- ♪ **Art Tatum:** *20th Century Piano Genius* (Verve).

Mysteriosos

"Fame made me do it!" Perhaps this phrase explains why three of the world's greatest pianists so mysteriously went from having their names up in lights to having "Do Not Disturb" signs affixed to their doors.

Van Cliburn

Van Cliburn (born in Texas in 1934) was fortunate to find a first piano teacher in his own mother. After attending the Juilliard School of Music and winning competitions, his career highlight came at the age of 24 when he won the first Tchaikovsky Competition in Russia. The competition, meant to prove the superiority of Russian pianists to the rest of the world, was turned upside down when this long, tall Texan suddenly won!

After his recording of the Tchaikovsky *Piano Concerto No. 1* became an all-time best seller, Cliburn became an international hit with frequent sold-out concerts. But in 1979, he suddenly retired from public performance for ten years. Upon his return, his playing was consistent with his old style, but his concert appearances are sporadic. It's still questionable whether or not he will resurrect his once-considerable career.

Glenn Gould

Canadian-born Glenn Gould (1932–1982) began studying piano at the age of 3. Seven years later, he was accepted to the Royal Conservatory in Toronto. At the age of 14, he was the youngest graduate ever from the Conservatory. He signed a recording contract with Columbia Records shortly after his U.S. debut, and his first recording, *The Goldberg Variations,* became a landmark. In 1964, feeling like "a vaudeville performer," he abandoned all live performances and limited his career to recordings, radio, and television. A reputation is hard to hide; although his recordings and radio programs were sensational in both content and number, he is perhaps best remembered today for being eccentric and reclusive.

Sviatoslav Richter

Sviatoslav Richter (1915–1997) started performing and recording in his teens, but the recordings of this Russian pianist were not heard in the West until the mid 1950s. They became immediate collector's items. Known for canceling concerts on a whim and playing brilliant but unusual interpretations of well-known pieces, Richter was quickly labeled a mystery man. Considered a real keyboard maverick, his management went so far as to call him "the pianist of the century." Now that's a manager I'd like to have.

Five habits for a promising musical career

Want a recipe for success? Some of the world's greatest pianists have adopted some perplexing, sometimes neurotic, habits over the years:

♪ Wear gloves at all times when not playing the piano.

♪ Never open doors or drawers with your hands.

♪ Always wear an overcoat, even in the heat of the summer.

♪ Insist on using only your *own* piano at every concert.

♪ After you make the big time, cancel engagements, stop returning calls, and drop out of society until the public begs your return . . . and I mean *begs!*

Find a habit that suits your fancy and you, too, may tempt the Fates into bestowing you with a monumental career.

Not-so-mysterious recordings

Fortunately, these performers often hid behind the doors of a recording studio, from which they produced these gems:

♪ **Van Cliburn:** Tchaikovsky, *Piano Concerto No. 1*, with Karil Kondrashin and the RCA Symphony (RCA); Prokofiev, *Piano Concerto No. 3*, Walter Hendl and the Chicago Symphony (RCA).

♪ **Glenn Gould:** Bach, *The Goldberg Variations* (CBS); Hindemith, *3 Sonatas* (CBS).

♪ **Sviatoslav Richter:** Mozart, *3 Sonatas* (Philips); Prokofiev, *Piano Concerto No. 5*, with Witold Rowicki and the Warsaw Philharmonic (DG).

Wild Ones

Notorious for their stage antics, extroverted personalities, wild costumes, and sometimes even pyrotechnics, these performers have given new meaning to the musical phrase "pulling out all the stops." (See Chapter 1 to understand the pipe organ term *pulling stops*.)

Jerry Lee Lewis

Jerry Lee Lewis (born in Louisiana in 1935) took to the piano at the age of 8. His first public performance was at the age of 14 with a country and western band. Upon arriving in Memphis in 1956, he auditioned for Sam Phillips at

Sun Records. (Sam is also credited with discovering Elvis.) Sam encouraged him to switch to rock 'n' roll, which led to such classics as "Great Balls of Fire" and "Whole Lotta Shakin' Going On." Never afraid of controversy, Lewis had a style of fast chord slamming, would often set his piano on fire in concert, and even married his 13-year-old cousin.

Liberace

Wladziu Valentino Liberace (1919–1987) moved from Wisconsin to New York in his early twenties, where he frequently performed in clubs and theaters. He moved to Los Angeles and appeared on television in 1951, and a legend was born. His expensive wardrobe, ornate candelabra, toothy smile, and florid piano style was Must See TV and led to a highly successful syndicated program. Always a good sport about being impersonated, he once said of a satirical parody, "I cried all the way to the bank." His home in Las Vegas is a well-attended museum. Visit the museum in person or on the World Wide Web at www.liberace.org. You'll be glad you did.

Little Richard

Many consider Little Richard Wayne Penniman (born in Georgia in 1932) to be the originator of rock 'n' roll. He learned piano at church, singing and playing gospel music, but at the age of 13 he was thrown out of the house for playing "the devil's music." Soon after, he signed with RCA Records and recorded several innovative records. In 1955, he signed with Specialty Records and recorded his first big hit, "Tutti Frutti." Surprisingly, he quit the music business in 1957 to become a minister, making sporadic returns to rock 'n' roll from 1964 to the present. Little Richard was one of the first ten performers to be inducted into the Rock and Roll ("Devil's Music") Hall of Fame.

Wild about their recordings

Even without a live audience, these flashy performers couldn't contain themselves when they played. A recording studio simply became another venue to showcase their talents:

> ♪ **Jerry Lee Lewis:** *All Killer, No Filler* (Rhino).
>
> ♪ **Liberace:** *16 Most Requested Songs* (CBS).
>
> ♪ **Little Richard:** *The Specialty Sessions* (Specialty).

Chart-Toppers

Turn on the radio and, within a half an hour or so, you're likely to hear a song performed by one of these chart-topping pianists. Each has his or her own distinct style, and these artists have helped blur the lines between pop and rock music.

Tori Amos

Myra Ellen Amos (born in North Carolina in 1963) studied classical piano as a child and attended the prestigious Peabody Conservatory at the age of five. When she insisted on playing her own compositions for the school examination board — a real no-no — her scholarship was not renewed. At the ripe old age of 13, she began playing in clubs in Washington, D.C., followed by a move to Los Angeles in 1984. Three years later, she was signed to Atlantic Records, but her first album was considered a failure. Finally, with a solo album called *Little Earthquakes,* Amos received the fame she deserves.

Billy Joel

Not your average kid, Bill Joel (born in New York in 1949) was a classically-trained musician, member of a street gang, and a boxer. He once broke his nose in the boxing ring, but I'm sure it had absolutely nothing to do with the piano-playing thing. His first album, released in 1971, was titled *Cold Spring Harbor.* After its release, he moved to the West Coast and played in piano bars. Appropriately enough, his first big seller was a song titled "Piano Man," followed by "The Entertainer." He continues to sell out concerts around the world and has recently focused his attention on composing concert music for the piano, a slightly less aggressive career than boxing, wouldn't you say?

Elton John

At the age of 11, Reginald Kenneth Dwight (born in England in 1947) studied piano at the Royal Academy of Music. He auditioned for Liberty Records, who suggested he team with another auditioner, lyricist Bernie Taupin. Publisher Dick James signed the songwriting team as house songwriters. Since his American debut in 1970, John has set many chart-topping records: first album to enter the charts at #1, first artist since The Beatles to have four albums in the Top Ten at once, and best-selling single record in the history of recorded music for "Candle in the Wind 1997." Not too shabby, huh? His highly acclaimed work on Disney's animated film, *The Lion King,* won an Oscar for Best Original Song.

Topping the charts

You can't have a #1 record without recording one first. The following list features some of the albums that won these artists the gold:

♪ **Tori Amos:** *Little Earthquakes* (Atlantic); *From the Choirgirl Hotel* (Atlantic).

♪ **Billy Joel:** *Greatest Hits, Volumes I & II* (Columbia).

♪ **Elton John:** *Greatest Hits* (MCA); *The One* (MCA).

Southern Stars

New Orleans is well known for Mardi Gras, crawfish, and a particular brand of jazz. But what about the rest of the South? Get on the bus and travel to other Southern locales that have given the world some unforgettable pianists, new musical styles, and . . . rhubarb pie.

Ray Charles

Blind since childhood, Ray Charles Robinson (born in Georgia in 1930) began playing piano at the age of 5. He attended the St. Augustine School for the Blind and learned to read music in Braille. In 1945, he left school and toured with a band through Florida. As his notoriety grew, he decided to shorten his name to Ray Charles to avoid any confusion with boxer Sugar Ray Robinson. In 1955, he had his first big hit, titled "I've Got a Woman." He is credited as the main influence behind the transformation of R&B into what's now considered Soul music. Through his music, Charles is a legend; with his trademark smile, he is an icon.

Floyd Cramer

Upon graduation from high school in Arkansas, young Cramer (1933–1997) moved to Shreveport, Louisiana, and joined a band for the radio show *The Louisiana Hayride*. Soon after, he became a highly sought-after session player for such legendary artists as Elvis Presley, Patsy Cline, Roy Orbison, and The Everly Brothers. Wisely taking the advice of Chet Atkins, he moved to Nashville in the mid-1950s and quickly established himself as a legend — he will be forever remembered as the person who successfully adapted country guitar style to the piano . . . and without plucking the strings!

Dr. John

Malcolm (Mac) Rebennack (born in Louisiana in 1942) grew up playing piano and guitar. A session player in high demand, he began producing and arranging in his early twenties. A move to Los Angeles brought session work with the legendary producer Phil Spector. It's not difficult to see how being raised in New Orleans might lead to an interest in voodoo. And from this interest came the self-appointed alias Dr. John Creaux the Night Tripper. Such a big, exotic name garnered a big, exotic cult following. Over the years that followed, he has recorded with such artists as Eric Clapton, Jeff Beck, and Mike Bloomfield. His unique style is punctuated by a blend of blues, rock, boogie, and jazz.

Scott Joplin

As a teenager growing up in Texas, Scott Joplin (1868-1917) was known all over Texas and Arkansas for his improvisational piano skills. His specialty was a new form of piano music called *ragtime*, named for its "ragged" syncopated rhythms. His playing at the Maple Leaf Club inspired his first important composition, "The Maple Leaf Rag," an enormous hit all over the world. A few years later, a second hit was born in "The Entertainer." You may remember this song as the theme used in the motion picture *The Sting*. After his death in 1917, he and his music were all but forgotten until a 1950 book titled *They All Played Ragtime* first called attention to the genius that he was.

Cooking up a collection

Stir the beans, warm the cornbread, and mix up the following recordings in your stereo for a taste of Southern-fried masterpieces:

- ♪ **Ray Charles:** *Genius and Soul — 50th Anniversary* (Rhino).
- ♪ **Floyd Cramer:** *Best* (BMG).
- ♪ **Dr. John:** *Anthology* (Rhino).
- ♪ **Scott Joplin:** *Complete Rags,* William Albright (Music Masters).

Mood Enhancers

New Age music's audience can be divided into two camps: those who love it and those who loathe it. A relatively new genre, this relaxing mood music generates sell-out records and sell-out concerts all around the world. And what instrument is better suited for relaxation than the piano or electric keyboard? Well, certainly not the drums.

George Winston

Not until after high school did George Winston (born in Montana in 1949) start playing keyboards. Influenced by blues, rock, and R&B, he became interested in the organ and electric piano. But after hearing Fats Waller play, he switched to the acoustic piano, where he has cultivated his own rural, folk piano style. His first solo album, *Ballads and Blues,* came out in 1972. Then, after many years of silence, he emerged with a Windham Hill recording contract and produced many highly successful albums. His major influences include Floyd Cramer, Ray Charles, and Vince Guaraldi (the man who gave us the Peanuts theme). In fact, Winston devotes part of every live show to the music of Guaraldi.

Yanni

Yanni Chryssomallis (born in Greece in 1954) was a member of the Greek National Swimming Team with little time for music or the piano. At the age of 14, he came to the U.S. After graduating from the University of Minnesota with a degree in psychology, he found work as a session player and even composed some commercial jingles. His first solo album, *Optimystique,* was released in 1980. Today, his albums and concert appearances are huge sellers worldwide. He is the first artist to ever perform a live concert at India's Taj Mahal palace. His compositions have been heard on ABC's *Wide World of Sports* and the Olympic Games. The degree in psychology? That's how he knows what the public wants to hear.

Enhancing your mood

Put one of these recordings in the CD player, sit back, relax, maybe even take a nice long nap:

♪ **George Winston:** *Winter Into Spring* (Windham Hill); *Linus and Lucy — The Music of Vince Guaraldi* (Windham Hill).

♪ **Yanni:** *Live at the Acropolis* (Private Music); *Tribute* (Virgin).

Song-Spinners

Sure, playing the piano is fun, but how can sitting around the house, banging away on the keys be considered a job? Perhaps it can when you produce the classic songs and classic shows that these three musicians did. With their piano as a desk, they went to work and have kept America singing ever since.

Duke Ellington

Some consider Edward Kennedy Ellington's arrival in New York from his birthplace in Washington D.C. to be the most important event in the jazz scene of the late 1920s. Initially aligning himself with the styles of James P. Johnson and Jelly Roll Morton, Ellington (1899–1974) could adapt to virtually any style, accompanying such distinct players as Coleman Hawkins and John Coltrane.

A true musical pioneer, he developed his own trademark style of jazz orchestration and led one of the most important bands of the swing era. Ellington wrote volumes of classic songs, including "Don't Get Around Much Anymore," "Sophisticated Lady," and "In a Sentimental Mood." Throughout a career spanning nearly five decades, Duke remained contemporary and surprisingly modern in his style and techniques.

George Gershwin

George Gershwin (1898–1937) got a late start, playing piano beginning at the age of 12. So consumed by music was young Gershwin, of New York, that he quit school to be a song-plugger (a person who sells songs) for the Remick Music Publishers. Tiring of this job, he sought work as a rehearsal pianist on Broadway. With his brother Ira as lyricist, he penned such classics as "I Got Rhythm" and "Let's Call the Whole Thing Off." He is the respected composer of successful Broadway shows, symphonic music, and the American opera, *Porgy and Bess.* More than any other composer before him, Gershwin pushed the boundaries of bringing commercial-sounding music into the snobbish concert hall. And, by the way, he was a darn good pianist, too!

Fats Waller

Thomas Wright Waller (1904–1943) played organ for his father's Baptist church services in New York. Mastering the organ's keys, he quickly took up piano, too. He was hired by the Lincoln Theatre in Harlem to accompany silent movies with his playing. At the age of 17, he began making piano rolls (see the sidebar "Roll me another piano"). A few years later, he began recording and broadcasting his own compositions. He teamed with lyricist Andy Razaf and the pair produced such hits as "Ain't Misbehavin'," "Black and Blue," and "Honeysuckle Rose." After successful records and tours around the world, he settled down and wrote a Broadway show, *Early to Bed.* I guess "settling down" is now defined as writing a Broadway show, not lying on the couch with a big glass of iced tea.

Roll me another piano

In the early 1900s, an invention called the *pianola*, or *player piano*, became the precursor to MIDI sequencing (see Chapter 16 for more on the World of MIDI). Perhaps that comparison is a stretch, but both have the same basic principle: making a keyboard play by itself.

The pianola holds a *piano roll*, a large roll of perforated paper containing holes punched in precise locations. As the piano roll turns, jets of air pass through the tiny holes and operate the hammers of the piano. When producing a piano roll, the pianist plays and causes the

perforations on a piano roll to be punched in a precise location, allowing you to hear exactly how that pianist played it.

In recent years, several record companies have released piano roll recordings of some of the great composers and pianists. Through the wonders of modern technology and old piano rolls, you can hear the likes of Rachmaninoff, Prokofiev, Ravel, and James P. Johnson playing their masterpieces the way they intended them to be played. It still doesn't rival a time machine, but I guess it will have to do.

They wrote the songs

Listen to these recordings and you'll realize who put the "show" in the word *showstoppers:*

♪ **Duke Ellington:** *The Essence of Duke Ellington* (CBS); *Piano Reflections* (Blue Note).

♪ **George Gershwin:** *George Gershwin Plays George Gershwin* (Pearl - UK); *Rhapsody in Blue*, Earl Wild with Arthur Fiedler and the Boston Pops (RCA).

♪ **Fats Waller:** *Turn On the Heat — The Fats Waller Piano Solos* (RCA).

Chapter 19

Ten Ways to Go Beyond This Book

In This Chapter

▶ Books, movies, and Web sites that can help you be a better player

▶ Playing with friends

▶ Listening to all types of music, whether live or recorded

▶ Enjoying the wider world of pianoness

Although this book certainly provides you with a basic understanding of how a piano works and how to start playing, I admit that it does not provide you with absolutely everything you need to know about the piano.

In your pursuit of eternal piano prowess, you may think, "What now?" This chapter gives you a few ideas of where to go from here — with one major exception. Hiring a piano teacher is such an important option that I devoted a whole chapter to it: Chapter 20.

Studying Method Books

If you're not ready to hire a piano teacher, an excellent resource for the beginning musician is what the industry calls *method books*.

A method book is an instructional book, or series of books, designed to teach you how to play a musical instrument in a strategic, proven, *methodical* manner. Countless volumes of these books exist, each featuring its own "method to the madness," whether old-fashioned or new-and-improved.

Like any series of "how-to" books, methods come in all shapes, sizes, and various levels of skill — from beginner to advanced. After reading *Piano For Dummies,* you should be ready for an intermediate-level method.

Visit a sheet music store, and you can find rock methods, classical methods, jazz methods, country methods — the list is endless. Pick one that's right for you and, most importantly, one that looks fun and interesting.

Although no book can replace a live, human teacher, I highly recommend method books as an inexpensive, viable option for continuing to master the piano. To get you started, the following method books are worth checking out:

♪ *FastTrack Keyboard 1 and 2,* by Blake Neely (that's me) and Gary Meisner (Hal Leonard)

♪ *Francis Clark Piano Library,* by Francis Clark (Warner Bros.)

♪ *Hal Leonard Student Piano Library,* by Barbara Kreader, Fred Kern, Phillip Keveren, and Mona Rejino (Hal Leonard)

♪ *The Jazz Piano Book,* by Mark Levine (Sher Music Co.)

♪ *You Can Teach Yourself Piano,* by Matt Dennis (Mel Bay)

Using Reference Books

In music stores and libraries, you find literally thousands of *music reference books,* sometimes called *supplementals,* about the piano. Books exist on everything from the history of keyboards to building your own piano (good luck!).

Don't be fooled: Reference books will not teach you how to play. They should be used *in addition to,* not instead of, a method book or teacher. Use these books to help you further understand a concept introduced by your method book or teacher. For example, when you first start to play chords (Chapter 12), you can buy a chord dictionary.

You'll find reference books on music theory, harmony, chords, scales, songwriting, the lives of the great composers, musical terms, orchestration, grooves, styles, and much more. My personal library contains the following books, which I can highly recommend:

♪ *1000 Keyboard Ideas,* edited by Ronald Herder (Ekay Music, Inc.)

♪ *The Art of the Piano,* by David Dubal (Harvest/Harcourt, Brace & Company)

♪ *Blues Riffs for Piano,* Ed Baker (Cherry Lane Music)

♪ *Chord Voicing Handbook,* by Matt Harris and Jeff Jarvis (Kendor Music, Inc.)

♪ *Complete Book of Modulations for the Pianist,* by Gail Smith (Mel Bay)

♪ *FastTrack Keyboard Chords & Scales,* by Blake Neely (who?) and Gary Meisner (Hal Leonard)

♪ *Five Centuries of Keyboard Music* (Dover)

♪ *The Great Pianists,* Harold C. Schonberg (Fireside/Simon & Schuster)

♪ *Musician's Guide to the Internet,* Gary Hustwit (Rockpress/Hal Leonard)

♪ *Pocket Music Dictionary* (Hal Leonard)

Those of you who are on the World Wide Web (you know who you are) can buy music reference books online from Music Books Plus at www.vaxxine.com/mbp or at Amazon Books at www.amazon.com. (I talk about additional Web resources later in this chapter.)

Buying Music to Play

You are learning to play the piano for one simple reason: to play music. Okay, so maybe you're learning for another reason: to impress your friends. After you achieve the first goal, the second naturally just happens.

Unless you're playing strictly by ear, you'll need some music to read. Enter the concept of *printed music.*

Types of printed music

Thanks to five centuries worth of composers, you have a wealth of printed music from which to choose. Generally, you find it in three packages:

♪ **Sheet music:** Single songs printed on 2 to 12 pages, folded or stapled together.

♪ **Folios:** Collections of various songs, packaged together for a specific marketing reason.

♪ **Classical:** Most classical pieces are very long and require an entire little book to hold one piece.

For example, you can buy the sheet music to the song "Footloose," or you can buy a folio called "Movie Hits from the '80s," which contains "Footloose" as well as 50 others.

Buying folios is a great value. Sheet music sells for around $4.95 for one song, whereas a folio sells for around $16.95 and may have 50 to 100 songs. However, chances are that if it's a really new song, it will only be available as sheet music. It's your choice: Buy now, or wait, or both.

Varying formats

Printed music, whether sheets or folios, comes in many different formats. The different formats, called *arrangements,* allow the publisher to release the song in several levels of skill and for various keyboard instruments. It's the same song, but the publisher has arranged the notes and chords to suit your needs.

Using the "Footloose" example, you may want to play a very easy version of the song on an electronic organ, or you may want to play an advanced piano solo version on a grand piano. Both formats are probably available. And, of course, you can probably find every other level in between.

After you master a song, it's fun to try playing other arrangements of the same song. (I once learned to play 18 different versions of "Yankee Doodle," ranging from plain vanilla to rock 'n' roll. Thank goodness it was just a phase.) Your local sheet music dealer can help you find just the arrangement and style you want.

Fake books

A *fake book* is actually a real book. This is the music industry term for a printed music book, or folio, that gives you only the melody line, lyrics, and chords of a song. Compared to a piece of sheet music that has both hands written out and fully harmonized, the fake book acts as merely a road map of the song, allowing you to play the melody, sing the lyrics, and create your own left-hand accompaniment with the chords that are shown. (Chapter 14 gives you some great left-hand accompaniment ideas.)

Working pianists love fake books. They can take a request, flip to the song (usually printed in its entirety on one single page), and improvise the rest of the song. If they are accompanying a singer, even better. A fake book's streamlined form makes it easy to *transpose* (or change keys) a song on the spot to accommodate the singer's range. And that's why you put the little tip jar on your piano!

Some of my favorite fake books — based on content, usability, and price — are the following:

- ♪ *The Classical Fake Book,* over 600 themes and melodies (Hal Leonard)
- ♪ *Fake Book of the World's Favorite Songs* (Hal Leonard)
- ♪ *Keyboard Player Omnibus Edition* (Music Sales)
- ♪ *The New Real Book Vol. 1–3* (Sher Music Company)
- ♪ *The Real Ultimate Fake Book,* over 1200 songs (Hal Leonard)

Where to buy printed music

Printed music isn't as easy to find as CDs, tapes, or chewing gum, but there are several companies and several stores that specialize in it. More and more often these days, large bookstores and mass-market stores like K-mart and Target are beginning to stock sheet music. I guess it shows how many people are playing instruments. And that's a great thing.

You can also find printed music at a local music store that carries instruments. If all else fails, look in your local phone book under "Music - Sheet" or "Music - Instrument Retail."

The World Wide Web is a wonderful resource for finding just about anything. Simply do a search for "printed music," and you'll find what you need with a few clicks of the mouse. Check out Sheet Music Direct at www.sheetmusicdirect.com.

You can contact any of the following companies to get a catalog of their offerings:

- ♪ **Alfred Publishing Co., Inc.:** 16380 Roscoe Boulevard, P.O. Box 10003, Van Nuys, CA, 91410-0003; Phone: 818-891-5999. Web: www.alfredpub.com.

- ♪ **Carl Fischer, Inc.:** 62 Cooper Square, New York, NY, 10003; Phone: 212-777-0900. Web: www.carlfischer.com.

- ♪ **Cherry Lane Music Company:** 10 Midland Avenue, Port Chester, NY, 10573; Phone: 800-637-2852. Web: www.cherrylane.com.

- ♪ **Hal Leonard Corporation:** 7777 West Bluemound Road, Milwaukee, WI, 53213; Phone: 800-554-0626. Web: www.halleonard.com.

- ♪ **Mel Bay Publishing, Inc.:** #4 Industrial Drive, Pacific, MO, 63069-0066; Phone: 800-8-MEL-BAY (863-5229). Web: www.melbay.com.

- ♪ **Music Sales:** 257 Park Avenue South, New York, NY, 10010; Phone: 800-431-7187. Web: www.musicsales.com.

- ♪ **Sher Music Company:** P.O. Box 445, Petaluma, CA, 94953; Phone: 800-444-7437. Web: www.shermusic.com.

- ♪ **Warner Bros. Publications:** 15800 NW 48th Avenue, Miami, FL, 33014; Phone: 800-327-7643. Web: www.warnerbros.com.

Gigging with Others

Nothing teaches music better than playing music. After a while, you may feel in the mood for collaboration. Lucky for you the concept of piano duets, ensembles, and bands came along.

In any city, college, or university, you can easily find other musicians who simply love to play together, and I'm not talking about playing video games.

Piano duets

Find a friend, sibling, parent, or teacher who will share the piano bench with you and play the lower or upper part of a duet. Many songs are available in duet form, where each player gets their own printed music showing which part of the piano to play. But playing a duet is not a race. You start, stop, and play the song together.

Ensembles

Many ensembles require a pianist. In the world of classical music, a piano trio features a piano and two other instruments — typically a violin and a cello. In the world of jazz, a quartet might include a piano, drums, bass, and saxophone. Find friends who need a third or fourth wheel and climb on board.

Virtually every major composer has written specifically for trios, quartets, and other size ensembles, so the repertoire of pieces you and your friends can play is endless.

Bands

With you on keyboard, all you need is a drummer, bassist, guitarist, and maybe a singer, and you've got yourself a band. Whether you're just having fun in the garage or actually pursuing gigs, playing in a band can be fun and rewarding.

Everyone in a band should be on an equal playing field. Having band members with similar playing proficiency as you — that is, not much better or much worse — will keep those intra-band rivalries to a minimum.

Having trouble finding someone else to play with? Call a friend, buy her lunch, and drive to your local bookstore. As you approach the large display of black-and-yellow books, talk glowingly about the allure of fame, the glamour of touring, and the joys of forming a band. When you have your friend's attention, grab *Guitar For Dummies*, by Mark Phillips and Jon Chappel, published by IDG Books Worldwide, Inc., and head quickly toward the cash register.

As you and your band or ensemble improve, invite friends to come hear you practice. Play songs that your audience wants to hear, or make up your own. When you're convinced that you're really good, solicit interest from local venues — bars, restaurants, hotels, bridge clubs — and play for a bigger crowd. A hobby can easily become a career if you work at it hard enough.

Listening to CDs

Buy them, borrow them, just get your hands on some CDs that you like and listen, listen, listen! Read through Chapter 18 and find some artists and recordings that interest you.

Listening to other pianists gives you insight into the quality of your own playing as well as stylistic ideas you can borrow to liven up your performance. Plus, being inspired is always motivating.

Perusing record stores

You'll find a record store on nearly every major street in every major city — humans buy lots of records. Some of these can be expensive, but many record labels — especially the classical ones — offer varied price ranges. Make sure you check every listing under a particular artist, and you may find the same performance for much less money.

It pays to patronize record stores that allow in-store listening, allowing you to sample any CD in the store for as long as you like before you ever let a dime fall from your pocket. One bit of caution: Try not to sing out loud or dance provocatively until *after* you've purchased the CD.

If you can't find it, order it. Most any record store can order most any album you desire, as long as it is still in print. The store should have one or two ways to look up the album information:

♪ **Electronic kiosk:** Punch in the title, artist, label, or any other data you may know about the album, and in seconds you'll get a printed form with the right information.

♪ **Phonolog:** This is an alphabetical listing of virtually every record ever made. Look up the album you want by title, artist, or even individual songs.

Using either method, gather as much album information as you can, ask the store to order it, return home, have a donut, and wait for them to call you. Life can be so easy sometimes.

Shopping online

Avoid the traffic, stay in your pajamas, and shop for music from the comforts of your own home. That's right: The Internet has many sites for ordering music. Some of them even allow you to listen to a sample of the recording before purchasing. Have your credit card information handy and check out the following:

♪ **1-800-Music Now:** www.1800musicnow.com

♪ **Amazon:** www.amazon.com

♪ **CDNOW:** www.cdnow.com

♪ **CD Universe:** www.cduniverse.com

♪ **Every CD:** www.everycd.com

♪ **Tower Records:** www.towerrecords.com

Visit libraries

Libraries aren't just for books any more. Visit your local library and check out their collection of CDs. No, I mean literally *check out* their collection. That's why it's there.

After you find the Liberace CD you desire, the nice librarian will give you a set of headphones and a quiet place to sit and listen. Some libraries even let you take CDs home, but you'll have to leave the headphones.

When a record store fails to locate an out of print CD, a library is the place to go. Of course, you probably won't be able to take these hard-to-find ones home, but you still get a nice comfortable listening room.

Believe it or not, recorded music did exist before CDs. Many albums from the olden days still haven't made it to CD. Your library is likely to have some of these recordings on LP, cassette, or *(gulp!)* 8-track. Many audiophiles and historians actually prefer the sound of analog to digital . . . er, LP to CD.

Join record clubs

If you want to build a CD collection, record clubs are the way to go. You've seen these "13 CDs for 1¢" offers, right? They're real! The club will send you a basket of CDs for one penny. You just have to agree to buy five more at regular price over the next three years, or something like that.

Do the math; it's not a bad value. You want to build your collection anyway, right? You're likely to buy five CDs at regular price from a store in the next three years. So, this way you get 18 CDs for around $75.01 (don't forget that penny!). This calculates to roughly $4.00 per CD. Beat that! Of course, you have to pay for shipping and handling (around $3.00 per CD), but this is a small price to pay for the savings you garner.

Make sure to always mail back the little card each month, whether you want to order music or not. It only costs you a single stamp. Otherwise, the club sends you the featured selection and charges you for it.

Most clubs offer a variety of genres: classical, jazz, pop, rock, New Age, easy listening, and everything else. A few clubs are genre-specific: classical only, jazz only, and so on. Here are a couple of good starting places for you:

♪ **Berkshire Record Outlet, Inc.:** Route 102, Pleasant Street, Lee, MA, 01238-9804; Phone: 413-243-4080. Web: www.berkshirerecordoutlet.com

♪ **Musical Heritage Society:** 1710 Highway 35, Ocean, NJ, 07712; Phone: 908-531-7003

Borrow from friends

My favorite way to build a collection is to borrow from friends. With the old "bait and switch" routine, chances are you'll have a free CD for as long as you need it. Don't stray from the following script, except to change the CD names to suit your needs:

You: "Can I borrow your *Complete Bill Evans* boxed set, Fred?"

Fred: "You must be crazy!"

You: "Oh, come on, please?"

Fred: "You're not *that* good a friend."

You: "Well [*dramatic pause*] . . . how 'bout this little *Thelonious Monk at Carnegie* disc?"

Fred: "Whatever. But not my Bill Evans boxed set!"

Got it? Enough said . . . enjoy the free music.

Attending Live Concerts

If you have a symphony orchestra in your city, buy a ticket. If not, it's worth driving to the closest town that does have one. They will invite at least one pianist to appear as guest soloist each season. To see and hear a pianist live is wholly different from listening to a recording.

Listening to a recording gives you the most important part of the performance but not the entire picture. *Watching* a pianist play, you gain insight into playing habits, posture, finger dexterity, intensity, emotions, and overall skill. You subconsciously take this gained knowledge home with you and apply it to your own playing technique.

If you aren't into classical music, find a jazz club, go to a hotel bar, visit a shopping mall during the holidays, or attend a rock concert. Just find live piano players, other than your Uncle Dave — unless, of course, his last name happens to be Brubeck — and watch them play.

Exploring the Internet

The World Wide Web is a fabulous and mysterious place. Full of sites and home pages no one even knows about, it's always fun and informative to just start surfing.

Among the many music-specific sites on the Internet, a plethora of piano and keyboard Web pages exist. The following sites are some of the best in both content and entertainment value:

♪ **Piano Parlour:** www.hits.net/~pianists/piano.html

♪ **Piano Education Page:** www.unm.edu/~loritaf/pnoedmn.html

♪ **Piano Page:** www.ptg.org

♪ **Piano Home Page:** www.serve.com/marbeth/piano.html

♪ **Billy Taylor Jazz Lectures:** www.town.hall.org/Archives/radio/Kennedy/Taylor

♪ **Jazz Central Station:** www.jazzcentralstation.com

If you author a Web page on pianos or keyboards, or if you find a really cool one that I haven't listed, please e-mail me at BlakeNeely@aol.com. I'll look forward to catching a wave over to your site.

In addition to Web pages, many newsgroups center around the topics of pianos, performance, electric keyboards, MIDI gear, audio recording, and more. Subscribe to these newsgroups (usually free) and make friends who care about what you care about:

♪ alt.music.midi

♪ rec.music.classical.recordings

♪ rec.music.makers.marketplace

Pianos at the Movies

Hollywood has made many, many movies with the piano, or a piano player, prominently featured. Whether it's a mute woman who speaks through her piano or a deaf composer who can't hear his, movie makers sure can make a dramatic story out of 88 keys.

Check out these fine films:

♪ ***Thirty Two Short Films About Glenn Gould***: One of them is less than one minute long; the other 31 give you insight into this reclusive and mysterious virtuoso performer.

♪ ***Amadeus***: It's about that Mozart guy.

♪ ***Casablanc***a: Bogart didn't say "Play it, Sam" to a tuba player!

♪ ***The Competition***: Amy Irving and Richard Dreyfuss are pianists competing for the same prize and falling in love.

♪ ***The Fabulous Baker Boys***: Jeff and Beau Bridges play duet cocktail pianos and search for a singer. They find one in Michelle Pfeiffer, who manages to crawl across a piano like no one has before.

♪ ***Five Easy Pieces***: Jack Nicholson is a piano player with five easy pieces to play.

♪ ***Immortal Beloved***: Gary Oldman plays Beethoven, and Beethoven plays his "Moonlight Sonata."

♪ ***Impromptu***: The story of Chopin's love affair with author George Sand.

♪ ***Madame Sousatzka***: Shirley MacClaine plays a reclusive but passionate piano teacher in London.

♪ ***The Piano***: Holly Hunter plays a mute woman who expresses herself through her clarinet . . . no, wait, I mean piano.

♪ **Shine**: David Helfgott practices Rachmaninoff's concerto so much that he goes a little loco.

♪ **Song Without End**: In the height of Lisztomania, Franz has an affair with a countess and ponders giving up performing. Oh, the humanity!

♪ **Thelonious Monk: Straight, No Chaser**: Documentary on the great jazz legend, featuring films shot during his 1968 sessions and tour.

Realizing You're Not Alone

I thought it would be fun to give you a sample list of famous people who also play (or played) the piano. Now you know that you're not alone in your quest for piano perfection:

♪ Steve Allen, comedian – former host of TV's *The Tonight Show*

♪ William F. Buckley, writer

♪ Clint Eastwood, actor-director

♪ Jeff Goldblum, actor

♪ Jack Lemmon, actor

♪ Denny MacLaine (organ), former pitcher for the Detroit Tigers

♪ Dudley Moore, actor

♪ Richard M. Nixon, former U.S. President

♪ Paul Reiser, comedian-actor

♪ Fred (Mister) Rogers, beloved children's TV personality

♪ John Tesh, recording artist–former host of TV's *Entertainment Tonight*

♪ Harry S. Truman, former U.S. President

Chapter 20

Blake's Ten Teacher-Tracking Tips

* *

In This Chapter
▶ Finding a great teacher
▶ Asking a candidate the right questions

* *

*A*fter you decide to hire a private teacher, your next step is to find one, a *good* one. Oh, sure, you think it's easy, but finding a good teacher takes time, commitment, and patience. Many pianists change teachers three or four times in the span of a career. Personally, I've had five different teachers.

Before you take a single lesson, it is perfectly acceptable, and highly advisable, to interview each candidate and discover their strengths and weaknesses. Don't be afraid to ask questions. Just remember, you are the boss — *you* are hiring the teacher, not the other way around.

To help you ask the right questions of a prospective teacher, use this chapter as a checklist. Go ahead and take this book along with you on the interview.

Question #1: Whom Else Have You Taught?

Possible answers:

♪ "I've had several students over the years and would be happy to give you their names and numbers to contact."

♪ "Just a few: Leonard Bernstein, Rudolf Serkin, and André Watts."

♪ "No one. You'll be my first."

You should get a list of references from the teacher candidate and contact each of them, if possible. If you were referred to the candidate by a friend or relative, it's still okay to ask for another reference.

Assess your teacher's overall abilities by asking current and former students what they like and don't like about the teacher.

Question #2: How Long Have You Been Teaching and Playing?

Possible answers:

♪ "Over 25 years, and I love it."

♪ "I retired from public performance three years ago and decided to start teaching."

♪ "Since lunch."

Whether it's years of playing, years of studying, or years of teaching, experience is a must for any good teacher. Without it, you'll both be learning as you go, but you won't be the one getting paid by the hour.

You may also want to know where the candidate received his education, what awards he won, or if he enjoyed a previous career as a performer.

Question #3: What Do You Think of Mozart?

Possible answers:

♪ "A wonderful 18th-century composer of symphonic, chamber, and keyboard music."

♪ "An overrated, questionable child prodigy who wrote some works considered classic today."

♪ "Oh, isn't that the mayor's boy?"

A teacher who is knowledgeable about music is a teacher who can answer the myriad questions that you are bound to have. Knowledge of the great composers or music history is not the defining characteristic of a good teacher, but it tells a lot about their education and repertoire.

Other questions to test a candidate's general music knowledge might include:

♪ What is the difference between a piano and harpsichord? (See Chapter 1.)

♪ What style of music did Bill Evans play? (See Chapter 18.)

♪ What is the key signature for the key of C-sharp major? (See Chapter 11.)

Question #4: Would You Mind Playing Something for Me?

Possible answers:

♪ "Sure, what key would you like it in?"

♪ "Well, I would be happy to play for you. How about a bit of Fats Waller?"

♪ "I don't really play. I'm just a good teacher."

How well does your candidate play? Ask her to play something for you, nothing too tricky but nothing too easy — perhaps Bach, Chopin, or even Scott Joplin. Your ears will tell you the answer. Are you impressed with the candidate's skill, or can your friends play just as well?

Don't head for the door if you get the third answer. Surprisingly, even someone who can't play very well can still be a good teacher. They may be very skilled in listening and correcting your technique without being able to make their own fingers play the music. If you like the answers the candidate gives you to the other questions in this chapter, he may be a good candidate despite not playing well for you.

Question #5: What Repertoire Do You Teach?

Possible answers:

♪ "I like all music. We'll start with the classics and work our way up to today's Top Ten."

♪ "The three Bs: Bach, Beethoven, and The Beatles."

♪ "Come again?"

Most likely, you have an idea of the pieces you want to play. It's important for every pianist to be able to play the classics — Bach, Mozart, Chopin — but, of course, they aren't the only composers. And classical isn't the only genre of music. (Chapter 15 introduces you to several styles of music.)

If you want to play rockabilly or jazz or R&B, find out if your teacher is willing to teach you those styles. Granted, you have to work your way up to playing these other styles by starting with the classics. But as you improve, make sure your teacher will let you pick your own repertoire to some extent.

Question #6: How Do You Feel about Wrong Notes, Mistakes, or Lack of Practice?

Possible answers:

> ♪ "To err is human."
>
> ♪ "Mistakes are the path toward learning."
>
> ♪ *[Fist pounds the table]* "I abhor imperfection."

Patience is a virtue, and patience is an absolute must in teaching anyone anything. Learning to play piano is no exception. You want your teacher to teach you at your pace, regardless of how many mistakes you make.

Question #7: What Methods Do You Use to Teach Piano?

Possible answers:

> ♪ "I use the internationally respected blankety-blank method."
>
> ♪ "My method varies depending on the needs of each student. We can begin with. . . ."
>
> ♪ "Let's just see what happens."

Each teacher has his or her own method of teaching. It may be a tried and true approach, finely honed over the years. It may be a new method she just read about in a book. (Read more about method books in Chapter 19.) Whatever the method, your teacher should teach piano in a way you are comfortable with.

True story: I once had a teacher who thought the "shock treatment" approach could apply to piano. By rapping my knuckles with a yardstick every time I played a wrong note, my teacher expected that the outcome would be perfection. The outcome was intimidation, resulting in more wrong notes, red knuckles, and a new teacher for me. It really does pay to find out about a candidate's methods and avoid getting sore knuckles.

Question #8: Where Will the Lessons Be Given?

Possible answers:

♪ "Right here in my living room at my Steinway."

♪ "I am happy to teach at your home if you have a keyboard and feel more relaxed in a familiar environment."

♪ "In the alley behind the stadium after midnight."

As with real estate, location is everything. You don't want any excuses to skip piano lessons. And, believe me, on hot summer days with a new movie blockbuster opening at the theater down the street, you dream up a wealth of excuses. Don't let location be one of them.

Question #9: How Much Do You Charge?

Possible answers:

♪ "I require $35 per hour lesson. We'll meet once a week, and I ask that you give me plenty of notice if you must cancel."

♪ "We'll schedule four lessons per month, and you pay me $200."

♪ "How can you put a price on art?"

On average, most teachers charge between $30 and $50 per hour. However, depending on a number of economic factors, including notoriety and demand, your teacher may command upwards of $100 per hour.

Question #10: Do You Have Annual Student Recitals?

Possible answers:

♪ "Yes. I rent the college concert hall and have a recital for all of my students. You can invite as many guests as you like, and I serve soft drinks and cookies at intermission."

♪ "No, but that's an excellent idea for this year."

♪ "Sure, if Dad will let me use the barn."

Playing for an audience is fun and, for many, the main reason to play the piano. A teacher can help build your audience (and courage) through annual, or semi-annual, public performances called *recitals*. Your teacher will plan the recital, find the venue, advertise, and prepare you. Without a teacher, you're left to self-promote your public debut.

Appendix A
Glossary of Musical Terms

. . . .

*M*any of the terms in this glossary are explained at length in this book. However, when you encounter an unfamiliar musical term, you can find a brief explanation in this appendix.

a tempo: Literally means "at time." Return to original tempo. Usually appears after an *accelerando* or *ritardando*.

accelerando: Gradually get faster, like when you push the accelerator in a car. Sometimes abbreviated as *accel*.

accidental: Not on purpose; or a sign such as a sharp, flat, or natural, used to raise, lower, or return a tone to its natural pitch.

acoustic: Not electric.

adagio: Slow and easy.

allegro: Fast and lively.

andante: Medium speed, in between *adagio* and *allegro*.

arpeggio: Literally means "harp-like." Notes of a chord played in succession but not simultaneously. Commonly known as a *broken chord*.

arrangement: Adaptation of a piece of music.

articulation: Marking that indicates how to perform a musical note, such as short, long, heavy, light, and so on.

augmented: Raised by one half step. A major chord becomes an augmented chord when the 5th interval is raised one half step.

backbeat: Emphasis on beats 2 and 4; most common in rock and reggae music.

bar: A place to buy alcoholic beverages. See also *measure.*

barline: People waiting to buy drinks; or a vertical line that divides the musical staff into measures.

bass: Pronounced one way, it's a type of fish; pronounced another way, it's the lower-sounding part in music.

bass clef: Symbol placed on the fourth line of the staff designating that line to be the tone F. Corresponds to the F below middle C.

beam: Horizontal line that connects and replaces the flags on a group of short notes such as eighth notes or sixteenth notes.

beat: A single unit of musical time.

blues: A style of music employing 12-bar form, shuffle rhythms, and specific chord progressions.

broken chord: See *arpeggio.*

chord: Three or more different notes played simultaneously.

chord progression: Movement from one chord to another.

clef: A symbol placed on the music staff to indicate the pitch represented by each staff line and space.

coda: Literally means "tail." The ending section of a song, indicated by a target-looking sign.

common time: 4/4 meter.

concerto: What you might be playing one day; a composition for a featured soloist and an orchestra.

crescendo: Gradually get louder.

cut time: Pays less than full-time; or 2/2 meter

da capo: Literally means "from the beginning;" often abbreviated as *D.C. al Coda* or *D.C. al Fine*, meaning to play again from the beginning to the coda, or end.

dal segno: Literally means "from the sign;" often abbreviated as *D.S. al Coda* or *D.S. al Fine*, meaning to play again from the dollar-looking sign to the coda, or end.

damper: Little felt pads that stop the piano strings from vibrating.

D.C.: Home of the United States government; see *da capo*.

decrescendo: See *crescendo* and do the opposite.

diminished: Lowered by one half step. A minor chord becomes a diminished chord when the 5th interval is lowered one half step.

diminuendo: Gradually get softer.

dissonant: Not pleasant to hear; unresolved tonality.

double barline: See *barline* and add another one; indicates the end of a section in the music.

D.S.: See *dal segno*.

dynamics: Music's volume indications. See *mezzo*.

enharmonics: Two tones that are the same pitch but have different names, such as C-sharp and D-flat.

F clef: See *bass clef*.

fermata: To hold a note or rest for an undetermined amount of time.

fine: The end.

flat: What you hope your tires aren't; or a half-step lower.

forte: The number after 39 (just kidding!); or literally means strong or loud.

fortissimo: Very loud and forceful.

G clef: See *treble clef*.

glissando: Literally means "gliding." A musical effect produced by sliding the fingers rapidly across the keys between two notes.

grace note: A note with no rhythmic value played just slightly before another note, so that the effect is "sliding" into the note.

grand staff: Two staves joined together, using treble and bass clefs, allowing left-hand and right-hand notes to be shown simultaneously.

half step: The smallest interval on a keyboard, from one key to the next closest key; also known as a minor second interval.

hammer: An essential tool to have around the house; or a felt-covered mechanism inside a piano used to strike the strings to produce sounds.

harmony: The sound created by two or more different tones played together.

harpsichord: Keyboard instrument with strings that are plucked, rather than hammered; precursor to the *pianoforte*.

heavy metal: Iron or steel; or a type of rock music with hard-edged sound.

interval: The distance between any two tones.

inversion: Upside down; or a chord that does not have the root as its bass note.

jazz: American musical form with emphasis on harmonic complexity, rhythm, and improvisation.

key: Those things you press on a piano; or those things you use to get in your house; or the tonal center of a piece of music.

key signature: Small grouping of insecure sharps or flats at the beginning of each staff line, telling you which key the song is in.

largo: Very slow and broad.

ledger line: Little lines that extend the music staff in either direction, used for notes that exceed the pitches represented by the lines and spaces of the staff.

legato: Smooth.

lento: What comes out of your pockets in the dryer; or slow tempo.

maestoso: Literally means "majestically." To play with lots of emotion.

manual: Type of hard labor; or a set of keys on an organ or harpsichord.

march time: What follows "Hup, 2, 3, 4" in a parade; or 2/4 meter.

measure: To see how long something is; or the space between two barlines on a musical staff in which a specific number of beats are placed.

melody: A hummable line of music; or an organized sequence of single notes and rhythms.

meter: About 36 inches long; or the division of music and rhythm into measures by defining the number of beats and the length of one beat for each measure; also called *time signature*.

metronome: A device that clicks, beeps, or flashes the correct tempo in beats per minute (bpm).

mezzo: Literally means "medium." Used with other dynamics such as *piano* and *forte*, so that *mezzo-forte* means "medium loud."

MIDI: Acronym for "musical instrument digital interface." A system used to connect an electric keyboard to another MIDI device such as a computer, sequencer, or other electric keyboards.

moderato: A tempo indication, which literally means "moderate."

modulation: Changing keys, or the transition between two keys.

multitimbral: On electric keyboards, the ability to produce more than one sound simultaneously.

note: The representation of a musical tone and rhythmic value, such as a *quarter note G* or an *eighth note A-flat*.

octave: An interval spanning eight tones with the top and bottom tone having the same name.

organ: Acoustic keyboard instrument with a set of keys that trigger air to be sent through a series of pipes to produce sounds; or an electric version which sounds similar but without the air.

pedal: A mechanism controlled by the foot, commonly found on pianos, organs, and bicycles.

pentatonic: Literally means "five tones." A scale found in Asian folk music, heavy metal, country, pop, and other music.

perfect pitch: The coveted ability to hear and identify a musical tone correctly without the aid of a musical instrument or device.

pianissimo: Very soft.

piano: The instrument you're playing; literally means "soft."

pianoforte: Literally means "soft-loud." Keyboard instrument with a set of 88 keys that trigger hammers to strike strings to produce sounds.

pianola: A "player piano." A piano affixed with a mechanical drum that spins a roll of paper perforated with holes corresponding to specific keys, air, and other complicated things.

pickup measure: An incomplete measure at the beginning of a song, which allows the music to begin on a beat other than beat 1.

pitch: To throw a baseball; or the highness or lowness of a musical tone.

plectrum: A mechanism inside a harpsichord or other stringed instrument that plucks the strings to produce sounds.

polyphonic: Sounding more than one musical tone at once.

prepared piano: A piano with the sound altered by placing objects such as screws, bolts, pillows, and so on between or on the strings.

presto: What a magician says; or very fast tempo.

rallentando: Gradually get slower but more than *ritardando*.

reggae: A musical style from Jamaica, emphasizing beats 2 and 4.

relative minor: Underage kinfolk; or a minor chord or scale related to a major chord or scale with the same tones.

rest: A musical beat without sound.

rhythm: The result of putting lots of beats together.

ritardando: Gradually get slower.

rubato: Freely, or an unsteady tempo at the player's discretion.

sampler: Electric keyboard instrument that makes recordings, or "samples," of sounds and assigns the resulting tones to appropriate keys.

scale: A specific sequence of musical tones, rising or falling in pitch, in accordance with a strict system of intervals.

sequencer: Device that records a stream of MIDI data to be played back.

sharp: What you hope your knives are; or a half step higher than natural pitch.

shuffle: What every dealer should do to a new deck of cards; or a rhythm marked by the feel of long-short, long-short; commonly found in blues, rock, and jazz music.

slash chord: Chord symbol indicating a specific bass note to play.

sostenuto: Literally means "sustain." Also the middle pedal on a piano that sustains a specific note, or group of notes, allowing the player to play successive notes without sustain.

staccato: Literally means "detached." An articulation indicated by a dot under or above the note, telling the player to give that note less than its full rhythmic value.

staff: A hard-working team of employees; or a set of five lines and four spaces on which musical notes are written.

stem: Flower part; or the vertical line extending from a notehead.

subito: Literally means "suddenly;" used with a dynamic or tempo change, such as *subito piano* or *subito allegro*.

swing: Frequent act performed by a golfer; or a rhythm similar to shuffle where two eighth notes are played as a quarter-eighth triplet.

syncopation: Playing off the beat. Rhythm that emphasizes beats other than the downbeat.

synthesizer: Electric keyboard instrument that mimics other sounds by manipulating the shape of a sound wave.

tempo: Literally means "time;" more commonly referred to as musical speed.

tenuto: Literally means "held." An articulation indicated by a short line under or above the notehead, telling the player to give that note its full rhythmic value and then some.

tie: Common gift for dads, uncles, and bosses; or a curved line connecting two notes, telling the player to hold the tone for the combined rhythmic value of both notes.

time signature: Two numbers placed on the music staff to indicate the *meter*.

tone: A sound, whether musical or other, with pitch; the opposite of noise.

transposition: Changing a piece of music from one key to another.

treble clef: Symbol placed on the second line of the staff designating that line to be the tone G above middle C.

tremolo: Musical effect created by rapidly alternating between two notes separated by more than a 2nd interval.

trill: Musical effect created by rapidly alternating between two notes of close proximity.

tuning: Correcting the pitch of a piano string or other acoustic instrument.

vivace: Lively and quick.

voicing: Giving your opinion; or the vertical arrangement of notes in a chord.

waltz time: The point in the festivities when everyone dances; or 3/4 meter.

whole step: Two half steps; also known as a major second interval.

xylophone: Percussion instrument that looks like a keyboard but is played with mallets. (Hey, I needed an "x" on this list.)

yodel: A type of singing, originally from Switzerland, where the voice jumps between natural and very high-pitched (falsetto) tones.

zapateado: A Spanish dance in triple meter, characterized by rhythmic heel stamping. (What's a glossary without a "z?")

Appendix B
About the CD

● ●

*T*he audio CD that comes with this book features all of the great songs you play in *Piano For Dummies*. I recorded most of the songs with a piano sound. (How appropriate.) But give the CD a whirl, and you also hear some surprises.

That's right. Many of the CD tracks use various synthesizer sounds to create the illusion of a band or orchestra playing along with you. But you can still hear the keyboard part loud and clear above the rest of the music.

Each CD track is preceded by one full measure of "clicks." These clicks tell you how fast to play and help you synchronize with the recording. Think of the clicks as your own personal drummer counting off the beats of the song for you.

Here's a comprehensive list of all the stuff that you find on the audio CD:

Track Number	Track Title	Chapter
1	*Three Gymnopédies* and *Maple Leaf Rag*	1
2	*The Well-Tempered Clavier*	1
3	*Toccata and Fugue in D minor*	1
4	Sounds of a synthesizer	1
5	*Here Comes the Bride*	1
6	Mixing up all the notes	5
7	Faster, faster alley cat	5
8	Congrats! You have triplets	5
9	*Hot Time in the Old Town Tonight*	5
10	*The Beautiful Blue Danube*	5
11	*Can Can*	5
12	*Changing It Up*	5

(continued)

Track Number	*Track Title*	*Chapter*
13	*Add-Ons*	5
14	*Waiting for a Note*	6
15	*When the Saints Go Marching In*	6
16	*Oh, Susannah*	6
17	Tying up the notes	6
18	*Scheherazade*	6
19	*I've Been Working on the Railroad*	6
20	*Swanee River*	6
21	Swinging a straight beat	6
22	*The Kitchen Sync*	6
23	*Frere Jacques*	7
24	*Ode to Joy*	7
25	*Skip to My Lou*	7
26	*Kum-bah-yah*	7
27	*Chiapanecas*	7
28	*This Old Man*	7
29	*Minuet*	7
30	*Row, Row, Row Your Boat*	7
31	*Danny Boy*	8
32	*Jesu, Joy of Man's Desiring*	8
33	*House of the Rising Sun*	8
34	*The Farmer in the Dell*	8
35	*Greensleeves*	8
36	*Swing Low, Sweet Chariot*	9
37	*Little Brown Jug*	9
38	*Yankee Doodle*	9
39	*On Top of Old Smoky*	9
40	*America, The Beautiful*	10
41	*Piano (Shenandoah)*	10
42	*Marianne*	10
43	*I'm Called Little Buttercup*	10

Track Number	Track Title	Chapter
44	Aura Lee	10
45	Auld Lang Syne	10
46	Good Night Ladies (in C)	11
47	Good Night Ladies (in F)	11
48	Destination unknown	11
49	Worried Man Blues (in G)	11
50	Worried Man Blues (in D)	11
51	The Star-Spangled Banner	11
52	Red River Valley	12
53	Down by the Station	12
54	To a Wild Rose	12
55	Rags and Riches	12
56	A little suspension tension	12
57	Lullaby	12
58	Bingo	12
59	Camptown Races	13
60	Pop! Goes the Weasel	13
61	Trumpet Voluntary	13
62	To Gliss Is Bliss	13
63	Also Sprach Zarathustra	13
64	Polovtsian Dance	13
65	Varied rhythm chords in the left hand	14
66	Arpeggios are great-sounding and easy	14
67	Picking and Grinning	14
68	Octaves in the Left	14
69	Lumping Octaves	14
70	Rockin' Intervals	14
71	Berry-Style Blues	14
72	Bum-Ba-Di-Da	14
73	Boogie-Woogie Bass Line	14
74	The "Get Ready, Here We Go" intro	14

(continued)

Track Number	Track Title	Chapter
75	The "Rockin' Jam" intro	14
76	The "Sweet Ballad" intro	14
77	The "Killing Time" intro	14
78	The "Saloon Salutations" intro	14
79	The "I Love You, You Left Me" outro	14
80	The "Let's Load Up the Bus" outro	14
81	The "Last Call" outro	14
82	The "Shave and a Haircut" outro	14
83	"Bernstein Would've Been Proud" riff	14
84	"Love Me Like You Used To" riff	14
85	"Classic Boogie" riff	14
86	"Hank the Honky-Tonk" riff	14
87	"Chopsticks" riff	14
88	*This Old Man Wore a Wig*	15
89	*Dixie a la Grieg*	15
90	*Jerry Had a Little Lamb*	15
91	*Sadder Blues, Softer Shoes*	15
92	*Michael, Ride Your Horse Ashore*	15
93	*Go Tell Aunt Rhody You Love Her*	15
94	*Home on the Motown Range*	15
95	*For He's a Funky Good Fellow*	15
96	*Yankee Doodle Went to a Jazz Club*	15
97	*Merrily We Roll Along*	15

Index

(continued)

(continued)

WWW.DUMMIES.COM

Discover Dummies Online!

The Dummies Web Site is your fun and friendly online resource for the latest information about *For Dummies®* books and your favorite topics. The Web site is the place to communicate with us, exchange ideas with other *For Dummies* readers, chat with authors, and have fun!

Ten Fun and Useful Things You Can Do at www.dummies.com

1. Win free *For Dummies* books and more!
2. Register your book and be entered in a prize drawing.
3. Meet your favorite authors through the IDG Books Worldwide Author Chat Series.
4. Exchange helpful information with other *For Dummies* readers.
5. Discover other great *For Dummies* books you must have!
6. Purchase Dummieswear® exclusively from our Web site.
7. Buy *For Dummies* books online.
8. Talk to us. Make comments, ask questions, get answers!
9. Download free software.
10. Find additional useful resources from authors.

Link directly to these ten fun and useful things at
http://www.dummies.com/10useful

For other technology titles from IDG Books Worldwide, go to
www.idgbooks.com

Not on the Web yet? It's easy to get started with *Dummies 101®: The Internet For Windows® 98* or *The Internet For Dummies®* at local retailers everywhere.

IDG BOOKS WORLDWIDE

Find other *For Dummies* books on these topics:

Business • Career • Databases • Food & Beverage • Games • Gardening • Graphics • Hardware
Health & Fitness • Internet and the World Wide Web • Networking • Office Suites
Operating Systems • Personal Finance • Pets • Programming • Recreation • Sports
Spreadsheets • Teacher Resources • Test Prep • Word Processing

IDG BOOKS WORLDWIDE
BOOK REGISTRATION

We want to hear from you!

Visit **http://my2cents.dummies.com** to register this book and tell us how you liked it!

- ✔ Get entered in our monthly prize giveaway.

- ✔ Give us feedback about this book — tell us what you like best, what you like least, or maybe what you'd like to ask the author and us to change!

- ✔ Let us know any other *For Dummies*® topics that interest you.

Your feedback helps us determine what books to publish, tells us what coverage to add as we revise our books, and lets us know whether we're meeting your needs as a *For Dummies* reader. You're our most valuable resource, and what you have to say is important to us!

Not on the Web yet? It's easy to get started with *Dummies 101*®: *The Internet For Windows*® *98* or *The Internet For Dummies*® at local retailers everywhere.

Or let us know what you think by sending us a letter at the following address:

For Dummies Book Registration
Dummies Press
10475 Crosspoint Blvd.
Indianapolis, IN 46256

BESTSELLING BOOK SERIES